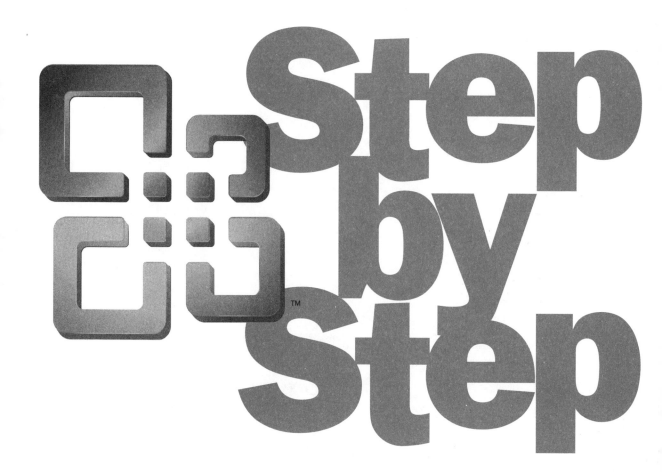

Microsoft® Office
Word 2003

Online Training Solutions, Inc.

PUBLISHED BY
Microsoft Press
A Division of Microsoft Corporation
One Microsoft Way
Redmond, Washington 98052-6399

Library of Congress Cataloging-in-Publication Data
Microsoft Office Word 2003 Step by Step / Online Training Solutions, Inc.
     p. cm.
    Includes index.
    ISBN 0-7356-1523-3
    1. Microsoft Word. 2. Word processing. I. Online Training Solutions (Firm)

   Z52.5.M52M47   2003
   652.5'5369--dc21   2003052664

Printed and bound in the United States of America.

8 9   QWE   8 7

Distributed in Canada by H.B. Fenn and Company Ltd.

A CIP catalogue record for this book is available from the British Library.

Microsoft Press books are available through booksellers and distributors worldwide. For further information about international editions, contact your local Microsoft Corporation office or contact Microsoft Press International directly at fax (425) 936-7329. Visit our Web site at www.microsoft.com/mspress. Send comments to *mspinput@microsoft.com*.

Acquisitions Editor: Alex Blanton
Project Editor: Aileen Wrothwell

Body Part No. X09-71472

Contents

Contents

1   Working with Documents   1

2   Editing and Proofreading Documents   24

3   Changing the Appearance of Text   50

4   Arranging and Printing Documents   80

Contents

What's New in Microsoft Office Word 2003

You'll notice some changes as soon as you start Microsoft Office Word 2003. The user interface has been updated with a fresh new look.

New in Office 2003

Many of the features that are new or improved in this version of Word won't be apparent to you until you start using the program. To help you quickly identify features that are new or improved with this version, this book uses the icon in the margin whenever those features are discussed or shown.

The following table lists the new features that you might be interested in, as well as the chapters in which those features are discussed.

To learn how to	Using this feature	See
View and read the document as it will appear on paper without needing to print it	Reading Layout view	Chapter 1
View small images of each page in a document	Thumbnails	Chapter 1
Display a menu of options for performing common tasks	Smart Tags	Chapter 2
Locate supporting information in local reference materials or on the Internet	Research service	Chapter 2
Mark up the document with comments, highlighting, and revisions	Reading Mode Markup toolbar	Chapter 8
Specify that insertions be marked with a different color from deletions	Setting insertions and deletions to different colors	Chapter 8
Make handwritten comments in Word documents	Support for handwriting	Chapter 8
Turn off display of balloons for revisions and display the balloons for comments only	Control revision and comment balloons separately	Chapter 8
Specify that only specific individuals have permission to modify a document	Control who can edit and format documents	Chapter 8

To learn how to	Using this feature	See
Send a file as an attachment and automatically create a Windows SharePoint Services Web site, with a task list and other information that's pertinent to the document	Shared workspace	Chapter 9
Access tools for creating XML documents and using XML data in Word documents	XML capabilities	Chapter 9
Extract the key points of the document	AutoSummarize feature	Chapter 12
View document statistics such as the average number of characters in a word, the average number of words in a sentence, and the reading level of the document.	Readability Statistics	Chapter 12

Getting Help

Every effort has been made to ensure the accuracy of this book and the contents of its CD-ROM. If you do run into problems, please contact the appropriate source for help and assistance.

Getting Help with This Book and Its CD-ROM

If your question or issue concerns the content of this book or its companion CD-ROM, please first search the online Microsoft Press Knowledge Base, which provides support information for known errors in or corrections to this book, at the following Web site:

www.microsoft.com/mspress/support/search.asp

If you do not find your answer at the online Knowledge Base, send your comments or questions to Microsoft Press Technical Support at:

mspinput@microsoft.com

Getting Help with Microsoft Office Word 2003

If your question is about Microsoft Office Word 2003, and not about the content of this Microsoft Press book, your first recourse is Word's Help system. This system is a combination of help tools and files stored on your computer when you installed The Microsoft Office System 2003 and, if your computer is connected to the Internet, help files available from Microsoft Office Online.

To find out about different items on the screen, you can display a *ScreenTip*. To display a ScreenTip for a toolbar button, for example, point to the button without clicking it. Its ScreenTip appears, telling you its name. In some dialog boxes, you can click a question mark icon to the left of the Close button in the title bar to display the Microsoft Office Word Help window with information related to the dialog box.

When you have a question about using Word, you can type it in the "Type a question for help" box at the right end of the program window's menu bar. Then press Enter to display a list of Help topics from which you can select the one that most closely relates to your question.

Another way to get help is to display the Office Assistant, which provides help as you work in the form of helpful information or a tip. If the Office Assistant is hidden when a tip is available, a light bulb appears. Clicking the light bulb displays the tip, and provides other options.

If you want to practice getting help, you can work through this exercise, which demonstrates two ways to get help.

BE SURE TO start Word before beginning this exercise.

1 At the right end of the menu bar, click the **Type a question for help** box.

2 Type How do I get help?, and press `Enter`.

A list of topics that relate to your question appears in the Search Results task pane.

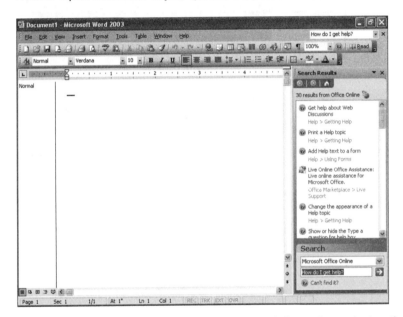

You can click any of the help topics to get more information or instructions.

3 In the **Search Results** task pane, scroll down the results list, and click **About getting help while you work**.

The Microsoft Office Word Help window opens, displaying information about that topic.

Maximize

4 At the right end of the Microsoft Office Word Help window's title bar, click the **Maximize** button, and then click **Show All**.

The topic content expands to provide in-depth information about getting help while you work.

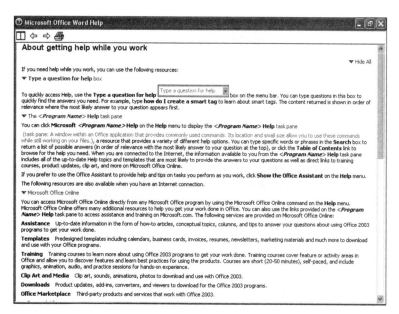

Close

5 At the right end of the Microsoft Office Word Help window's title bar, click the **Close** button, to close the window.

6 On the **Help** menu, click **Microsoft Office Word Help**.

The Word Help task pane opens.

7 In the task pane, click **Table of Contents**.

8   The task pane now displays a list of help topics organized by category, like the table of contents in a book.

Back

9   On the toolbar at the top of the task pane, click the **Back** button.

Notice the categories of information that are available from the Microsoft Office Online Web site. You can also reach this Web site by clicking Microsoft Office Online on the Help menu.

More Information

If your question is about a Microsoft software product, including Word 2003, and not about the content of this Microsoft Press book, please search the appropriate product support center or the Microsoft Knowledge Base at:

support.microsoft.com

In the United States, Microsoft software product support issues not covered by the Microsoft Knowledge Base are addressed by Microsoft Product Support Services. The Microsoft software support options available from Microsoft Product Support Services are listed at:

support.microsoft.com

Outside the United States, for support information specific to your location, please refer to the Worldwide Support menu on the Microsoft Product Support Services Web site for the site specific to your country:

support.microsoft.com

Using the Book's CD-ROM

The CD-ROM included with this book contains all the practice files you'll use as you work through the exercises in this book. By using practice files, you won't waste time creating sample content with which to experiment—instead, you can jump right in and concentrate on learning how to use Microsoft Office Word 2003.

What's on the CD-ROM?

In addition to the practice files, the CD-ROM contains some exciting resources that will really enhance your ability to get the most out of using this book and Word 2003, including the following:

- *Microsoft Office Word 2003 Step by Step* in e-book format.
- *Insider's Guide to Microsoft Office OneNote 2003* in e-book format.
- *Microsoft Office System Quick Reference* in e-book format.
- *Introducing the Tablet PC* in e-book format.
- *Microsoft Computer Dictionary, Fifth Edition* in e-book format.
- 25 business-oriented templates for use with programs in The Microsoft Office System.
- 100 pieces of clip art.

Important The CD-ROM for this book does not contain the Word 2003 software. You should purchase and install that program before using this book.

Minimum System Requirements

To use this book, you will need:

- **Computer/Processor**

  Computer with a Pentium 133-megahertz (MHz) or higher processor; Pentium III recommended
- **Memory**

  64 MB of RAM (128 MB recommended) plus an additional 8 MB of RAM for each program in The Microsoft Office System (such as Word) running simultaneously

■ **Hard Disk**

Hard disk requirements will vary depending on configuration; custom installation choices may require more or less hard disk space

■ 245 MB of available hard disk space with 115 MB on the hard disk where the operating system is installed

■ An additional 20 MB of hard disk space is required for installing the practice files.

■ **Operating System**

Microsoft Windows 2000 with Service Pack 3 (SP3) or Microsoft Windows XP or later

■ **Drive**

CD-ROM drive

■ **Display**

Super VGA (800 × 600) or higher-resolution monitor with 256 colors

■ **Peripherals**

Microsoft Mouse, Microsoft IntelliMouse, or compatible pointing device

■ **Software**

Microsoft Office Word 2003, Microsoft Office Outlook 2003, and Microsoft Internet Explorer 5 or later

Installing the Practice Files

You need to install the practice files on your hard disk before you use them in the chapters' exercises. Follow these steps to prepare the CD's files for your use:

1 Insert the CD-ROM into the CD-ROM drive of your computer.

The Step by Step Companion CD End User License Agreement appears. Follow the on-screen directions. It is necessary to accept the terms of the license agreement in order to use the practice files. After you accept the license agreement, a menu screen appears.

Important If the menu screen does not appear, start Windows Explorer. In the left pane, locate the icon for your CD-ROM drive and click this icon. In the right pane, double-click the StartCD executable file.

2 Click **Install Practice Files**.

3 Click **Next** on the first screen, and then click **Yes** to accept the license agreement on the next screen.

4   If you want to install the practice files to a location other than the default folder (*My Documents\Microsoft Press\Word 2003 SBS*), click the **Browse** button, select the new drive and path, and then click **OK**.

5   Click **Next** on the **Choose Destination Location** screen, click **Next** on the **Select Features** screen, and then click **Next** on the **Start Copying Files** screen to install the selected practice files.

6   After the practice files have been installed, click **Finish**.

      Within the installation folder are subfolders for each chapter in the book.

7   Close the Step by Step Companion CD window, remove the CD-ROM from the CD-ROM drive, and return it to the envelope at the back of the book.

Using the Practice Files

Each exercise is preceded by a paragraph or paragraphs that list the files needed for that exercise and explains any file preparation you need to take care of before you start working through the exercise, as shown here:

BE SURE TO start Word before beginning this exercise.
USE the *CreateList* document in the practice file folder for this topic. This practice file is located in the *My Documents\Microsoft Press\Word 2003 SBS\ChangingText\CreatingList* folder and can also be accessed by clicking *Start/All Programs/Microsoft Press/Word 2003 Step by Step*.
OPEN the CreateList document.

Usually you will be instructed to open the practice files from within the application in which you are working. However, you can also access the files directly from Windows by clicking the Start menu items indicated. Locate the file in the chapter subfolder and then double-click the file to open it.

The following table lists each chapter's practice files.

Chapter	Folder	Subfolder	Files
Chapter 1: Working with Documents	WorkingDoc	OpeningDoc	ExistDoc
			OpenDoc
		DecidingView	ViewDoc
Chapter 2: Editing and Proofreading Documents	EditingProof	EditingDoc	EditDoc
		UsingShort	EntryAuto
		FindingWord	Thesaurus
		UsingOutline	OutlineText
		FindingText	ReplaceText
		CheckingSpell	SpellCheck

Chapter	Folder	Subfolder	Files
Chapter 3: Changing the Appearance of Text	ChangingText	ChangingChar ChangingPara CreatingList AutoFormatting ChangingStyle	FormatText FormatPara CreateList FormatAuto FormatStyle
Chapter 4: Arranging and Printing Documents	ArrangingDoc	ChangingBack ChangingTheme PreviewingDoc ControllingPage	FormatBackground FormatTheme ViewPages FormatPage
Chapter 5: Pesenting Information in Tables and Columns	PresentingInfo	PresentingTable FormattingTable WorkingData PresentingColumn	CreateTable FormatTable DataTable InsertTable CreateColumn
Chapter 6: Working with Graphics	WorkingGraphic	CreatingDiag InsertingPic AligningPic CreatingArt DrawingShape	OrgChart InsertPics AlignPics WordArt DrawShape
Chapter 7: Working with Charts	WorkingChart	InsertingChart ModifyingChart ImportingData	AddChart ModChart ImportData FileImport
Chapter 8: Collaborating with Others	CollaboratingOther	TrackingChange AddingComment ProtectingDoc PreventingEdit SendingDoc ComparingDoc	TrackChange RevComment ProtectDoc PreventDoc Send Attach1 Attach2 CompareMerge Merge1 Merge2
Chapter 9: Creating Documents for the Web	Creating Web	CreatingWebDoc AddingLink CreatingXML	CreateWeb HyperWeb OtherLogos AttachSchema

Chapter	Folder	Subfolder	Files
Chapter 10: Creating Forms	CreatingForm	SettingUp ModifyingForm UsingForm	CreateForm ModifyForm UseForm
Chapter 11: Creating Form Letters and Labels	CreatingMail	PreparingData PreparingLetter MergingData CreatingLabel	FormLetter Data FormLetter2 Data2 FormLetter3 Data3 Data4
Chapter 12: Making Information in Longer Documents Accessible	MakingAvail	ManagingMaster AddingBook CreatingContents CreatingIndex SummarizingDoc	Master Bookmark TableContents CreateIndex SummarizeDoc
Chapter 13: Increasing Efficiency	IncreasingEfficiency	CustomizingMenu CustomizingTool ChangingSetting CreatingMacro EditingMacro	CustomMenu CustomToolbar SettingsDoc RecordMacro ModifyMacro

Uninstalling the Practice Files

After you finish working through this book, you should uninstall the practice files to free up hard disk space.

1   On the Windows taskbar, click the **Start** button, and then click **Control Panel**.

2   In Control Panel, click **Add or Remove Programs**.

3   In the list of installed programs, click **Microsoft Office Word 2003 Step By Step**, and then click the **Remove** or **Change/Remove** button.

4   In the **Uninstall** dialog box, click **OK**.

5   After the files are uninstalled, click **Finish**, and then close the Add or Remove Programs window and Control Panel.

Important   If you need additional help installing or uninstalling the practice files, please see "Getting Help" earlier in this book. Microsoft Product Support Services does not provide support for this book or its CD-ROM.

Conventions and Features

You can save time when you use this book by understanding how the *Step by Step* series shows special instructions, keys to press, buttons to click, and so on.

Convention	Meaning
Microsoft Office Specialist	This icon indicates a topic that covers a Microsoft Office Specialist exam objective.
New in Office 2003	This icon indicates a new or greatly improved feature in Microsoft Office Word 2003.
	This icon indicates a reference to the book's companion CD.
BE SURE TO	These words are found at the beginning of paragraphs preceding or following step-by-step exercises. They point out items you should check or actions you should carry out either before beginning an exercise or after completing an exercise.
USE OPEN	These words are found at the beginning of paragraphs preceding step-by-step exercises. They draw your attention to practice files that you'll need to use in the exercise.
CLOSE	This word is found at the beginning of paragraphs following step-by-step exercises. They give instructions for closing open files or programs before moving on to another topic.
1 2	Numbered steps guide you through hands-on exercises in each topic.
●	A round bullet indicates an exercise that has only one step.
Troubleshooting	These paragraphs show you how to fix a common problem that might prevent you from continuing with the exercise.
Tip	These paragraphs provide a helpful hint or shortcut that makes working through a task easier.
Important	These paragraphs point out information that you need to know to complete a procedure.

Convention	Meaning
🖫 Save	The first time you are told to click a button in an exercise, a picture of the button appears in the left margin. If the name of the button does not appear on the button itself, the name appears under the picture.
Ctrl + Home	A plus sign (+) between two key names means that you must hold down the first key while you press the second key. For example, "press Ctrl+Home" means "hold down the Ctrl key while you press the Home key."
Black bold characters	In steps, the names of program elements, such as buttons, commands, and dialog boxes, are shown in black bold characters.
Blue bold characters	Anything you are supposed to type appears in blue bold characters.
Blue italic characters	Terms that are explained in the glossary at the end of the book are shown in blue italic characters.

Taking a Microsoft Office Specialist Certification Exam

As desktop computing technology advances, more employers rely on the objectivity and consistency of technology certification when screening, hiring, and training employees to ensure the competence of these professionals. As a job seeker or employee, you can use technology certification to prove that you have the skills businesses need, and can save them the trouble and expense of training. Microsoft Office Specialist is the only Microsoft certification program designed to assist employees in validating their Microsoft Office System skills.

About the Microsoft Office Specialist Program

A Microsoft Office Specialist is an individual who has demonstrated worldwide standards of Microsoft Office skill through a certification exam in one or more of The Microsoft Office System desktop programs including Microsoft Word, Excel, PowerPoint®, Outlook®, Access and Project. Office Specialist certifications are available at the "Specialist" and "Expert" skill levels. Visit *www.microsoft.com /officespecialist/* to locate skill standards for each certification and an Authorized Testing Center in your area.

What Does This Logo Mean?

This Microsoft Office Specialist logo means this courseware has been approved by the Microsoft Office Specialist Program to be among the finest available for learning Word 2003. It also means that upon completion of this courseware, you might be prepared to become a Microsoft Office Specialist.

Selecting a Microsoft Office Specialist Certification Level

When selecting the Microsoft Office Specialist certification(s) level that you would like to pursue, you should assess the following:

- The Office program ("program") and version(s) of that program with which you are familiar

- The length of time you have used the program

- Whether you have had formal or informal training in the use of that program

Candidates for Specialist-level certification are expected to successfully complete a wide range of standard business tasks, such as formatting a document or spreadsheet. Successful candidates generally have six or more months of experience with the program, including either formal, instructor-led training or self-study using Microsoft Office Specialist-approved books, guides, or interactive computer-based materials.

Candidates for Expert-level certification are expected to complete more complex, business-oriented tasks utilizing the program's advanced functionality, such as importing data and recording macros. Successful candidates generally have one or more years of experience with the program, including formal, instructor-led training or self-study using Microsoft Office Specialist-approved materials.

Microsoft Office Specialist Skill Standards

Every Microsoft Office Specialist certification exam is developed from a set of exam skill standards that are derived from studies of how the Office program is used in the workplace. Because these skill standards dictate the scope of each exam, they provide you with critical information on how to prepare for certification.

Microsoft Office Specialist Approved Courseware, including the Microsoft Press Step by Step series, are reviewed and approved on the basis of their coverage of the Microsoft Office Specialist skill standards.

The Exam Experience

Microsoft Office Specialist certification exams for Office 2003 programs are performance-based exams that require you to complete 15 to 20 standard business tasks using an interactive simulation (a digital model) of a Microsoft Office System program. Exam questions can have one, two, or three task components that, for example, require you to create or modify a document or spreadsheet:

Modify the existing brochure by completing the following three tasks:

1   Left-align the heading, *Premium Real Estate.*

2   Insert a footer with right-aligned page numbering. (Note: accept all other default settings.)

3   Save the document with the file name **Broker Brochure** in the My Documents folder.

Candidates should also be aware that each exam must be completed within an allotted time of 45 minutes and that in the interest of test security and fairness, the Office Help system (including the Office Assistant) cannot be accessed during the exam.

Passing standards (the minimum required score) for Microsoft Office Specialist certification exams range from 60 to 85 percent correct, depending on the exam.

The Exam Interface and Controls

The exam interface and controls, including the test question, appear across the bottom of the screen.

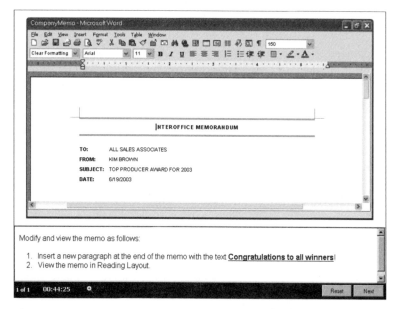

- The **Counter** is located in the left corner of the exam interface and tracks the number of questions completed and how many questions remain.

- The **Timer** is located to the right of the Counter and starts when the first question appears on the screen. The Timer displays the remaining exam time. If the Timer is distracting, click the Timer to remove the display.

Important Transition time between questions is not counted against total allotted exam time.

- The **Reset** button is located to the left of the **Next** button and will restart a question if you believe you have made an error. The **Reset** button will not restart the entire exam nor extend the total allotted exam time.

- The **Next** button is located in the right corner. When you complete a question, click the **Next** button to move to the next question. It is not possible to move back to a previous question on the exam.

Test-Taking Tips

- Follow all instructions provided in each question completely and accurately.

- Enter requested information as it appears in the instructions, but without duplicating the format. For example, all text and values that you will be asked to enter will appear in the instructions with bold and underlined text formats (for example, **text**), however, you should enter the information without applying these formats unless you are specifically instructed to do otherwise.

- Close all dialog boxes before proceeding to the next exam question unless you are specifically instructed otherwise.

- There is no need to close task panes before proceeding to the next exam question unless you are specifically instructed otherwise.

- There is no need to save your work before moving on to the next question unless you are specifically instructed to do otherwise.

- For questions that ask you to print a document, spreadsheet, chart, report, slide, and so on, please be aware that nothing will actually be printed.

- Responses are scored based on the result of your work, not the method you use to achieve that result (unless a specific method is indicated in the instructions), and not the time you take to complete the question. Extra keystrokes or mouse clicks do not count against your score.

- If your computer becomes unstable during the exam (for example, if the exam does not respond or the mouse no longer functions) or if a power outage occurs, contact a testing center administrator immediately. The administrator will restart the computer and return the exam to the point where the interruption occurred with your score intact.

Certification

At the conclusion of the exam, you will receive a score report, which you can print with the assistance of the testing center administrator. If your score meets or exceeds the passing standard (the minimum required score), you will be mailed a printed certificate within approximately 14 days.

College Credit Recommendation

The American Council on Education (ACE) has issued a one-semester hour college credit recommendation for each Microsoft Office Specialist certification. To learn more, visit *www.microsoft.com/traincert/mcp/officespecialist/credit.asp*.

For More Information

To learn more about Microsoft Office Specialist certification, visit *www.microsoft.com /officespecialist/*.

To learn about other Microsoft Office Specialist approved courseware from Microsoft Press, visit *www.microsoft.com/mspress/certification/officespecialist/*.

Microsoft Office Specialist Skill Standards

Each Microsoft Office Specialist certification has a set of corresponding skill standards that describe areas of individual, Microsoft Office program use. You should master each skill standard to prepare for the corresponding Microsoft Office Specialist certification exam.

Microsoft Office Specialist

This book will fully prepare you for the Microsoft Office Specialist certification at the Specialist and Expert levels. Throughout this book, content that pertains to a Microsoft Office Specialist skill standard is identified with the logo shown in the margin.

Specialist	Skill	Page
WW03S-1	**Creating Content**	
WW03S-1-1	Insert and edit text, symbols and special characters	4, 26, 31, 36, 45
WW03S-1-2	Insert frequently used and pre-defined text	26
WW03S-1-3	Navigate to specific content	11, 42
WW03S-1-4	Insert, position and size graphics	133, 144
WW03S-1-5	Create and modify diagrams and charts	129, 151, 156
WW03S-1-6	Locate, select and insert supporting information	38
WW03S-2	**Organizing Content**	
WW03S-2-1	Insert and modify tables	108, 114
WW03S-2-2	Create bulleted lists, numbered lists and outlines	38, 68
WW03S-2-3	Insert and modify hyperlinks	200
WW03S-3	**Formatting Content**	
WW03S-3-1	Format text	52, 74
WW03S-3-2	Format paragraphs	58
WW03S-3-3	Apply and format columns	124
WW03S-3-4	Insert and modify content in headers and footers	99

Microsoft Office Specialist Skill Standards

Specialist	Skill	Page
WW03S-4	**Collaborating**	
WW03S-4-1	Circulate documents for review	184
WW03S-4-2	Compare and merge document versions	187
WW03S-4-3	Insert, view and edit comments	173
WW03S-4-4	Track, accept and reject proposed changes	168
WW03S-5	**Formatting and Managing Documents**	
WW03S-5-1	Create new documents using templates	82
WW03S-5-2	Review and modify document properties	272
WW03S-5-3	Organize documents using file folders	4
WW03S-5-4	Save documents in appropriate formats for different uses	4
WW03S-5-5	Print documents, envelopes and labels	93, 242
WW03S-5-6	Preview documents and Web pages	194
WW03S-5-7	Change and organize document views and windows	11, 16

Expert	Skill	Page
WW03E-1	**Formatting Content**	
WW03E-1-1	Create custom styles for text, tables and lists	52
WW03E-1-2	Control pagination	99
WW03E-1-3	Format, position and resize graphics using advanced layout features	133, 137
WW03E-1-4	Insert and modify objects	119
WW03E-1-5	Create and modify diagrams and charts using data from other sources	162
WW03E-2	**Organizing Content**	
WW03E-2-1	Sort content in lists and tables	68, 108
WW03E-2-2	Perform calculations in tables	119
WW03E-2-3	Modify table formats	108, 114, 119

Expert	Skill	Page
WW03E-2-4	Summarize document content using automated tools	272
WW03E-2-5	Use automated tools for document navigation	272
WW03E-2-6	Merge letters with other data sources	254
WW03E-2-7	Merge labels with other data sources	229, 236, 239
WW03E-2-8	Structure documents using XML	204, 242
WW03E-3	**Formatting Documents**	
WW03E-3-1	Create and modify forms	214, 220
WW03E-3-2	Create and modify document background	87, 91
WW03E3-3	Create and modify document indexes and tables	259, 265
WW03E-3-4	Insert and modify endnotes, footnotes, captions, and cross-references	254, 258, 264
WW03E-3-5	Create and manage master documents and subdocuments	250
WW03E-4	**Collaborating**	
WW03E-4-1	Modify track changes options	187
WW03E-4-2	Publish and edit Web documents in Word	194
WW03E-4-3	Manage document versions	168
WW03E-4-4	Protect and restrict forms and documents	178, 182
WW03E-4-5	Attach digital signatures to documents	185
WW03E-4-6	Customize document properties	272
WW03E-5	**Customizing Word**	
WW03E-5-1	Create, edit, and run macros	294, 298
WW03E-5-2	Customize menus and toolbars	281, 286
WW03E-5-3	Modify default Word settings	82, 292, 294

About the Authors

Online Training Solutions, Inc. (OTSI)

OTSI is a traditional and electronic publishing company specializing in the creation, production, and delivery of computer software training. OTSI publishes the Quick Course® series of computer and business training products. The principals of OTSI are:

Joyce Cox has over 20 years' experience in writing about and editing technical subjects for non-technical audiences. For 12 of those years she was the principal author for Online Press. She was also the first managing editor of Microsoft Press, an editor for Sybex, and an editor for the University of California.

Steve Lambert started playing with computers in the mid-seventies. As computers evolved from wire-wrap and solder to consumer products, he evolved from hardware geek to programmer and writer. He has written over 14 books and a wide variety of technical documentation and has produced training tools and help systems.

Gale Nelson honed her communication skills as a technical writer for a SQL Server training company. Her attention to detail soon led her into software testing and quality assurance management. She now divides her work time between writing and data conversion projects.

Joan Preppernau has been contributing to the creation of excellent technical training materials for computer professionals for as long as she cares to remember. Joan's wide-ranging experiences in various facets of the industry have contributed to her passion for producing interesting, useful, and understandable training materials.

The OTSI publishing team includes the following outstanding professionals:

Susie Bayers
Jan Bednarczuk
Keith Bednarczuk
RJ Cadranell
Liz Clark
Nancy Depper
Leslie Eliel
Joseph Ford
Jon Kenoyer
Marlene Lambert
Aaron L'Heureux
Lisa Van Every
Michelle Ziegwied

For more information about Online Training Solutions, Inc., visit *www.otsi.com*.

Perspection, Inc.

Microsoft Word Version 2002 Step by Step, on which this book was based, was created by the professional trainers and writers at Perspection, Inc. Perspection writes and produces software training books, and develops multimedia and Web-based training.

Quick Reference

Chapter 1 **Working with Documents**

Page 2 **To start Word**

- On the taskbar, click **Start**, point to **All Programs**, point to **Microsoft Office**, and then click **Microsoft Office Word 2003**.

6 **To insert a symbol into text**

1 Click the document where you want the symbol to appear.

2 On the **Insert** menu, click **Symbol**.

3 On the **Symbol** tab of the **Symbol** dialog box, scroll through the list until you find the symbol you want to insert.

4 Click the symbol, click the **Insert** button, and then click the **Close** button.

6 **To save a document for the first time**

1 On the Standard toolbar, click the **Save** button.

2 In the **Save As** dialog box, click the down arrow to the right of the **Save in** box, and navigate to the location where you want to save the file.

3 If you want to create a new folder for the file, click the **Create New Folder** button, and in the **New Folder** dialog box, type the new folder's name, and click **OK**.

4 Select the text in the **File name** box, and type a new name.

5 Click **Save**.

6 **To save a document with a new name**

1 On the **File** menu, click **Save As**.

2 In the **Save As** dialog box, select the text in the **File name** box, and type a new name.

3 Click **Save**.

10 **To save a file for use in another program**

1 On the **File** menu, click **Save As**.

2 In the **Save As** dialog box, click the down arrow to the right of the **Save As Type** box, and click the file format to which you want to save the file.

3 Click **Save**.

11 **To open an existing file**

1 On the Standard toolbar, click the **Open** button.

2 In the **Open** dialog box, navigate to the folder that contains the file you want to open.

3 Double-click the file you want to open.

11 **To move the insertion point to the beginning or end of the document**

● Press `Ctrl`+`Home` or `Ctrl`+`End`.

11 **To show all formatting and hidden text**

● On the Standard toolbar, click the **Show/Hide ¶** button.

17 **To view thumbnails of a document**

1 In the lower-left corner of the window, click the **Start Reading** button, or on the **View** menu, click **Reading Layout**.

2 On the Reading Mode toolbar, click the **Thumbnails** button.

17 **To view the Document Map**

● On the Reading Mode toolbar, click the **Document Map** button.

17 **To change the zoom (magnification) level**

● On the Standard toolbar, click the down arrow to the right of the **Zoom** box, and click the zoom level you want.

Chapter 2 **Editing and Proofreading Documents**

Page 26 **To select a word**

● Double-click the word.

26 **To select a line**

● Click the selection area to the left of the line.

26 **To select a sentence**

● Click anywhere in the sentence while holding down the `Ctrl` key.

26 **To select a paragraph**

● Double-click the selection area to the left of the paragraph.

● Triple-click anywhere in the paragraph.

26 **To delete text**

● Select the text and click `Del` or `Backspace`.

26 **To undo or redo a command**

- On the Standard toolbar, click the **Undo** or **Redo** button.

26 **To undo or redo multiple commands**

1 Click the down arrow to the right of the **Undo** or **Redo** button.

2 Select the actions you want to undo, and click once.

26 **To copy or cut and paste text**

1 Select the text.

2 On the Standard toolbar, click the **Copy** or **Cut** button, place the insertion point, and click **Paste**.

26 **To paste text**

1 Position the insertion point where you want the cut or copied text to appear.

2 On the Standard toolbar, click the **Paste** button.

32 **To create text abbreviations using AutoText**

1 On the **Tools** menu, click **AutoCorrect Options**.

2 Enter information in the appropriate text boxes to create your abbreviations, and click **OK**.

32 **To insert a date or time field**

1 On the Insert menu, click **Date and Time**.

2 Click the date or time format you want, and click **OK**.

36 **To use the thesaurus**

1 Double-click the word you want to replace.

2 On the **Tools** menu, click **Language**, and then click **Thesaurus**.

3 Click the down arrow to the right of the word you want to insert in place of the selected word, and click **Insert**.

38 **To arrange text using Outline view**

1 On the **View** menu, click **Outline**.

2 Change the level of text or headings by clicking the **Promote** or **Demote** button on the Outlining toolbar.

3 Move headings up or down by clicking the **Move Up** or **Move Down** button on the Outlining toolbar.

42   To use the Find and Replace feature for quick text replacement

1   On the **Edit** menu, click **Replace**.

2   Specify the text you want to find and the text you want to replace it with.

3   Click **Find Next**.

4   Click **Replace** to replace the first instance of the text, **Replace All** to replace all instances, or **Find Next** to leave that instance unchanged and move to the next instance.

5   Click **Close** to close the dialog box.

45   To check spelling and grammar

1   On the Standard toolbar, click the **Spelling and Grammar** button.

2   In the **Spelling and Grammar** dialog box, click the appropriate buttons to correct the errors Word finds or to add words to the custom dictionary or AutoCorrect list.

3   Click **OK** when Word reaches the end of the Spelling and Grammar check.

Chapter 3   Changing the Appearance of Text

Page 52   **To change to a different font**

1   Select the text you want to change.

2   On the Formatting toolbar, click the down arrow to the right of the **Font** box, and click the name of the font you want to apply.

52   To change the font size

1   Select the text you want to change.

2   On the Formatting toolbar, click the down arrow to the right of the **Font Size** box, and click the font size that you want to apply.

52   To display the formatting of selected text

1   Select the text whose formatting you want to display.

2   On the **Format** menu, click **Reveal Formatting**.

52   To apply text effects

1   Select the text to which you want to add an effect.

2   On the **Format** menu, click **Font**.

3   Select the check box of the effect you want to apply, and click **OK**.

52   To change the character spacing of text

1   Select the text whose spacing you want to change.

2   On the **Format** menu, click **Font**.

3   Click the **Character Spacing** tab.

4   Click the down arrow to the right of the **Spacing** box, and click **Expanded** or **Condensed**.

5   Click the up or down arrow to the right of the **By** box to specify how much the spacing should be expanded or condensed, and then click **OK**.

52   To clear text formatting

1   Select the text whose formatting you want to clear.

2   In the **Reveal Formatting** task pane, point to the **Selected** text box at the top of the task pane, click the down arrow that appears to its right, and then click **Clear Formatting**.

52   To change the color of text

1   Select the text whose color you want to change.

2   On the Formatting toolbar, click the down arrow to the right of the **Font Color** button, and then on the color palette, click the box for the color you want.

52   To highlight text with a color

1   Select the text you want to highlight.

2   On the Formatting toolbar, click the down arrow to the right of the **Highlight** button, and then click the box for the color you want.

52   To select all text that has the same formatting

1   Select one instance of the formatted text.

2   In the **Reveal Formatting** task pane, point to the **Selected** text box, click the down arrow to its right, and then click **Select All Text With Similar Formatting**.

52   To format text as bold, italic, or underlined

1   Select the text you want to format.

2   On the Formatting toolbar, click the **Bold**, **Italic**, or **Underline** button.

57   To add an animation effect

1   Select the text you want to animate.

2   On the **Format** menu, click **Font**.

3   Click the **Text Effects** tab.

4   In the **Animations** box, select the animation effect that you want to add to the selected text, and click **OK**.

58   To show or hide formatting marks

●   On the Standard toolbar, click the **Show/Hide ¶** button.

58 **To align paragraphs**

1 Select the text you want to align.

2 On the Formatting toolbar, click the **Align Left**, **Center**, **Align Right**, or **Justify** button.

58 **To indent paragraphs**

1 Click anywhere in the paragraph you want to indent.

2 On the horizontal ruler, drag the **Left Indent** or **Right Indent** marker to where the indent should be.

58 **To set a tab stop**

● Click the **Tab** button until it displays the type of tab you want, and then click the horizontal ruler where you want to set the tab stop.

58 **To format paragraphs**

1 Click the paragraph you want to format.

2 On the **Format** menu, click **Paragraph**.

3 Select the formatting options you want to apply, and click **OK**.

58 **To copy one paragraph's formatting to another paragraph**

1 Select the paragraph whose formatting you want to copy.

2 On the Standard toolbar, click the **Format Painter** button.

3 Select the paragraph that you want to format.

58 **To put a border around a paragraph**

1 Click the paragraph to which you want to add a border

2 On the **Format** menu, click **Borders and Shading**.

3 On the **Borders** tab, click the icon of the border style you want to apply, and click **OK**.

58 **To shade the background of a paragraph**

1 Click the paragraph to which you want to add shading.

2 On the **Format** menu, click **Borders and Shading**.

3 On the **Shading** tab, click the box of the color you want on the color palette, and click **OK**.

68 **To format paragraphs as a list**

1 Select the paragraphs you want to make into a list.

2 On the Formatting toolbar, click the **Bullets** or **Numbering** button.

74 **To delete a style**

1 In the **Styles and Formatting** task pane, point to the style you want to delete, click the down arrow that appears to the right, and click **Delete**.

2 Click **Yes** to confirm the deletion.

Chapter 4 Arranging and Printing Documents

Page 82 **To create a document based on a template**

1 On the **View** menu, click **Task Pane**, if necessary, and display the **New Document** task pane.

2 In the **Templates** area of the **New Document** task pane, click **On my computer** to open the **Templates** dialog box.

3 Click the tab that contains the type of document you want to create.

4 Double-click the icon of the template for that type of document.

5 Delete the placeholder text, and fill in the template.

82 **To save a document as a template**

1 On the **File** menu, click **Save As**.

2 In the **Save in** box, choose the location where you will save the template.

3 In the **File name** box, type a name for the template.

4 Click the down arrow to the right of the **Save as type** box, and click **Document Template**.

87 **To add a background color to a document**

1 In the lower-left corner of the window, click the **Web Layout View** button.

2 On the **Format** menu, point to **Background**, and then on the color palette, click the background color you want.

87 **To add a text watermark**

1 In the lower-left corner of the window, click the **Print Layout View** button.

2 On the **Format** menu, point to **Background**, and then click **Printed Watermark**.

3 Select the **Text Watermark** option.

4 Click the Text box's down arrow, and click the text you want.

5 Format the text as you like by clicking the down arrows to the right of the **Font**, **Size**, and **Color** boxes and making your selections.

6 Select a layout option, clear the **Semitransparent** check box, and click **OK**.

91 **To add a picture watermark**

1 In the lower-left corner of the window, click the **Print Layout View** button.

2 On the **Format** menu, point to **Background**, and click **Printed Watermark**.

3 Select the **Picture watermark** option, and then click the **Select Picture** button.

4 Double click the picture you want to insert as a watermark.

5 Click the down arrow to the right of the **Scale** box, and then choose how big or small you want the watermark picture to appear in the document.

6 For a more vibrant picture, clear the **Washout** check box.

7 Click **OK**.

91 **To add a theme to a document**

1 On the **Format** menu, click **Theme**.

2 In the **Choose a Theme** list, click the theme you want to apply.

3 Select the **Vivid Colors** check box to brighten the colors in the theme.

4 Click **OK**.

93 **To preview how a document will look before printing it**

1 On the Standard toolbar, click the **Print Preview** button.

2 On the Print Preview toolbar, click the **Multiple Pages** button, and drag the pointer to select the number of pages you want to view. Or click the **One Page** button.

3 Click the **Close Preview** button.

93 **To zoom in and out in Print Preview**

● Position the Magnifying Glass pointer over the document, click to zoom in, and click again to zoom out.

93 **To adjust page margins or orientation**

1 On the **File** menu, click **Page Setup**.

2 In the **Margins** area, type new values in the **Top**, **Bottom**, **Left**, and **Right** boxes.

3 Click the icon for the orientation you want.

4 Click **OK**.

93 **To print a document with the default print settings**

● On the Standard toolbar, click the **Print** button.

93 **To print a document and specify the print settings**

1 On the **File** menu, click **Print**.

2 Modify the settings as needed, and then click **OK**.

98 **To print an envelope or label**

1 On the **Tools** menu, point to **Letters and Mailings**, and click **Envelopes and Labels**.

2 Click the **Envelopes** tab or the **Labels** tab.

3 Type the address, and make any other necessary selections.

4 Click **Print**.

99 **To prevent widows and orphans**

1 Select the paragraphs you want to format.

2 On the **Format** menu, click **Paragraph** to display the **Paragraph** dialog box, and click the **Line and Page Breaks** tab, if necessary.

3 Select the **Widow/Orphan control** check box and the **Keep lines together** check box.

4 Click **OK**.

99 **To insert a page break**

1 Click to the left of the text where you want to add the page break.

2 On the **Insert** menu, click **Break** to display the **Break** dialog box.

3 In the **Break types** area, verify that the **Page break** option is selected, and then click **OK**.

99 **To insert a section break**

1 Position the insertion point to the left of the text where you want to insert a section break.

2 On the **Insert** menu, click **Break** to open the **Break** dialog box, and select the **Next page** option in the **Section break types** area.

3 Click **OK**.

99 **To insert a header**

1 On the **View** menu, click **Header and Footer**.

2 Type the text you want to appear in the header.

3 On the **Header and Footer** toolbar, click **Switch Between Header and Footer**.

4 Type the text you want to appear in the footer.

5 On the **Header and Footer** toolbar, click the **Close Header and Footer** button.

104 **To insert and format page numbers**

1 On the **Insert** menu, click **Page Numbers**.

2 Specify the Position and Alignment settings.

3 Click the **Format** button.

4 Click the down arrow to the right of the **Number Format** box, and click the number format you want.

5 Select any other options you want to apply, and then click **OK**.

6 Click **OK**.

Chapter 5 Presenting Information in Tables and Columns

Page 108 **To insert a table**

1 Click where you want to position the table.

2 On the **Table** menu, point to **Insert**, and then click **Table**.

3 Enter the dimensions of the table in the **Number of columns** and **Number of rows** boxes, and click **OK**.

108 **To merge table cells**

1 Select the cells you want to merge.

2 On the **Table** menu, click **Merge Cells**.

108 **To convert text to a table**

1 Select the text you want to convert.

2 On the **Table** menu, point to **Convert**, and then click **Text to Table**.

3 Enter the dimensions of the table, and click **OK**.

108 **To sort a table**

1 Click anywhere in the table you want to sort.

2 On the **Table** menu, click **Sort**.

3 Click the down arrow to the right of the **Sort by** box, click the column by which you want to sort, select the option to sort in descending or ascending order, and click **OK**.

115 **To apply a Table AutoFormat**

1 Click anywhere in the table you want to format.

2 On the **Table** menu, click **Table AutoFormat**.

3 Scroll down the **Table styles** list, click the table style you want to apply, and then click **Apply**.

119 **To use a formula to total a column of values in a table**

1 Click the cell where you want the result of the formula to appear.

2 On the **Table** menu, click **Formula** to open the **Formula** dialog box.

3 Click **OK** to total the values.

119 **To insert a file created in another program into a document**

1 Click the location where you want to insert the file.

2 On the **Insert** menu, click **Object** to open the **Object** dialog box, and then click the **Create from File** tab.

3 Click **Browse**, navigate to the file you want to insert, and double-click it.

4 Click **OK**.

121 **To embed a new object in a document**

1 Click in the location where you want to insert the embedded object.

2 On the **Insert** menu, click **Object** to open the **Object** dialog box, and then click the **Create New** tab.

3 In the **Object type** list, click the type of object you want to embed.

4 Select the **Display as icon** check box if you want the embedded object to appear in the document as an icon.

5 Click **OK**.

6 Create the new object, and then click a blank area of the document to deselect it.

124 **To format text in multiple columns**

1 Click anywhere in the document to format all the text, or select the part of the document you want to format in columns.

2 On the **Format** menu, click **Columns**.

3 Choose the number and style of columns you want, and then click **OK**.

124 **To insert a column break**

1 Click the place in the text where you want to break the text.

2 On the **Insert** menu, click **Break** to open the **Break** dialog box, select the **Column break** option, and then click **OK**.

Chapter 6 Working with Graphics

To insert an organization chart

1 Click where you want the organization chart to appear.

2 On the Drawing toolbar, click the **Insert Diagram or Organization Chart** button.

3 Make sure **Organization Chart** is the selected diagram type, and click **OK**.

4 Fill in the organization chart's text boxes.

To insert a picture

1 Click where you want the picture to appear.

2 On the **Insert** menu, point to **Picture**, and then click **From File**.

3 Navigate to the folder where the picture's file is stored, and then double-click the file.

To size an object

1 Click the object.

2 Point to one of the handles surrounding the object, and drag until the object is the size you want.

To insert clip art

1 On the Drawing toolbar, click the **Insert Clip Art** button.

2 In the **Search for text** box in the **Clip Art** task pane, type a keyword that describes the type of picture you want, and click **Go**.

3 In the task pane, click the drawing that you want.

To move an object

1 Click the object to select it.

2 Point to the object, and when the pointer changes to the four-headed arrow, drag the object where you want.

To quickly copy an object

● Hold down Ctrl, click the object, and then drag it to the location where you want the copy to appear.

To modify the position and text wrapping attributes of a picture

1 Click the picture to select it.

2 On the **Format** menu, click **Picture**.

3 Click the **Layout** tab, and then click **Advanced**.

4 Select the options for the attributes you want to apply, and then click **OK** twice to close both dialog boxes.

4   Select the options you want to apply.

5   Click **OK** to close the **Fill Effects** dialog box, and then click **OK** to close the **Format Data Series** dialog box.

To toggle a chart's horizontal gridlines on and off

●   On Graph's Standard toolbar, click the **Value Axis Gridlines** button.

To change the position of the legend or format data labels in a chart

1   On Graph's Chart menu, click **Chart Options**.

2   Click the appropriate tab, and then select the options you want.

To toggle the legend on and off

●   On Graph's Standard toolbar, click the **Legend** button.

To show or hide a datasheet

●   On Graph's Standard toolbar, click the **View Datasheet** button.

To insert an Excel worksheet into a chart

1   Select cells into which you want to insert the worksheet.

2   On Graph's Standard toolbar, click the **Import File** button.

3   Navigate to the file, and double-click it.

4   Choose the data that you want to import.

5   Clear the **Overwrite existing cells** check box to prevent the incoming data from overwriting your existing chart data.

6   Click **OK**.

Chapter 8   **Collaborating with Others**

To turn on change tracking

1   On the **View** menu, point to **Toolbars,** and then click **Reviewing**.

2   On the Reviewing toolbar, click the **Track Changes** button.

To accept or reject a change

1   With the cursor positioned somewhere before the change, on the Reviewing toolbar, click the **Next** button to select the next change.

2   On the Reviewing toolbar, click either the **Accept Change** button or the **Reject Change/Delete Comment** button.

173 To insert a comment in a document

1 On the Reviewing toolbar, click the **Insert Comment** button.

2 Type your comment in the comment balloon or the Reviewing pane.

3 Click a blank area of the document.

173 To view comments and markup in Print Layout view

1 On the **View** menu, make sure **Markup** is active. (If it is, the icon to its left will have a square blue border and a tan background. If it's not active, click it.)

2 Scroll down to view the comment balloons, or click the **Next Comment** button on the Reviewing toolbar.

173 To review comments in a document

1 On the Reviewing toolbar, click the **Reviewing Pane** button to open that pane at the bottom of the Word window.

2 If necessary, adjust the height of the pane by pointing to its top border until the pointer becomes a two-headed arrow, and then dragging the border upward. You can also scroll down to see all the comments.

173 To close the Reviewing pane

● On the Reviewing toolbar, click the **Reviewing Pane** button.

173 To delete a comment in a document

● Right-click anywhere in the word that is marked with a comment, and then click **Delete Comment**.

173 To edit a comment in a document

● Right-click the word that is marked with a comment, and click **Edit Comment**.

173 To hide comments in Print Layout view

● On the Reviewing toolbar, click the down arrow to the right of the **Show** button, and then click **Comments** to hide them.

178 To protect a document by setting a password

1 On the **Tools** menu, click **Options**.

2 In the Options dialog box, click the **Security** tab to display security options.

3 In the **Password to modify** or **Password to open** box, type your password, and click **OK**.

4 In the **Confirm Password** dialog box, type the password again, and click **OK**.

5 Click the **Save** button to save the document.

178 **To remove password protection**

    1   On the **Tools** menu, click **Options**.

    2   On the **Security** tab of the **Options** dialog box, delete the contents of the **Password to open** or **Password to modify** box, and then click **OK**.

    3   On the Standard toolbar, click the **Save** button to save the document.

182 **To set editing and formatting restrictions for others**

    1   On the **Tools** menu, click **Protect Document**.

    2   In the **Protect Document** task pane's **Formatting restrictions** area, select the **Limit formatting to a selection of styles** check box, and then click **Settings**.

    3   In the **Formatting Restrictions** dialog box, scroll through the list of styles in the **Checked styles are currently allowed** box, click **Recommended Minimum**, and scroll through the list again.

    4   Modify the list, or click **OK** to implement the restricted set of styles.

    5   Click **Yes** when Word asks if you want to remove directly-applied formatting.

    6   In the **Editing restrictions** area of the task pane, select the **Allow only this type of editing in the document** check box.

    7   Click the down arrow to the right of the box below, and click **Tracked changes** in the drop-down list.

    8   Click the **Yes, Start Enforcing Protection** button, entering a password if you want to protect the document still further.

    9   Click **OK**, and then, with some text selected, click **Format** on the menu bar to check that most of the formatting commands are not available, indicating that the formatting restrictions are in effect.

184 **To attach a document to an e-mail message**

    1   On the **File** menu, point to **Send To**, and then click **Mail Recipient**.

    2   If the **Choose Profile** dialog box appears with information about your Internet or network profile, click **OK**.

    3   In the **To** box, type the recipient's e-mail address.

    4   Click the **Insert File** button, and if the right folder does not appear in the **Insert File** dialog box, navigate to the document's location.

    5   Click the document you want to attach, and then click **Insert**.

    6   On the message window's toolbar, click the **Send** button.

1 Click **Options** on the **Tools** menu, and click the **Security** tab.

2 Click **Digital Signatures**, and in the **Digital Signature** dialog box, click **Add**.

3 In the **Select Certificate** dialog box, click a certificate in the list, and click **OK**.

4 Click **OK** twice to close the **Digital Signature** and **Options** dialog boxes.

5 On the Standard toolbar, click the **Save** button to save the document.

1 Click **Options** on the Tools menu, and click the **Security** tab.

2 Click **Digital Signatures** to open the **Digital Signature** dialog box, where you can view a list of signers and see who issued their digital IDs.

3 Click **OK** twice to close the **Digital Signature** and **Options** dialog boxes.

1 With the document you want to compare to open, click **Compare and Merge Documents** on the **Tools** menu.

2 In the **Compare and Merge Documents** dialog box, navigate to the folder that has the document with which you want to make a comparison.

3 Click **Merge1**, click the down arrow to the right of the Merge button, and then click **Merge into current document**.

4 Check the changes from the **Merge1** document that have now been transferred to the current document. (Each reviewer's changes are a different color.)

1 On the **Tools** menu, click **Options**.

2 Click the **General** tab, if necessary, and then click **Web Options**.

3 Click the **Browsers** tab, if necessary, click the down arrow to the right of the **People who view this Web page will be using** box, and then click the appropriate browser.

4 In the **Options** list, verify that the **Disable features not supported by these browsers** check box is selected, and then click **OK** to close the **Web Options** dialog box.

5 Click **OK** to close the **Options** dialog box.

● On the **File** menu, click **Web Page Preview**.

194   **To save a document as a Web page**

1   On the **File** menu, click **Save as Web Page**.

2   Navigate to the folder where you want to save the document, and then type a name in the **File name** box.

3   Click the down arrow to the right of the **Save as type** box, and then click **Web page**.

4   Click **Save**.

194   **To add a frame**

1   On the **Format** menu, point to **Frames**, and then click **New Frames Page**.

2   On the Frames toolbar, click the frame you want to add.

194   **To size a frame**

●   Point to the border between the two frames, and when the pointer changes to a double-headed arrow, drag until the frame is the size you want.

194   **To modify text in a Web document or frame**

1   Select the text you want to modify.

2   Click the toolbar buttons and menu commands to format the text the way you want.

200   **To add a hyperlink**

1   Right-click the item into which you want to add a hyperlink, and then click **Hyperlink**.

2   In the **Insert Hyperlink** dialog box, make a selection from the **Link to** bar, click the file you want to link to, and then click **Target Frame**.

3   Set your target frame and click **OK** to close the **Insert Hyperlink** dialog box.

200   **To open a hyperlink**

●   Hold down the Ctrl key, and click the link.

200   **To edit a hyperlink**

1   Right-click the hyperlink, and then click **Edit Hyperlink**.

2   In the **Address** box, select the text and type the new address.

3   Click **OK** to close the **Edit Hyperlink** dialog box.

204   **To save a Word document as an XML document**

1   On the **File** menu, click **Save As**.

2   Click the down arrow to the right of the **Save as type** box, and click **XML Document**.

3   Click **Save**.

Chapter 10 Creating Forms

Page 214 To display the Forms toolbar

- On the **View** menu, point to **Toolbars**, and then click **Forms**.

214 To insert a text form field

1 Position the mouse pointer where you want to insert the field.

2 On the **Forms** toolbar, click the **Text Form Field** button.

214 To enter a date form field

1 Position the mouse pointer where you want to insert the field.

2 On the **Forms** toolbar, click the **Text Form Field** button and then the **Form Field Options** button.

3 In the **Text Form Field Options** dialog box, click the down arrow to the right of the **Type** box, and then click **Date**.

4 Click the down arrow to the right of the **Date format** box, click a date format, and then click **OK**.

214 To insert a check box form field

1 Position the mouse pointer where you want to insert the field.

2 On the **Forms** toolbar, click the **Check Box Form Field** button and then the **Form Field Options** button.

3 In the **Check box size** area, select a sizing option, click the up or down arrows to specify the size, if necessary, and then click **OK**.

214 To insert a drop-down form field

1 Position the mouse pointer where you want to insert the field.

2 On the **Forms** toolbar, click the **Drop-Down Form Field** button.

3 On the **Forms** toolbar, click the **Form Field Options** button to open the **Drop-Down Form Field Options** dialog box.

4 In the **Drop-down item** box, type an entry that will appear in the list, and then click **Add**.

5 Repeat step 4 until all entries have been created, and then click **OK**.

220 To rearrange entries in a drop-down form field

- In the **Drop-down item** box, select the item that you want to move, and click either the **Move Up** or **Move Down** arrow button.

To add a border to a form field

1 Click the shaded area text form field.

2 On the Formatting toolbar, click the down arrow to the right of the **Border** button, and click the border type you want.

To change the default value for a check box form field

1 Double-click the check box.

2 In the **Check Box Form Field Options** dialog box, in the **Default value** area, select an option for the check box's default value, and then click **OK**.

To remove an item from a drop down form field menu

1 Double-click the first drop-down form field.

2 In the **Drop-Down Form Field Options** dialog box, in the **Items in drop-down list** box, click the item you want to remove, click **Remove**, and then click **OK**.

To move and size a text form field

1 Click the text form field, and on the **Forms** toolbar, click the **Insert Frame** button.

2 Drag the text box field where you want it, and then drag a selection handle to size the form field.

To remove form shading

● On the **Forms** toolbar, click the **Form Field Shading** button.

To protect or unprotect a form

● On the **Forms** toolbar, click the **Protect Form** button.

To protect a form with a password

1 Click **Protect Document** on the **Tools** menu.

2 In the **Editing restrictions** area of the **Protect Document** task pane, select **Allow only this type of editing in the document**, click the down arrow to the right of the text box, and then click **Filling in forms**.

3 In the **Start enforcement** area, click **Yes, Start Enforcing Protection** to open the **Start enforcing protection** dialog box, then set the password and click **OK**.

Chapter 11 Creating Form Letters and Labels

To start the Mail Merge Wizard

● On the **Tools** menu, point to **Letters and Mailings**, and then click **Mail Merge**.

To insert a data list from an existing file

   1 On the **Tools** menu, point to **Letters and Mailings**, and then click **Mail Merge**.

   2 In the **Mail Merge** task pane, select an option in the **Select recipients** area, and then click **Next: Starting document** at the bottom of the pane.

   3 Select the **Use the current document** option, if necessary, and then click **Next: Select recipients** at the bottom of the pane.

   4 Select the **Use an existing list** option, if necessary, and then click **Browse** in the **Use an existing list** area.

   5 Navigate to the folder containing the data list, and double click the data list.

To add a record to a data list

   1 On the **Tools** menu, point to **Letters and Mailings**, and then click **Mail Merge**.

   2 In the **Mail Merge** task pane, select an option in the **Select recipients** area, and then click **Next: Starting document** at the bottom of the pane.

   3 Select the **Use the current document** option, if necessary, and then click **Next: Select recipients** at the bottom of the pane.

   4 Select the **Use an existing list** option, if necessary, and then click **Browse**.

   5 Navigate to the folder containing the data list, and double click the data list.

   6 In the **Mail Merge Recipients** dialog box, click any field, and then click **Edit** to open the **Data Form** dialog box.

   7 Click **Add New**, if necessary, to clear the data fields.

   8 Enter the information into the fields.

   9 Click **Close** to close the **Data Form** dialog box.

To sort data in a data file

   1 On the **Tools** menu, point to **Letters and Mailings**, and then click **Mail Merge**.

   2 In the **Mail Merge** task pane, click the **Next** link, if necessary, until Step 3 appears in the wizard.

   3 Click **Select a different list** in the **Use an existing list** area to open the **Select Data Source** dialog box.

   4 Navigate to the data file and double-click it.

   5 Click the down arrow for the field by which you want to sort, and then click **Advanced**.

   6 Click the **Sort Records** tab to display the sorting options.

7   Click the down arrow to the right of the **Sort by** box, and then click the field by which you want to sort.

8   Select the **Ascending** or **Descending** option, and then click **OK**.

229   **To filter records in a data file**

1   On the **Tools** menu, point to **Letters and Mailings**, and then click **Mail Merge**.

2   In the **Mail Merge** task pane, if necessary, click the **Next** link until Step 3 appears in the wizard.

3   Click **Select a different list** in the **Use an existing list** area to open the **Select Data Source** dialog box.

4   Navigate to the data file and double-click it.

5   Click the down arrow for the field by which you want to sort, and then click **Advanced**.

6   Click the down arrow to the right of the **Field** box, and then click the files by which you want to filter.

7   Click the down arrow to the right of the **Comparison** box, and then, if necessary, click **Equal to**.

8   In the **Compare to** box, type the text that the record must match.

9   Click **OK** twice to close both dialog boxes.

235   **To use Outlook data in a form letter**

1   On the **Tools** menu, point to **Letters and Mailings**, and then click **Mail Merge** to open the **Mail Merge** task pane.

2   In the **Mail Merge** task pane, select the **Letters** option, if necessary, and then click **Next: Starting document** at the bottom of the pane.

3   Select the **Use the current document** option, if necessary, and then click **Next: Select recipients** at the bottom of the pane.

4   Select the **Select from Outlook contacts** option, and then click **Next: Write your letter** at the bottom of the pane.

5   Click **OK**, if necessary, to select your Outlook profile.

6   Click a contact list, and then click **OK**.

7   Clear the check boxes in the left column to exclude contacts from the mail merge.

8   Click **OK** to close the **Mail Merge Recipients** dialog box.

9   In the **Mail Merge** task pane, click **Next: Write your letter** at the bottom of the pane.

236 **To insert a merge field into a form letter**

1   On the **Tools** menu, point to **Letters and Mailings**, and then click **Mail Merge**.

2   In the **Mail Merge** task pane, if necessary, click the **Next** link until Step 3 appears in the wizard.

3   Click **Select a different list** in the **Use an existing list** section to open the **Select Data Source** dialog box.

4   Navigate to the data file, and double-click it.

5   Click **OK** to close the **Mail Merge Recipients** dialog box.

6   In the **Mail Merge** task pane, click **Next: Write your letter** at the bottom of the pane.

7   On the Standard toolbar, if necessary, click the **Show/Hide** ¶ button to show formatting marks.

8   In the document window, click the location where you want to insert the merge field, and then in the **Mail Merge** task pane, click the kind of field you want to insert.

9   Click **OK** to accept the default settings.

239 **To merge a data list into a form letter**

1   On the **Tools** menu, point to **Letters and Mailings**, and then click **Mail Merge**.

2   In the **Mail Merge** task pane, if necessary, click the **Next** link until Step 3 appears in the wizard.

3   Click **Select a different list** in the **Use an existing list** area to open the **Select Data Source** dialog box.

4   Navigate to the data file, and double-click it.

5   Click **OK** to close the **Mail Merge Recipients** dialog box.

6   In the **Mail Merge** task pane, click the **Next** link until Step 5 appears in the wizard.

239 **To add a merge field into the body of a form letter**

1   In the document window, scroll down to the location where you want to insert the merge field, and click to place the insertion point.

2   In the **Mail Merge** task pane, click **More items** in the **Write your letter** section.

3   Select the **Database Fields** option, and then in the **Fields** box, click the name of the field you want to add.

4   Click **Insert**, and then click **Close**.

242 **To create labels from a data file**

1   On the Standard toolbar, click the **New Blank Document** button.

2 On the **Tools** menu, point to **Letters and Mailings**, and then click **Mail Merge** to open the **Mail Merge** task pane showing Step 1 in the wizard.

3 In the **Mail Merge** task pane, select the **Labels** option, and then click **Next: Starting document** to proceed to Step 2.

4 In the **Mail Merge** task pane, select the **Change document layout** option, if necessary, and then click **Label options** in the **Change document layout** area.

5 Scroll down the **Product number** list, click the format you want for the labels, and then click **OK**.

6 In the **Mail Merge** task pane, click **Next: Select recipients** to proceed to Step 3.

7 In the **Mail Merge** task pane, select the **Use an existing list** option, if necessary, and then click **Browse** to open the **Select Data Source** dialog box.

8 Navigate to the data file, and double-click it.

9 Make sure that all the recipient check boxes are selected in the first column, and then click **OK**.

10 In the **Mail Merge** task pane, click **Next: Arrange your labels** to proceed to Step 4.

11 Click **Address block**.

12 Click **OK**, and then in the **Mail Merge** task pane, click the **Update all labels** button in the **Replicate labels** area.

13 Click **Next: Preview your labels** to proceed to Step 5.

14 Click **Next: Complete the merge**.

242 **To print labels**

1 After creating the label document, in the **Mail Merge** task pane, click **Print**.

2 Click **OK** to open the Print dialog box.

3 Select a printer, if necessary, and then click **OK**.

Chapter 12 **Making Information in Longer Documents Accessible**

Page 250 **To create subdocuments in a master document**

1 In Outline view, select the heading and text you want to include in the subdocument.

2 On the Outlining toolbar, click the **Create Subdocument** button.

254 **To insert a bookmark**

1 Place the insertion point where you want to insert the bookmark.

2 On the **Insert** menu, click **Bookmark** to open the **Bookmark** dialog box.

3   In the **Bookmark name** box, type a name for the bookmark (do not use spaces).

4   Click **Add**.

254   **To insert a cross-reference**

1   Place the insertion point where you want to insert the cross-reference.

2   Type introductory text for the cross-reference, for example, For more information, see.

3   On the **Insert** menu, point to **Reference**, and click **Cross-reference**.

4   Click the down arrow to the right of the **Reference type** box, and click the type of reference you are creating.

5   Click the down arrow to the right of the **Insert reference to** box, and click the type of item you are referencing to, if necessary.

6   In the **For which** list, click the item you are referencing to.

7   Click **Insert**, and then click **Close**.

258   **To create a footnote or endnote**

1   Place the insertion point where you want to insert the footnote reference mark.

2   On the **Insert** menu, point to **Reference**, and then click **Footnote**.

3   In the **Location** area, select either the **Footnotes** or **Endnotes** option and then choose a location from the drop-down list.

4   In the **Format** area, click the down arrow to the right of the **Number format** box, select a number format, and click **Insert**.

5   Type the note text.

258   **To convert an endnote to a footnote**

1   Right-click anywhere in the endnote to open a shortcut menu.

2   Click **Convert to Footnote**.

259   **To create a table of contents**

1   Assuming that the document headings have already been styled as such, place the insertion point where you want the table of contents to appear, type Table of Contents, and then press the ⌷Enter key.

2   On the **Insert** menu, point to **Reference**, and then click **Index and Tables**.

3   Click the **Table of Contents** tab to display table of contents settings.

4   Click the down arrow to the right of the **Formats** box, and then click the format you want.

5   Click the down arrow to the right of the **Tab leader** box, click the tab leader you want, and then click **OK**.

To create a table of authorities

1 Assuming that citations have already been marked in the document, on the **Insert** menu, point to **Reference**, and then click **Index and Tables**.

2 Click the **Table of Authorities** tab.

3 In the **Category** list, click the category you want to include in your table of authorities, or click **All** to include all categories.

4 Select formatting options for the table, and then click **OK** to close the **Index and Tables** dialog box and insert the table of authorities.

To create a table of figures

1 Place the insertion point where you want to insert the table of figures.

2 On the **Insert** menu, point to **Reference**, and click **Index and Tables**.

3 Click the **Table of Figures** tab, click the down arrow to the right of the **Caption label** box, and click the type of caption you want to include in the table.

4 Click the down arrow to the right of the **Formats** box, and click the format you want for the table.

5 Select any other table options you want, and then click **OK** to close the **Index and Tables** dialog box and insert the table of figures.

To mark an index entry

1 Select the word you want to mark.

2 Press [Ctrl]+[Alt]+[X].

3 In the **Mark Index Entry** dialog box, select any options and formatting you want, and then click **Mark** or **Mark All**.

To insert an index

1 Place the insertion point where you want the index to appear.

2 On the **Insert** menu, point to **Reference**, and then click **Index and Tables**.

3 Click the **Index** tab to display index settings.

4 Click the down arrow to the right of the **Formats** box, click an index format, select any other options you want, and click **OK**.

Increasing Efficiency

To add a command to a menu

1 In the **Customize** dialog box, click the **Commands** tab, and then in the **Categories** list, click the name of the toolbar on which the command is located.

2 Scroll down in the **Commands** list, click the command you want to add, and then drag it to the menu without releasing the mouse button.

3   When the menu opens, drag to position the insertion bar to the location on the menu where you want to place the command, and then release the mouse button to lock this position.

4   Click the menu to close it.

5   In the **Customize** dialog box, click **Close**.

281   **To create a new menu on the menu bar and then change its name**

1   In the **Customize** dialog box, click the **Commands** tab, scroll down to the end of the **Categories** list, and then click **New Menu**.

2   Drag **New Menu** from the **Commands** list to the menu bar.

3   On the menu bar, right-click **New Menu**.

4   In the **Name** box on the shortcut menu, select the text *New Menu*, and then type a name for the menu.

5   Press the Enter key to change the menu name and close the menu.

281   **To add a command to a custom menu**

1   Open the Customize dialog box.

2   In the **Categories** list of the Customize dialog box, click the name of the toolbar that contains the command you want to add.

3   In the **Commands** list, drag the command you want to add onto the empty menu.

286   **To display Standard and Formatting toolbars on two rows**

1   On the right edge of the Standard toolbar, click the **Toolbar Options** button.

2   Click **Show Buttons on Two Rows**.

286   **To add or remove buttons on a toolbar**

1   On the toolbar, click the **Toolbar Options** button.

2   Point to **Add or Remove Buttons**, and then point to the name of the toolbar you want to change.

3   Clear the check boxes for the buttons you want to remove and select the check boxes for the buttons you want to add.

286   **To restore a toolbar to its default settings**

●   On the Standard toolbar, click the **Toolbar Options** button, point to **Add or Remove Buttons**, point to the name of the toolbar you want to restore, and then click **Reset Toolbar**.

286   **To create a custom toolbar**

1   Right-click any toolbar, and then click **Customize** to open the **Customize** dialog box.

2   Click the **Toolbars** tab, and then click **New** to open the **New Toolbar** dialog box.

3 In the **Toolbar name** box, type a name for the new toolbar.

4 Click the down arrow to the right of the **Make toolbar available to** box, click the name of the current document to make the new toolbar available only to this document, and then click **OK**.

286 **To add a button to a custom toolbar**

1 In the **Customize** dialog box, click the **Commands** tab.

2 In the **Categories** list of the **Customize** dialog box, click the name of the toolbar that contains the command you want to add.

3 In the **Commands** list, drag the button you want to add to the blank toolbar.

292 **To change the default location where templates are stored**

1 On the **Tools** menu, click **Options**.

2 Click the **File Locations** tab.

3 In the **File types** list, click **User templates**, and then click **Modify**.

4 Navigate to where you want to store templates, and then click **OK**.

5 Click **OK** to close the **Options** dialog box.

294 **To create a macro**

1 On the **Tools** menu, point to **Macro**, and then click **Record New Macro** to open the **Record Macro** dialog box.

2 In the **Macro name** box, type a name for the macro.

3 Click the down arrow to the right of the **Store macro in** box, and then click the name of the document or template where you want the macro to be stored.

4 In the document, perform the steps that you want recorded in the macro.

5 On the **Macro** toolbar, click the **Stop Recording** button.

294 **To run a macro**

1 Place the insertion point where you want the result of the macro to appear.

2 On the **Tools** menu, point to **Macro**, and then click **Macros**.

3 In the list of macros, click the name of the macro you want to run, and then click **Run**.

298 **To edit an existing macro**

1 On the **Tools** menu, point to **Macro**, and then click **Macros** to open the **Macros** dialog box.

2 In the list of macros, click the name of the macro you want, and then click **Edit**.

3 Make the changes to the macro in the code window.

4 On the **File** menu, click **Close and Return to Microsoft Word**.

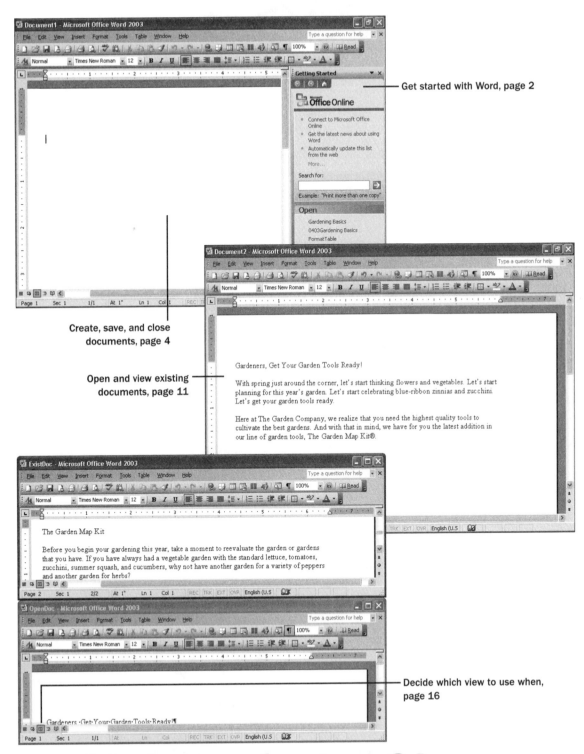

Get started with Word, page 2

Create, save, and close documents, page 4

Open and view existing documents, page 11

Decide which view to use when, page 16

Chapter 1 at a Glance

1 Working with Documents

In this chapter you will learn to:

✔ Get started with Word.

✔ Create, save, and close documents.

✔ Open and view existing documents.

✔ Decide which view to use when.

When you use a computer program to create, edit, and produce text documents, you are *word processing*. Word-processing programs help you create professional-quality documents because you can type and format text, correct errors, and preview your work before you print or distribute a document.

Microsoft Office Word 2003 is one of the most sophisticated word-processing programs available today. You can use Word to compose and update a wide range of business and personal documents. In addition, Word includes many *desktop publishing* features that you can use to enhance the appearance of documents so that they are appealing and easy to read. Whether you need to create a letter, memo, fax, annual report, or newsletter, Word has the power and flexibility to produce professional documents quickly and easily.

In this chapter, you'll start by entering text to create a document, and then you'll save the document as a *file*. While saving the document, you'll create a *folder* in which to store it. You'll also open other documents so that you can see how to move around in them and switch between them. Finally, you'll explore the different ways you can view documents in Word.

See Also   Do you need only a quick refresher on the topics in this chapter? See the Quick Reference entries on pages xxxi–xxxii.

 On the CD   Before you can use the practice files in this chapter, you need to install them from the book's companion CD to their default location. See "Using the Book's CD-ROM" on page xiii for more information.

Getting Started with Word

When you first start Word, the Word *program window* opens. This window includes many of the menus, tools, and other features found in every Microsoft Office System program window, as well as some that are unique to Office 2003 and some that are unique to Word.

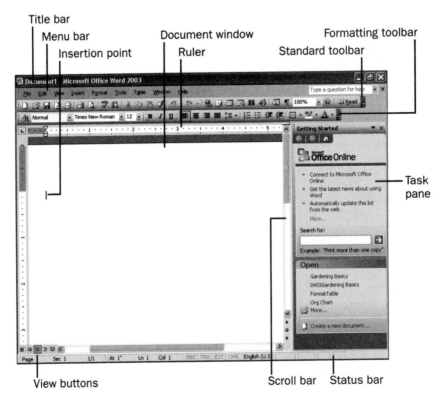

Tip What you see on your screen might not match the graphics in this book exactly. The screens in this book were captured on a monitor set to 800 x 600 resolution with 24-bit color and the Windows XP Standard color scheme. By default, the Standard and Formatting toolbars share one row, which prevents you from seeing all their buttons. To make it easier for you to find buttons, the Standard and Formatting toolbars in the graphics in this book appear on two rows. If you want to change your setting to match the screens in this book, click Customize on the Tools menu. On the Options tab, select the "Show Standard and Formatting toolbars on two rows" check box, and then click Close.

You enter and edit text in the *document window*, which is part of the Word program window. The *insertion point*, the blinking vertical line that appears in the document window, indicates where the text will appear when you begin to type.

Word organizes commands for common tasks in the *task pane*, a small window next to your document that opens when you are most likely to need it. For example, when you start Word, you see the Getting Started task pane, which includes commands for opening and creating documents. You can use the Getting Started task pane to open a saved or blank document, to create a document based on an existing one, or to create a document from a *template*, a file containing structure and style settings that help you create a specific type of document, such as a memo or résumé. You can show or hide a task pane whenever you like by clicking Task Pane on the View menu. Clicking the command hides the task pane if it is currently displayed or shows it if it is currently hidden. (This type of on/off command is called a *toggle*.) If you want to use a task pane other than the one that is currently displayed, you can select the one you want from the Other Task Panes menu on the task pane's title bar. If you no longer need the task pane, you can hide it. The document window then expands to fill the width of the program window.

Tip The Getting Started task pane opens each time you start Word. If you do not want the task pane to appear when you start Word, click Options on the Tools menu, click the View tab, clear the Startup Task Pane check box, and click OK.

In this exercise, you will start Word and then explore and close the task pane.

BE SURE TO start your computer, but don't start Word before beginning this exercise.

1 On the taskbar, click **Start**, point to **All Programs,** point to **Microsoft Office,** and then click **Microsoft Office Word 2003.**

The Word program window opens with a blank document in the document window and the Getting Started task pane displayed.

Tip You can also start Word by creating a shortcut icon on the Windows desktop. Simply double-click a shortcut icon to start its associated program. To create a shortcut, click the Start button, point to All Programs, point to Microsoft Office, right-click Microsoft Office Word 2003, point to Send To, and then click "Desktop (create shortcut)."

2 At the right end of the title bar of the **Getting Started** task pane, click the **Other Task Panes** down arrow.

The Other Task Panes menu opens.

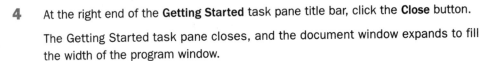

3 Press the [Esc] key, or click an empty place in the document.

Word closes the Other Task Panes menu.

Close

4 At the right end of the **Getting Started** task pane title bar, click the **Close** button.

The Getting Started task pane closes, and the document window expands to fill the width of the program window.

5 On the **View** menu, click **Task Pane** to open the task pane again.

Troubleshooting If you don't see the Task Pane command on the View menu, it is hidden. Word personalizes your menus and toolbars to reduce the number of menu commands and toolbar buttons you see on the screen. When you click a menu name on the View menu, a short menu appears, containing only the commands you use most often. To make the complete menu appear, you can leave the pointer over the menu name for a second or two (called *hovering*), double-click the menu name, or point to the chevrons (the double arrows) at the bottom of the short menu.

Creating, Saving, and Closing Documents

Microsoft Office Specialist

Creating a Word document is as simple as typing text. The insertion point indicates where the text will appear in the document. When the text you're typing goes beyond the right margin, Word "wraps" the text to the next line. Because of this *word wrap* feature, which is common in word-processing and desktop-publishing programs, you press [Enter] only to start a new paragraph, not a new line.

The text you type appears in the document window and is stored by the computer, but only temporarily. If you want to keep a copy of the text, you must save the document as a file. Specifying a name and location for the file ensures that you can retrieve the file later.

To save a new document in Word, you click the Save button on the Standard toolbar or click the Save As command on the File menu. Either action displays the Save As dialog box, where you can name the file and indicate where you want to save it.

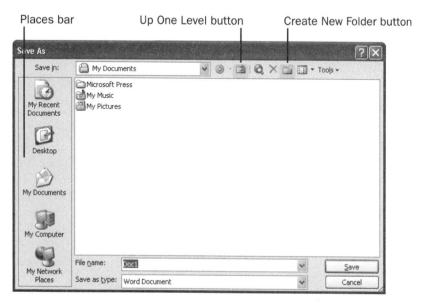

To help you locate the disk and folder where you want to store a new file, you can click the Up One Level button to move up one folder level, or you can use the Places bar on the left side of the dialog box to move to another location on your computer. The Places bar provides quick access to locations commonly used for storing files. For example, to save a file on a floppy disk, you click the My Computer icon on the Places bar, and then double-click 3½ Floppy (A:).

To keep your documents organized and easily accessible, you can store related documents in a folder. You can create folders ahead of time in Windows, or you can create them in Word by clicking the Create New Folder button in the Save As dialog box.

After you save a document once using the Save As dialog box, you can save subsequent changes by clicking the Save button on the Standard toolbar. Each time you do, the new version overwrites the previous version. To keep the new version without overwriting the original, you click the Save As command on the File menu and save the new version either in the same folder with a different name or in a different folder. You cannot store two documents with the same name in the same folder.

Tip You can tell Word to periodically save a document you are working on in case the program stops responding or you lose power. Word saves the changes in a recovery file according to the time interval specified in the AutoRecover option. To turn on the AutoRecover option and specify a time interval for automatic saving, click Options on the Tools menu, click the Save tab, select the "Save AutoRecover info every" check box, specify the period of time, and then click OK. If your power fails or if Word stops responding while you have documents open, the next time you start Word, the Document Recovery task pane appears with a list of recovered documents. From there you can open a document, view any repairs, and compare recovered versions.

In this exercise, you'll enter text in a new document, add a symbol, save your new document, and then close it.

New Blank
Document

1 On the Standard toolbar, click the **New Blank Document** button.

A new document window opens.

Toolbar Options

Troubleshooting If a button mentioned in this book doesn't appear on the specified toolbar on your screen, it is probably hidden. You can display the rest of that toolbar's buttons by clicking the Toolbar Options button at the right end of the toolbar, pointing to Add or Remove Buttons, then pointing to the toolbar's name and clicking the button you want. You can also double-click the move handle (the four vertical dots) at the left end of a toolbar to quickly expand it.

2 With the insertion point at the beginning of the new document, type Gardeners, Get Your Garden Tools Ready!, and then press Enter .

The text appears in the new document.

3 Press Enter again to insert a blank line below the heading.

4 Type With spring just around the corner, let's start thinking flowers and vegetables. Let's start planning for this year's garden. Let's start celebrating blue-ribbon zinnias and zucchini. Let's get your garden tools ready.

Notice that you did not need to press Enter when the insertion point reached the right margin because the text wrapped to the next line.

Important   If a colored wavy line appears under a word or phrase, Word is flagging a possible error: red indicates spelling, green indicates grammar, and blue indicates inconsistent formatting. A dotted purple line indicates a Smart Tag, which recognizes certain types of text as data that you can use with other programs. For example, Word tags a person's name as data that you can add to an electronic address book. For now, ignore any errors.

5   Press Enter two times to insert a blank line between paragraphs, and then type **Here at The Garden Company, we realize that you need the highest quality tools to cultivate the best gardens. And with that in mind, we have for you the latest addition in our line of garden tools, The Garden Map Kit.**

6   Press the ← key to move the insertion point one character to the left, between the letter *t* and the period.

7   On the **Insert** menu, click **Symbol**.

Word displays the Symbol dialog box.

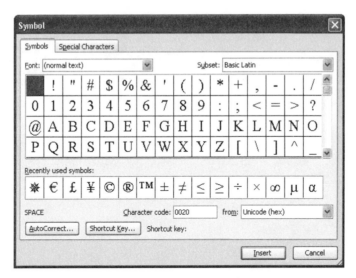

8 In the **Recently used symbols** area of the **Symbols** tab, click ® (the registered sign); or scroll through the list of symbols until you find this sign, and then click it.

9 Click the **Insert** button, and then click the **Close** button.

Word places the registered sign before the period in your document.

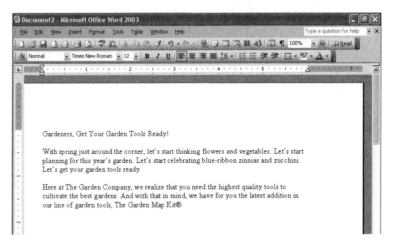

Tip You can insert some common symbols either by using the Symbol dialog box or by typing characters that Word recognizes as representing the symbol. For example, if you type two consecutive dashes followed by a word and a space, Word changes the two dashes to a professional-looking em-dash—like this one. (This symbol gets its name from the fact that it was originally the width of the character *m*.)

Save

10 On the Standard toolbar, click the **Save** button.

The Save As dialog box appears, displaying the contents of the My Documents folder.

11 In the list of the folder and file names stored in your *My Documents* folder, double-click the *Microsoft Press* folder, double-click the *Word 2003 SBS* folder, and then double-click the *WorkingDoc* folder.

The contents of the folder for this chapter appear in the Save As dialog box.

12 Click the New Folder icon on the toolbar. Names this new folder "CreatingDoc" and press Enter. Double-click the *CreatingDoc* folder.

You can see that the CreatingDoc folder is currently empty. Word has entered the word *Gardeners*, the first word in the document, in the "File name" box as a suggested name for this file.

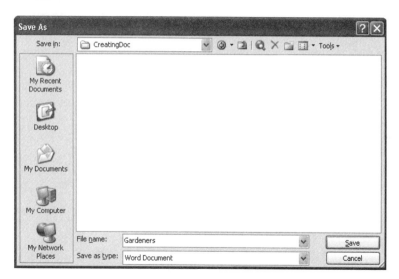

Tip Word uses the first few characters (or words) in the document to suggest a file name. You can accept this suggested name or type a new one. Depending on your Windows setup, file names might appear with an *extension*, which is a period followed by a three-letter program identifier. For Word, the extension is *.doc*. You don't have to type the extension after the file name in the Save As dialog box.

Create New
Folder

13 On the toolbar to the right of the **Save in** box, click the **Create New Folder** button.

The New Folder dialog box appears so that you can create a new folder within the CreatingDoc folder.

14   Type NewFolder, and click **OK**.

NewFolder becomes the current folder.

15   In the **File name** box, double-click *Gardeners*, type FirstSave, and click the **Save** button.

The Save As dialog box closes, and the name of the document, FirstSave, appears in the program window's title bar.

Close Window

16   At the right end of the menu bar (not the title bar), click the **Close Window** button.

The FirstSave document closes.

Saving a File for Use in Another Program

Microsoft Office Specialist

You can save a document in a *file format* other than the Word document format. A file format is the way that a program stores a file so that the program can open the file later. Saving a document in another format is important if you share documents with people who use previous versions of Word (such as Word 6.0/95) or other programs that have a different file format (such as WordPerfect). For example, if you use Word 6.0 on your home computer, you can create a document in Word 2003 at the office, save it in the Word 6.0 format, and then open and edit the document on your home computer.

If you want to save a Word document in a format that can be opened by the widest variety of programs, you can use one of the following formats:

- Rich Text Format (*.rtf). Save the document in this format if you want its formatting to be preserved.

- Text Only (*.txt). Save the document in this format if you want only the text of the document to be preserved.

If you are not sure of the format of a document, you can use the Properties dialog box to display the document's format information, including the version, type, and creator of the file. On the File menu, click Properties, and then click the General tab to display the document format information.

To save a document in another file format:

1   On the **File** menu, click **Save As**.

The Save As dialog box appears.

2   In the **File name** box, type a new name for the document.

3   Click the down arrow to the right of the **Save as type** box, and click the file format you want to use.

4   Click **Save**.

Opening and Viewing Existing Documents

Microsoft Office Specialist

After you save a document as a file, you can open the document again at any time. To open an existing document, you can use the Getting Started task pane. To create a new document based on an existing one, you can use the New Document task pane. This is useful when you want to take existing text and use it in a new document without changing the original document.

You can also open a document by clicking the Open button on the Standard toolbar.

When you open a document, a program button with the Word program icon and the document's name appears on the taskbar. You can have many documents open at the same time, but only one is the current or active document. The program button of the active document is darker than the others. To move between open documents, click the program buttons on the taskbar, or use the Window menu, which lists all open documents and indicates the active document with a check mark to the left of its name.

You can use the vertical and horizontal scroll bars to move around the active document. Using the scroll bars does not move the insertion point—it changes only your view of the document in the window. For example, if you drag the vertical scroll box down to the bottom of the scroll bar, the end of the document comes into view, but the insertion point does not move. Here are some other ways to use the scroll bars:

- Click the up or down scroll arrow on the vertical scroll bar to move the document window up or down one line of text.

- Click above or below the scroll box to move up or down one windowful.

- Click the left or right scroll arrow on the horizontal scroll bar to move the document window to the left or right several characters at a time.

- Click to the left or right of the scroll box to move left or right one windowful.

You can also move around a document by moving the insertion point. You can click to place the insertion point at a particular location, or you can press a key or a *key combination* on the keyboard to move the insertion point. For example, pressing the End key moves the insertion point to the right end of a line of text, whereas pressing the Ctrl and End keys at the same time moves the insertion point to the end of the document. To use a key combination, you hold down the first key (for example, Ctrl) and then press the second key (for example, End). After the action takes place, you release both keys.

Tip The program window's status bar shows the location of the insertion point (by page, section, inch, line, and column).

The following table shows the keys and key combinations you can use to move the insertion point quickly.

Pressing this key	Moves the insertion point
←	Left one character at a time
→	Right one character at a time
↓	Down one line at a time
↑	Up one line at a time
Ctrl + ←	Left one word at a time
Ctrl + →	Right one word at a time
Home	To the beginning of the current line
End	To the end of the current line
Ctrl + Home	To the start of the document
Ctrl + End	To the end of the document
Ctrl + Page Up	To the beginning of the previous page
Ctrl + Page Down	To the beginning of the next page
Page Down	Up one screen
Page Up	Down one screen

If you create longer documents, you can use the Select Browse Object palette at the bottom of the vertical scroll bar to move quickly through a document. When you click the Select Browse Object button, a palette appears with browsing options, such as Browse by Page, Browse by Comment, and Browse by Graphic.

In this exercise, you will move around a document, switch between open documents, view nonprinting characters and text, and view documents in more than one window at the same time.

USE the *ExistDoc* and *OpenDoc* documents in the practice file folder for this topic. These practice files are located in the *My Documents\Microsoft Press\Word 2003 SBS\WorkingDoc\OpeningDoc* folder and can also be accessed by clicking *Start/All Programs/Microsoft Press/Word 2003 Step by Step*.

Open

1   On the Standard toolbar, click the **Open** button.

The Open dialog box appears, showing the contents of the folder you used for your last open or save action.

2   On the Places bar, click the **My Documents** icon to display the contents of that folder.

3   Double-click the *Microsoft Press* folder, double-click the *Word 2003 SBS* folder, double-click the *WorkingDoc* folder, and then double-click the *OpeningDoc* folder.

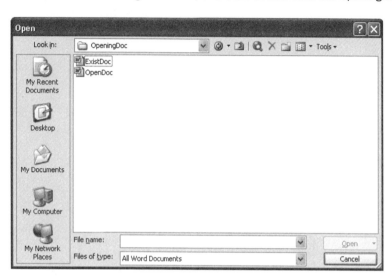

4   Click the *ExistDoc* file, and then click the **Open** button.

The ExistDoc document opens in the Word program window.

Troubleshooting   If you work on a network, documents might be stored in a common location so that more than one person can access them. If you try to open a document that is already open on another person's computer, Word gives you three options. You can open a Read Only copy that allows you to view the document but not save any changes in the same file, you can create and edit a copy of the document on your computer and merge your changes later, or you can ask to receive notification when the original copy becomes available.

5   In the greeting, click after the colon (:) to position the insertion point.

6   Press the ⎡Home⎤ key to move the insertion point to the beginning of the line.

7   Press the ⎡→⎤ key five times to move the insertion point to the beginning of the word *Garden* in the greeting.

8   Press the ⎡End⎤ key to move the insertion point to the end of the line.

9   Press ⎡Ctrl⎤+⎡End⎤ to move the insertion point to the end of the document.

10   Press ⎡Ctrl⎤+⎡Home⎤ to move the insertion point to the beginning of the document.

11 Drag the vertical scroll box to the bottom of the vertical scroll bar.

The end of the document comes into view. Note that the location of the insertion point has not changed—just the view of the document.

12 Click above the vertical scroll box to change the view of the document by one screen.

13 In the horizontal scroll bar, click the right scroll arrow twice so that the left side of the document scrolls out of view.

14 Drag the horizontal scroll box all the way to the left.

Select Browse Object

15 At the bottom of the vertical scroll bar, click the **Select Browse Object** button.

A palette of objects appears.

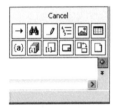

16 Move the pointer over the palette of objects.

The name of each object appears at the top of the palette as you point to it.

Browse by Page

17 Click the **Browse by Page** button.

The insertion point moves from the beginning of page 1 to the beginning of page 2.

18 On the Standard toolbar, click the **Open** button, and when the **Open** dialog box appears, double-click the *OpenDoc* file.

Troubleshooting If a document becomes corrupted and won't open, you can try to repair it. On the Standard toolbar, click the Open button, and click (don't double-click) the file you want to open. Then click the down arrow to the right of the Open button, and click Open and Repair on the menu of options.

The OpenDoc document opens in its own document window. If your taskbar is visible, it shows two program buttons, each with the name of an open document. The darker button indicates the active document, which is currently the OpenDoc document.

Tip If you have hidden your Windows taskbar to reduce screen clutter, you can display it at any time by pointing to the bottom of your screen. If you work with several open programs, you can reduce crowding on the taskbar by setting Word to show only one program button. On the Tools menu, click Options, and in the Show area of the View tab, clear the Windows in Taskbar check box, and click OK. You can then use the Window menu to switch between open documents.

Show/Hide ¶

19 On the Standard toolbar, click the **Show/Hide ¶** button.

The document changes to reveal formatting and hidden text.

Paragraph mark

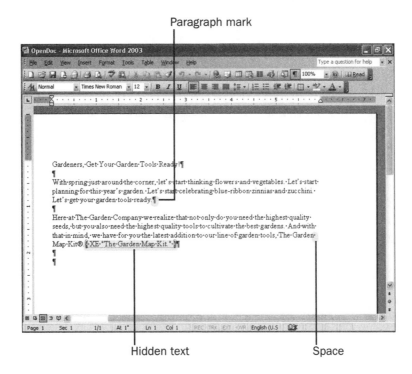

Hidden text   Space

Tip   When the Show/Hide ¶ button is turned off, Word hides text like the index code shown in the graphic on this page. You can hide any text by selecting it, clicking Font on the Format menu, selecting the Hidden check box, and clicking OK. When hidden text is visible, it is identified in the document by a dotted underline, as shown in the graphic above.

20 On the taskbar, click the **ExistDoc** program button to make its document active.

If your taskbar is hidden, first point to the bottom of the screen to display it.

21 On the menu bar, click **Window**.

The two open files are listed at the bottom of the Window menu.

22 On the **Window** menu, click **Arrange All**.

The two document windows are sized and stacked one on top of the other. Each window has a menu bar, toolbar, and scroll bars, so you can work on each document independently.

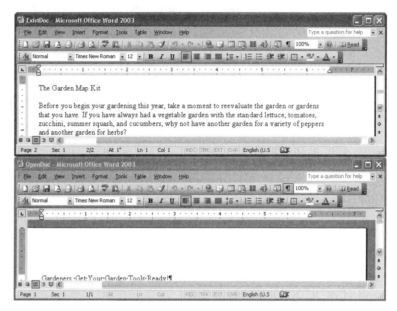

Maximize

23 At the right end of the ExistDoc window's title bar, click the **Maximize** button.

The document window expands to fill the program window.

24 On the **Window** menu, click **OpenDoc**, and then maximize its window.

CLOSE the *ExistDoc* and *OpenDoc* documents.

Close

Troubleshooting If you click the Close button at the end of the title bar instead of clicking the Close Window button at the end of the menu bar, you will close any open Word documents and quit the Word program. To continue working, start Word again.

Deciding Which View to Use When

Microsoft Office Specialist

In Word, you can view a document in a variety of ways:

■ *Print Layout view* displays a document on the screen the way it will look when printed. You can see elements such as margins, page breaks, headers and footers, and watermarks.

■ *Normal view* displays the content of a document with a simplified layout so that you can type and edit quickly. Page breaks are indicated only as dotted lines, and you cannot see layout elements such as headers and footers.

■ *Web Layout view* displays a document on the screen the way it will look when viewed in a Web browser. You can see backgrounds, AutoShapes, and other effects. You can also see how text wraps to fit the window and how graphics are positioned.

See Also   For information about Web documents, see "Creating and Modifying a Web Document" in Chapter 9.

■ *Outline view* displays the structure of a document as nested levels of headings and body text, and provides tools for viewing and changing its hierarchy.

See Also   For information about outlining, see "Using an Outline to Rearrange Paragraphs" in Chapter 2.

New in Office 2003

Reading Layout view and thumbnails

■ *Reading Layout view* (which is new in Word 2003) as much of the content of the document as will fit in the screen at a size that is comfortable for viewing. In this view, you have access to the Reading Layout and Reviewing toolbars, which you can use to adjust the view, display page thumbnails, search the document, and suggest changes.

See Also   For information about the Reviewing toolbar, see "Tracking and Managing Document Changes" in Chapter 8.

■ *Document Map* displays a list of your document's headings in a separate pane so that you can see the structure of the document while viewing and editing its text.

In this exercise, you explore Word's views so that you have an idea of which one is most appropriate for which task. After opening a document you switch between views, noticing the differences. You also zoom in and out, open up the Document Map, and work with thumbnails.

USE the *ViewDoc* document in the practice file folder for this topic. This practice file is located in the *My Documents\Microsoft Press\Word 2003 SBS\WorkingDoc\DecidingView* folder and can also be accessed by clicking *Start/All Programs/Microsoft Press/Word 2003 Step by Step*.
OPEN the *ViewDoc* document.

Normal View

1   If the Normal View button in the lower-left corner of the window is not already active, click the **Normal View** button, or on the **View** menu, click **Normal**.

2   Scroll through the document.

You can see the basic content of the document without any extraneous elements. The active area on the ruler indicates the width of the text column, dotted lines indicate page breaks, and scrolling is quick and easy.

The ruler indicates the width of the text column.

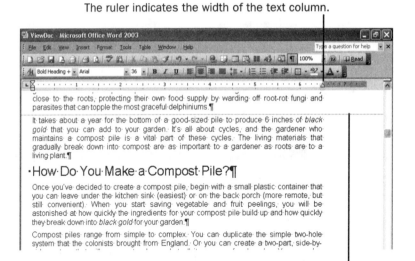

Page break

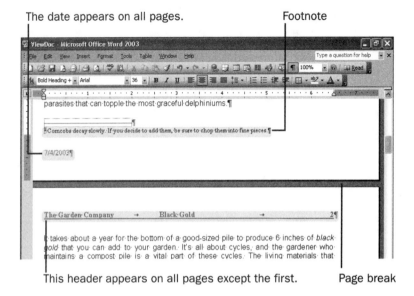

Web Layout
View

3 Press Ctrl+Home, and click the **Web Layout View** button in the lower-left corner of the window, or on the **View** menu, click **Web Layout**.

4 Scroll through the document.

In a Web browser, the text column fills the window and has no page breaks.

Print Layout
View

5 Press Ctrl+Home, and click the **Print Layout View** button in the lower-left corner of the window, or on the **View** menu, click **Print Layout**.

6 Scroll through the document.

The date appears on all pages.   Footnote

This header appears on all pages except the first.   Page break

As you can see, when printed the document will have footnotes, the date will be printed at the bottom of each page, and a header will appear on all pages except the first.

7 On the **Tools** menu, click **Options**. Then on the **View** tab, clear the **White space between pages** check box, and click **OK**.

The white space at the top and bottom of each page and the gray space between pages is hidden.

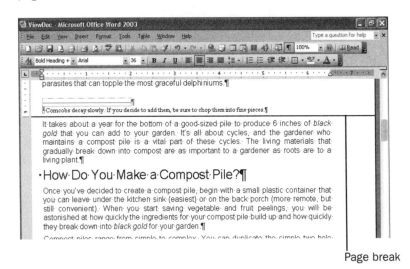

Page break

8 Restore the white space by clicking **Options** on the **Tools** menu, selecting the **White space between pages** check box, and clicking **OK**.

Tip You can also show or hide the white space by pointing between the pages until the Show White Space pointer or Hide White Space pointer appears, and then clicking.

Outline View

9 Press Ctrl+Home, and click the **Outline View** button in the lower-left corner of the window, or on the **View** menu, click **Outline**.

The screen changes to show the document's hierarchical structure, and the Outlining toolbar appears.

10 On the Outlining toolbar, click the down arrow to the right of the **Show All Levels** box, and click **Show Level 2**.

The document collapses to display only the Level 1 and Level 2 headings.

Outlining toolbar

11 In the lower-left corner of the window, click the **Reading Layout** button, or on the **View** menu, click **Reading Layout**. (You can also click the **Read** button on the Standard toolbar.)

The screen changes to display the document in Reading Layout view, and the Reading Layout and Reviewing toolbars appear.

Reading Layout toolbar   Reviewing toolbar

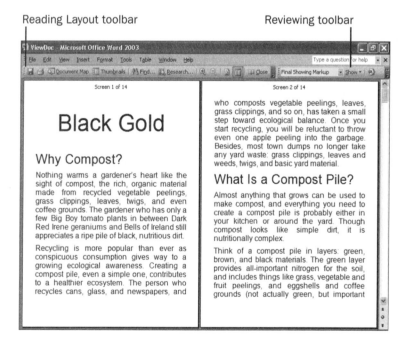

Allow
Multiple Pages

Troubleshooting If your screen doesn't look like ours, click all active buttons on the Reading Layout toolbar to toggle them off, and then click the Allow Multiple Pages button.

12 On the Reading Layout toolbar, click the **Allow Multiple Pages** button to toggle it off, and then click the **Thumbnails** button.

A pane opens on the left side of the screen showing each page of the document as a *thumbnail* image. You can use these thumbnails to quickly move around the document.

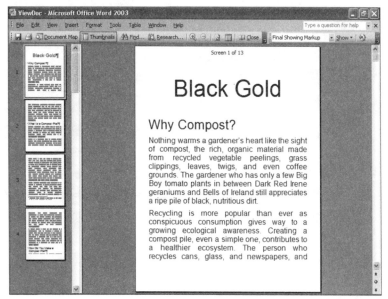

13 In the left pane, click the scroll bar below the scroll box, and then click thumbnail **8**.

The eighth page appears on the screen.

Actual Page

14 On the Reading Layout toolbar, click the **Actual Page** button.

The screen changes to show the same section of text as it will look when printed. The thumbnails still appear in the left pane, but they have changed to reflect the number of pages in the document in Print Layout view.

15 On the Reading Layout toolbar, click the **Document Map** button.

In the pane on the left side of the screen, an outline of the headings in the document replaces the thumbnails, and the first heading on the active page is highlighted.

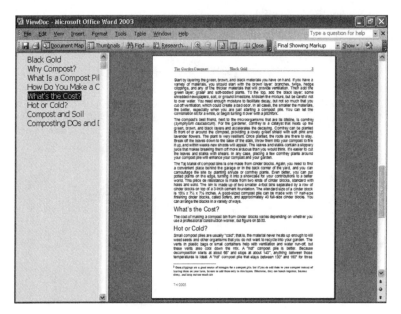

16 In the Document Map, click the *Black Gold* heading.

The page containing that heading is now displayed.

17 On the Reading Mode toolbar, click the **Document Map** button again to toggle it off, and then click the **Close** button.

18 In the lower-left corner of the window, click the **Print Layout View** button.

Zoom

19 On the Standard toolbar, click the down arrow to the right of the **Zoom** box, and click **50%**.

The screen changes to display the text of the document at half its size.

20 Click the **Zoom** box, type 40, and press Enter .

The first two pages of the document are now displayed.

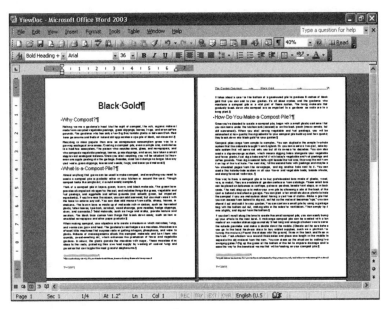

Next Page

21 On the right side of the window, click the **Next Page** button until the third and fourth pages of the document are displayed.

22 In the lower-left corner of the window, click the **Normal View** button.

Note that Normal view is still displayed at 100%. You can change the magnification in each view independently.

23 On the **View** menu, click **Print Layout**, and then return the **Zoom** setting to **100%**.

CLOSE the *ViewDoc* document, and if you are not continuing on to the next chapter, quit Word.

Key Points

- ■ You can open more than one Word document, and you can view more than one document at a time, but only one document can be active at a time.

- ■ You create Word documents by entering text and symbols at the insertion point, and you can move the insertion point to any location by clicking the document or by pressing keys and key combinations.

- ■ When you save a Word document, you can specify its name, location, and file format in the Save As dialog box.

- ■ You can view a document in a variety of ways, depending on your needs as you create the document and on the purpose for which you are creating it.

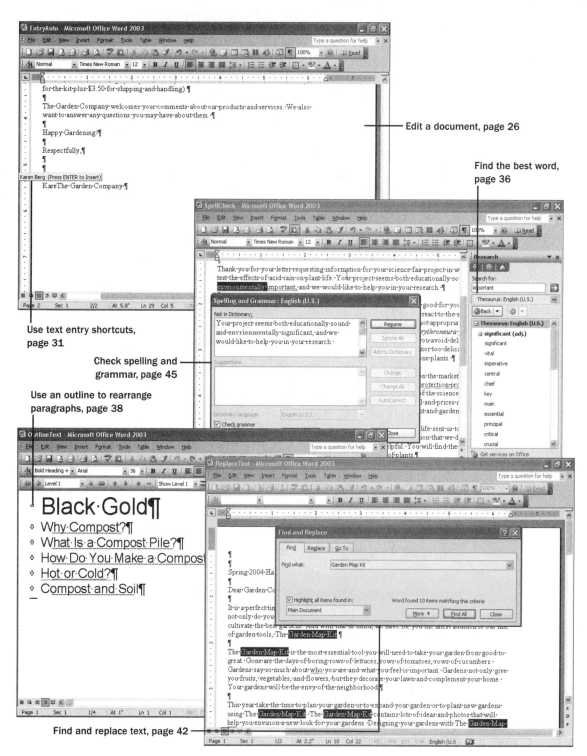

Edit a document, page 26

Find the best word, page 36

Use text entry shortcuts, page 31

Check spelling and grammar, page 45

Use an outline to rearrange paragraphs, page 38

Find and replace text, page 42

Chapter 2 at a Glance

2 Editing and Proofreading Documents

In this chapter you will learn to:

✔ Edit a document.

✔ Use text entry shortcuts.

✔ Find the best word.

✔ Use an outline to rearrange paragraphs.

✔ Find and replace text.

✔ Check spelling and grammar.

Unless the documents you create are intended for no one's eyes but your own, you need to be able to ensure that they are correct, logical, and persuasive. Whether you are a novice or an experienced writer, Microsoft Office Word 2003 has several tools that make creating professional documents easy and efficient:

■ Editing tools provide quick-selection techniques and drag-and-drop editing to make it easy to move and copy text anywhere you want it.

■ Shortcuts for handling often-used text enable you to save and recall specialized terms or proper names with the press of a key.

■ Reference and research tools include a thesaurus that makes it easy to track down synonyms and a research service that provides access to a variety of Internet reference materials.

■ Outlining tools allow easy rearranging of headings and text to ensure that your argument is logical.

■ Search tools can be used to locate and replace words and phrases, either one at a time or throughout a document.

■ Spelling and grammar features make it easy to correct typos and grammatical errors before you share the document with others.

In this chapter, you'll work with the text of a document to get it ready for distribution. You'll explore editing techniques, create and enter AutoText entries, ensure that the document is organized logically, and check that the language is precise and correct.

See Also   Do you need only a quick refresher on the topics in this chapter? See the Quick Reference entries on pages xxxii–xxxiv.

Important   Before you can use the practice files in this chapter, you need to install them from the book's companion CD to their default location. See "Using the Book's CD-ROM" on page xiii for more information.

Editing a Document

Microsoft Office Specialist

You will rarely write a perfect document that doesn't require any editing. You can edit a document as you create it, or you can write it first and then revise it. Or you might want to edit a document created for one purpose to create another document for a different purpose. For example, a marketing letter from last year might be edited to create a new letter for this year's marketing campaign. Editing encompasses many tasks, such as inserting and deleting words and phrases, correcting errors, and moving and copying text to different places in the document.

Inserting text is easy; you click to position the insertion point and simply begin typing. When you insert text, existing text moves to the right to accommodate the text that you are inserting, and the text that reaches the right margin wraps to the next line, if necessary.

Troubleshooting   If you have Word set to Overtype mode, existing text will not move to the right when you type new text. Instead, each character you type will replace an existing character. To determine whether Word is in Overtype mode or Insert mode, check the letters OVR in the status bar. If they are gray, Word is in Insert mode. If they are black, Word is in Overtype mode. To toggle between these modes, you can either double-click the letters OVR in the status bar or press the Insert key.

Deleting text is equally easy, but it helps to know how to *select* it. Selected text appears highlighted on the screen. You can select specific items as follows:

- To select a word, double-click it. The word and the space following it are selected. Punctuation following a word is not selected.

- To select a sentence, click anywhere in the sentence while holding down the Ctrl key. The first character in the sentence through the space following the ending punctuation mark are selected.

- To select a paragraph, triple-click it.

You can select adjacent words, lines, or paragraphs by positioning the insertion point at the beginning of the text you want to select, holding down the Shift key, and then pressing an arrow key or clicking at the end of the text that you want to select. To select blocks of text that are not adjacent in a document, you select the first block, hold down the Ctrl key, and then click to select the next block.

To select a block of text quickly, you can use the *selection area*, a blank strip to the left of the document's text column. When the pointer is in the selection area, it changes from an I-beam to a right-pointing arrow.

You can use the selection area to quickly select these items:

■   To select a line, click the selection area to the left of the line.

■   To select a paragraph, double-click the selection area to the left of the paragraph.

■   To select an entire document, triple-click the selection area.

Selection area

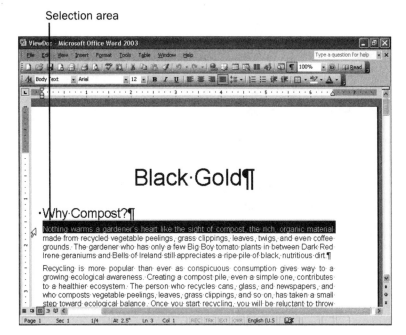

To deselect text, click anywhere in the document window except the selection area.

After selecting the text you want to work with, deleting it is an easy task: press the [Backspace] or [Del] key. If you want to delete only one or a few characters, you don't have to make a selection first: you can simply position the insertion point and then press [Backspace] or [Del] until the characters are all gone. Pressing [Backspace] deletes the character to the left of the insertion point. Pressing [Del] deletes the character to the right of the insertion point.

As you edit a document, Word keeps track of the changes you make so that you can easily reverse a change and restore your original text. This is useful when you make a mistake, such as inadvertently deleting a word. To undo the last action that you performed, click the Undo button on the Standard toolbar. To display the last five or six actions you have performed, click the down arrow to the right of the Undo button. To undo an action and all subsequent actions, click that action in the list.

If you undo an action, you can restore, or redo, the action by clicking the Redo button. You can click the down arrow to the right of the Redo button to restore multiple undone actions.

Tip Selecting an action from the Undo or Redo button's list undoes or redoes that action and all editing actions you performed after that one. You cannot undo or redo any single action except the last one you performed.

After selecting text, you can move it in one of the following ways:

- Use the Cut and Paste commands or buttons. Cut text disappears from the document but is temporarily stored in an area of your computer's memory called the *Office Clipboard*. After cutting the text, you reposition the insertion point and paste the text in a new location somewhere in the same document or in a different document.

- Use the Copy and Paste commands or buttons. Text that is copied rather than cut is also stored on the Office Clipboard but remains in its original location after it is pasted in the new location.

- Use *drag-and-drop editing*, which does not involve the Office Clipboard, when you need to move or copy text within a paragraph or line. To move selected text, you point to it, hold down the mouse button, drag the text to another place, and then release the mouse button. To copy selected text, you hold down the Ctrl key as you drag.

The Office Clipboard is useful for moving and copying information between pages and documents or for moving text in long documents. You can use the Office Clipboard to store items of information from one or more sources in one storage area that can be accessed by all Office programs.

In this exercise, you will edit text in the existing document. You'll insert and delete text, undo the deletion, copy and paste a phrase, and move a paragraph.

BE SURE TO start Word before beginning this exercise.
USE the *EditDoc* document in the practice file folder for this topic. This practice file is located in the *My Documents\Microsoft Press\Word 2003 SBS\EditingProof\EditingDoc* folder and can also be accessed by clicking *Start/All Programs/Microsoft Press/Word 2003 Step by Step*.
OPEN the *EditDoc* document.

1 Double-click the word *Early* at the top of the document to select it, and then press Enter to delete the word and replace it with a new blank paragraph.

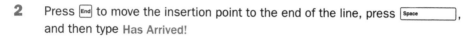

2 Press ⟨End⟩ to move the insertion point to the end of the line, press ⟨Space⟩, and then type Has Arrived!

The text appears at the end of the line.

3 Press the ⟨↓⟩ key four times, hold down ⟨Ctrl⟩, and then click anywhere in the first sentence of the first paragraph to select it.

4 Press ⟨Del⟩ to delete the sentence.

Undo

5 On the Standard toolbar, click the **Undo** button to restore the deleted text.

6 Click the down scroll arrow until the phrase *Happy Gardening!* appears, position the mouse pointer in the selection area to the left of the phrase, and click once to select the entire line of text.

Copy

7 On the Standard toolbar, click the **Copy** button.

The text is copied to the Clipboard.

Paste

8 Press ⟨Ctrl⟩+⟨Home⟩ to move to the beginning of the document, and on the Standard toolbar, click the **Paste** button.

Paste Options

Tip If a Paste Options button appears next to the pasted selection, you can ignore it for now. Clicking the Paste Options button displays a list of options that determine how the information is pasted into your document.

Cut

9 Select the new line of text, and on the Standard toolbar, click the **Cut** button.

The Clipboard task pane appears, displaying the current items in the Office Clipboard.

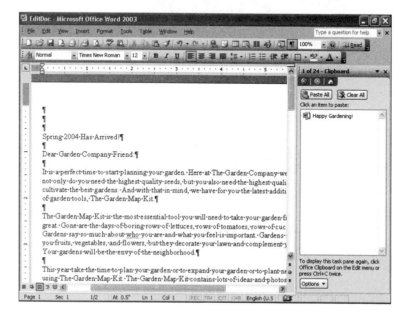

Clipboard icon

Tip You can paste the items listed in the Clipboard task pane into any Office program, either individually or all at once. You can choose not to have the Clipboard task pane appear when you cut or copy multiple items. You can also choose to display the Clipboard icon in the status area of the taskbar when the Office Clipboard is turned on. To access these options, click Options at the bottom of the Clipboard task pane. If the Clipboard task pane is turned off, you can open it by clicking Office Clipboard on the Edit menu.

10 Press Ctrl+End to move the insertion point to the end of the document, and then press Enter to insert a blank line.

11 In the **Clipboard** task pane, click the *Happy Gardening!* box to paste the text from the Clipboard in the document.

12 At the right end of the **Clipboard** task pane's title bar, click the **Close** button.

Close

13 If necessary, scroll up to the paragraph that begins *The Garden Company welcomes your comments*, and triple-click anywhere in the paragraph to select it.

14 Hold down the Shift key and press the ↓ key.

The blank paragraph is added to the selection.

15 Point to the selection, hold down the mouse button, and drag the paragraph down to the left of *Happy Gardening!*.

When you release the mouse, the text appears in its new location.

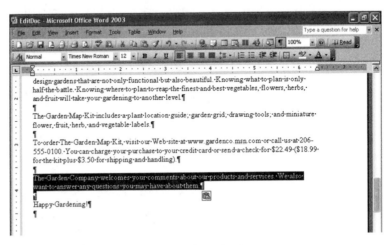

Save

16 On the Standard toolbar, click the **Save** button.

Word saves your changes to the document.

CLOSE: the *EditDoc* document.

Using Text Entry Shortcuts

Word provides several quick and easy ways to enter frequently used text in a document, including the following:

- *AutoCorrect* corrects commonly misspelled words so that you don't have to correct them yourself. You can also use this feature to insert text when you type an abbreviation.

- *AutoText* is similar to AutoCorrect but works only when you want it to, rather than automatically.

- *Date and time fields* supply the date and time from your computer's internal calendar and clock, so you don't have to look them up.

Have you noticed that Word automatically corrects some misspellings as you type them? For example, if you type *teh*, Word changes it to *the* as soon as you press `Space`. This is a feature of AutoCorrect. Besides relying on it to correct misspelled words, you can also use AutoCorrect to insert a phrase when you type an abbreviation. For example, you can set AutoCorrect to insert the words *The Garden Company* when you type the abbreviation *gc*. To accomplish this, you enter the abbreviation and the phrase in the AutoCorrect dialog box. You can also use this dialog box to check AutoCorrect options or to change or modify an AutoCorrect setting.

If you don't want Word to automatically change a misspelling or an abbreviation, you can reverse the change by clicking the Undo button before you type anything else, or you can turn off AutoCorrect options by pointing to the change and clicking the AutoCorrect Options button that appears below it. The AutoCorrect Options button first appears as a small blue box near the changed text and then becomes a button.

If you prefer to read and approve Word's changes before it automatically inserts them, you can use the AutoText feature to save time and create consistency in your documents. Word comes with built-in AutoText entries for commonly used items, such as the salutations and closings for letters, and you can create your own AutoText entries for the words and phrases you use repeatedly, such as your name, address, company, and job title.

To insert a built-in AutoText entry—for example, the closing of a letter—you click AutoText on the Insert menu, point to the category—for example, Closing—and then click the closing you want to insert in your document (for example, Respectfully yours,). To insert an AutoText entry you have created (for example, the name and address of Karen Berg, the owner of The Garden Company), you type the first four letters of the entry to display a ScreenTip of the full entry, press [Enter] to insert the entry in the document, and continue typing. If you are typing a different word with the same first four letters as the AutoText entry and you don't want to insert the entry, you just continue typing.

Besides commonly used words and phrases, you can also insert the date and the time, either as text entries or as date and time fields. If you insert a field, you can choose to have Word update the date and time whenever you open the document or whenever you print the document. Word uses your computer's internal calendar and clock as its source.

**New in
Office 2003**
Smart Tags

When you type certain information, such as the date and time, names, street addresses, telephone numbers, or the names of recent Microsoft Outlook e-mail message recipients, Word recognizes the information and displays a dotted line under the text to indicate that it has been flagged with a *Smart Tag*. Pointing to the underlined text displays the Smart Tag Actions button. You can click this button to display a menu of options for performing common tasks associated with that type of information. For example, if you type a name and address, Word flags it as a Smart Tag, and you can then add it to your Contacts list in Outlook.

In this exercise, you'll use AutoCorrect and change its settings. You will then insert a built-in AutoText entry and create and insert a custom AutoText entry. You'll also insert the date and examine actions you can perform using Smart Tags.

USE the *EntryAuto* document in the practice file folder for this topic. This practice file is located in the *My Documents\Microsoft Press\Word 2003 SBS\EditingProof\UsingShort* folder and can also be accessed by clicking *Start/All Programs/Microsoft Press/Word 2003 Step by Step.*
OPEN the *EntryAuto* document.

1   On the **Tools** menu, click **AutoCorrect Options**.

The AutoCorrect dialog box appears, displaying the AutoCorrect tab.

2   Clear the **Capitalize first letter of sentences** check box so that Word will not capitalize a lowercase letter or word that follows a period.

3   Click the **Replace** text box, and type gc.

4   Press the [Tab] key to move the insertion point to the **With** text box.

5   Type The Garden Company.

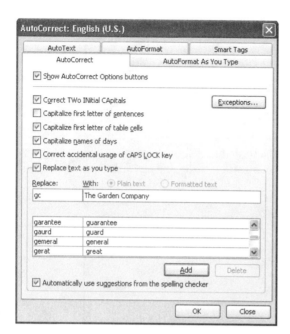

6   Click **Add** to add the entry to the correction list.

The text for the new AutoCorrect entry will now be inserted in a document each time you type its abbreviation and press [Space].

7   Click **OK** to close the **AutoCorrect** dialog box.

8   Press [Ctrl]+[End] to place the insertion point at the end of the document.

9   Type gc, and then press [Space].

The text gc changes to *The Garden Company*.

10 Press [Home] to move to the beginning of the line, and press [Enter] to start a new paragraph.

11 On the **Insert** menu, point to **AutoText**, point to **Closing**, and then click **Respectfully,**.

Word inserts this standard closing text at the location of the insertion point.

12 Press [Enter] four times to leave space for a signature.

13 On the **Insert** menu, point to **AutoText**, and then click **AutoText** on the submenu.

The AutoCorrect dialog box appears with the AutoText tab active.

14 In the **Enter AutoText entries here** text box, type Karen Berg.

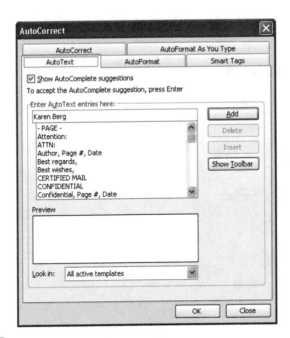

15   Click **Add**, and then click **OK**.

The AutoCorrect dialog box closes.

16   Type Kare.

A ScreenTip displays *Karen Berg (Press ENTER to Insert)*.

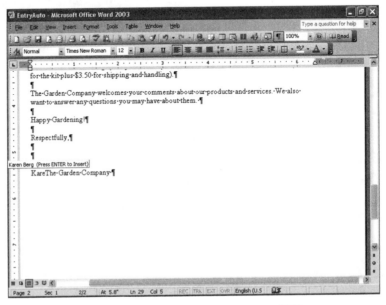

17   Press Enter to insert the full name, and then press Enter again.

18 Press ⌨Ctrl+⌨Home to move to the top of the document.

19 On the **Insert** menu, click **Date and Time**.

The Date and Time dialog box appears.

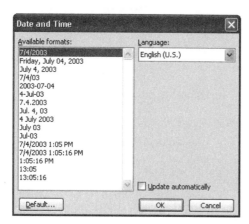

20 Click today's date with the **month dd yyyy** format, such as July 4, 2003, and click **OK**.

Word enters the current date in the document.

Smart Tag Actions

21 Point to the date, and when the **Smart Tag Actions** button appears, click it.

22 On the button's menu, click **Smart Tag Options**.

The AutoCorrect dialog box appears, displaying the Smart Tags tab.

You can use this dialog box to turn the Smart Tags feature on and off. Do not turn off the feature at this time.

23   Click **OK** to close the **AutoCorrect** dialog box.

24   On the Standard toolbar, click the **Save** button.

Word saves your changes to the document.

Save

CLOSE the *EntryAuto* document.

Finding the Best Word

Microsoft Office Specialist

Language is often contextual—the language you use in a letter to a friend is different from the language you use in business correspondence. To make sure you are using words that best convey your meaning in any given context, you can use Word's *Thesaurus* to look up alternative words or synonyms for a selected word. To use the Thesaurus, you select the word that you want to look up, and on the Tools menu, click Language and then Thesaurus. The Research task pane appears, displaying a list of synonyms with equivalent meanings.

In this exercise, you'll use the Thesaurus to replace one word with another.

USE the *Thesaurus* document in the practice file folder for this topic. This practice file is located in the *My Documents\Microsoft Press\Word 2003 SBS\EditingProof\FindingWord* folder and can also be accessed by clicking *Start/All Programs/Microsoft Press/Word 2003 Step by Step*.
OPEN the *Thesaurus* document.

1   Double-click the word **important** in the last line of the first paragraph.

2   On the **Tools** menu, click **Language**, and then click **Thesaurus**.

The Research task pane appears, listing synonyms for the word *important*.

3 Click the minus sign to the left of *significant*.

Word hides the list of synonyms under *significant*, bringing the synonym *valuable* and its own list of synonyms into view.

4 Click the plus sign to the left of *significant*, and then point to the word **significant** in the **Meanings** area just below it.

Word surrounds the meaning with a box containing a down arrow.

5 Click the down arrow to the right of the word *significant* (don't click the word itself), and click **Insert** on the drop-down menu.

Word replaces *important* with *significant*.

6 Close the **Research** task pane.

7 On the Standard toolbar, click the **Save** button.

Save

Word saves your changes to the document.

CLOSE the *Thesaurus* document.

Translating Text

Word provides a basic multi-language dictionary and translation feature so that you can look up text in the dictionary of a different language and translate words and phrases.

To translate text or look up words in another language:

1 If you want to translate a word or phrase, select it. If you want to look up a word or phrase, make sure nothing is selected.

2 On the **Tools** menu, point to **Language**, and then click **Translate**.

If you are prompted to install the feature, click Yes.

Start searching

3 If you want to look up a word or phrase, type it in the **Search for** box, and click the adjacent **Start searching** button.

If you are translating a selection, the word or phrase already appears in the "Search for" box.

4 In the **Translation** area of the **Research** task pane, change the dictionary settings in the **From** and **To** boxes as necessary.

The translated text appears in the bottom part of the pane.

Researching Information

Research
Service

In addition to the Thesaurus, the Research task pane provides access to a variety of informational resources, collectively known as the *Research service*, from within Word. You can enter a topic in the "Search for" text box and specify in the box below which resource Word should use to look for information regarding that topic. By clicking "Research options" at the bottom of the Research task pane, you can specify which of a predefined list of reference materials, such as Encarta and various Internet resources, will be available from a drop-down list, and you can add your own reference-material sources.

To use the Research service:

1   Display the **Research** task pane by clicking **Research** on the **Tools** menu.

2   In the **Search for** text box, type the topic you are interested in researching.

   For example, you might type *deer-proof plants*.

3   Click the down arrow to the right of the text box below, and select the resource you want to use to search for information.

   For example, you might click MSN Search.

Start searching

4   Click the **Start searching** button.

   The search results are displayed in the task pane.

5   Click the plus sign to the left of topics that interest you.

   You can click a hyperlink to a Web address to go to the Web to track down further information. You can also select part of a topic, right-click to display a shortcut menu, click Copy, and then paste the selection into your document. Or you can click Look Up on the shortcut menu to research information about the selection.

Using an Outline to Rearrange Paragraphs

Word provides a variety of ways in which to view a document. If you are creating a document that contains headings, you can format it with built-in heading styles that include outline levels. Then it is easy to view and organize the document by using Outline view. This view enables you to see only the headings of a document, level by level, and to rearrange the document as needed without scrolling through all the pages.

See Also   For more information about formatting with styles, see the topic "Changing the Look of Characters and Paragraphs with Styles" in Chapter 3.

To view a document in Outline view, click the Outline View button in the lower-left corner of the window. The screen displays the document and the Outlining toolbar. This toolbar includes buttons you can click to display a specific heading level, to *promote* or *demote* headings or body text to change their level, and to move headings and their text up or down in the document. The indentations and symbols in Outline view indicate the level of a heading or paragraph in the document's structure and do not appear in the document when you print it.

In this exercise, you'll switch to Outline view, promote and demote headings, move headings, and expand and collapse the outline.

USE the *OutlineText* document in the practice file folder for this topic. This practice file is located in the *My Documents\Microsoft Press\Word 2003 SBS\EditingProof\UsingOutline* folder and can also be accessed by clicking *Start/All Programs/Microsoft Press/Word 2003 Step by Step.*
OPEN the *OutlineText* document.

Outline View

1 In the lower-left corner of the window, click the **Outline View** button.

The screen changes to display the document in Outline view, and the Outlining toolbar appears.

Show Level

2 On the Outlining toolbar, click the down arrow to the right of the **Show Level** box, and click **Show Level 1**.

The document collapses to display only level 1 headings.

3 Click the *Hot or Cold?* heading.

Demote

4 On the Outlining toolbar, click the **Demote** button.

The *Hot or Cold?* heading changes to a level 2 heading.

5 On the Outlining toolbar, click the down arrow to the right of the **Show Level** box, and click **Show All Levels**.

The document expands to show the headings and their text. Note that the *Hot or Cold?* heading appears in a smaller font, and the body text under the heading is indented. When you restructure a heading in Outline view, the paragraphs below that heading are also restructured.

6 Press Ctrl + Home to move the insertion point to the beginning of the document.

7 On the Outlining toolbar, click the down arrow to the right of the **Show Level** box, and click **Show Level 2**.

The outline collapses to show all the first and second level headings.

Move Up

8 Click anywhere in the *Composting DOs and DON'Ts* heading, and then on the Outlining toolbar, click the **Move Up** button.

The heading moves above the *Compost and Soil* heading.

9 On the Outlining toolbar, click the down arrow to the right of the **Show Level** box, and click **Show All Levels**.

The document expands to show the *Composting DOs and DON'Ts* heading and its related paragraph, which is now above the *Compost and Soil* heading.

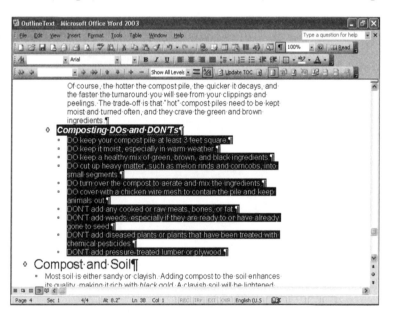

Promote

10 Press ⌃Ctrl+⌘Home to move the insertion point to the beginning of the document. Then on the Outlining toolbar, click the down arrow to the right of the **Show Level** box, and click **Show Level 2**.

11 Click anywhere in the *Hot or Cold?* heading, and on the Outlining toolbar, click the **Promote** button.

The heading changes to level 1.

Expand

12 On the Outlining toolbar, click the **Expand** button.

The paragraphs and headings under level 1 *Hot or Cold?* heading are now visible.

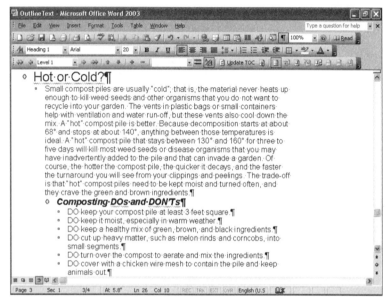

Collapse

13 On the Outlining toolbar, click the **Collapse** button.

14 On the **View** menu, click **Print Layout**.

The Outlining toolbar disappears, and you can now scroll through the document to see the effects of the reorganization.

CLOSE the *OutlineText* document without saving it.

Finding and Replacing Text

One way to ensure that the text in your documents is consistent and accurate is to use Word's Find command to search for every instance of a particular word or phrase. For example, the marketing director of The Garden Company might search for every instance of *The Garden Map Kit* to check that the capitalization is correct. If you know that you want to substitute one word or phrase for another, you can use the Replace command to find each occurrence of the text you want to change and replace it with different text.

Clicking the Find command on the Edit menu displays the Find tab of the Find and Replace dialog box, and clicking the Replace command displays the Replace tab, which is similar to the Find tab but has more options. After you enter the text you want to find in the "Find what" text box, you can click the Find Next button to locate the next occurrence of that text. On the Replace tab, you can then use the following buttons:

■ Click the Replace button to replace the selected occurrence with the text in the "Replace with" box and move to the next occurrence.

■ Click the Replace All button to replace all occurrences with the text in the "Replace with" box.

■ Click the Find Next button to leave the selected occurrence as it is and locate the next one.

You can use other options in the Find and Replace dialog box to carry out more complicated searches. Clicking the More button expands the box to make these additional options available.

Clicking the Less button hides the additional search options.

Find and Replace	? X

Find | **Replace** | Go To

Find what:

Replace with:

Less ± | Replace | Replace All | Find Next | Cancel

Search Options

Search: All

☐ Match case
☐ Find whole words only
☐ Use wildcards
☐ Sounds like (English)
☐ Find all word forms (English)

Replace

Format ▾ | Special ▾ | No Formatting

Using the options in the Search drop-down list, you can guide the direction of the search. You can select the "Match case" check box to match capitalization and select the "Find whole words only" check box to find only whole-word occurrences of the "Find what" text. If you want to check that your usage of two similar words, such as *effect* and *affect*, is correct, you can select the "Use wildcards" check box and then enter one of Word's *wildcard characters* in the "Find what" text box to locate variable information. The two most common wildcard characters are:

■ The ? wildcard stands for any single character in this location in the "Find what" text.

■ The * wildcard stands for any number of characters in this location in the "Find what" text.

Tip To see a list of the other available wildcards, use Help to search for *wildcards*.

Selecting the "Sounds like" check box finds occurrences of the search text that sound the same but are spelled differently, such as *there* and *their*. Selecting the "Find all word forms" check box finds occurrences of a particular word in any form, such as *plant, planted*, and *planting*. Finally, you can locate formatting, such as bold, or special characters, such as tabs, by selecting them from the Format or Special drop-down list.

In this exercise, you will find a phrase and replace some instances of it, and then you'll replace one phrase with another one throughout the entire document.

USE the *ReplaceText* document in the practice file folder for this topic. This practice file is located in the *My Documents\Microsoft Press\Word 2003 SBS\EditingProof\FindingText* folder and can also be accessed by clicking *Start/All Programs/Microsoft Press/Word 2003 Step by Step*.
OPEN the *ReplaceText* document.

1 With the insertion point at the beginning of the document, click **Find** on the **Edit** menu.

The Find and Replace dialog box appears with the Find tab displayed.

2 In the **Find what** text box, type Garden Map Kit, select the **Highlight all items found in** check box, and click **Find All**.

Word finds and selects all the occurrences of *Garden Map Kit* in the document.

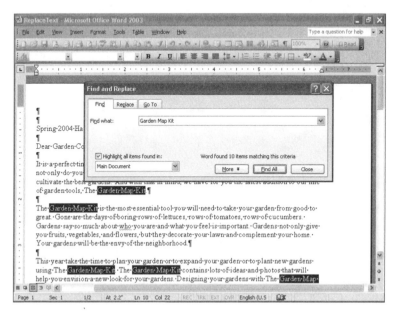

3 Click the document behind the **Find and Replace** dialog box, and then press Ctrl + Home to move the insertion point to the beginning of the document.

The occurrences of the "Find what" text are no longer highlighted.

Tip If a search reveals something amiss in a document, you can make editing changes on the fly without having to close the Find and Replace dialog box, by clicking the document, making the change, and then clicking the Find and Replace dialog box again to make it active.

4 In the **Find and Replace** dialog box, click the **Replace** tab.

The "Find what" text box retains the entry from the previous search.

5 Click the **Replace with** text box, type Interactive Garden, click **Find Next**, and then click **Replace**.

The selection is replaced with *Interactive Garden*, and the next occurrence of *Garden Map Kit* is selected.

6   Click **Replace All**.

Word displays a message box indicating that nine replacements were made.

7   Click **OK** to close the message box, and then click **Close** to close the **Find and Replace** dialog box.

Save

8   On the Standard toolbar, click the **Save** button.

Word saves your changes to the document.

CLOSE the *ReplaceText* document.

Checking Spelling and Grammar

Microsoft Office Specialist

Circulating a document that is filled with spelling and grammatical errors creates a poor impression on your readers. You should always proofread your documents before you print them or share them with others. Proofreading involves checking the spelling of words and correcting grammatical errors. You can use Word's *Spelling and Grammar* features to correct errors and maintain professional writing standards.

Tip   Although Word can help you eliminate misspellings and grammatical errors, its tools are not infallible. You should always read through your documents to catch the problems that Word's tools can't detect.

As you type the text of your document, by default Word underlines spelling and grammar errors with color-coded wavy lines:

■   A red line indicates that Word does not recognize the spelling of the word; that is, the word is not included in Word's online dictionary.

■   A green line indicates a possible grammar error.

To fix individual spelling and grammar errors quickly, you can right-click an underlined word to display a list of corrections from which you can choose.

In addition to correcting individual errors, you can check the entire document for spelling and grammar errors by clicking the Spelling and Grammar button on the Standard toolbar. When you start checking spelling and grammar, Word compares each word in the document with the words in its dictionary and analyzes sentences for breaches of grammatical rules. Word stops at each red or green wavy line and displays possible reasons for the error. For example, if a word is misspelled, the Spelling and Grammar dialog box provides a list of potential replacements. If a sentence appears to break a grammatical rule, the Spelling and Grammar dialog box identifies the rule and provides suggestions for correcting the error.

The options displayed in the Spelling and Grammar dialog box depend on the type of error Word encounters. The following table describes these options.

Button or Option	Function
Ignore Once	Leaves the highlighted error unchanged and finds the next spelling or grammar error. If you click the document to edit it, this button changes to Resume. After you finish editing, click Resume to continue checking the document.
Ignore All	Leaves all occurrences of the highlighted spelling error unchanged throughout the document and continues checking the document. Word ignores the spelling of this word in this document and in all documents whose spelling is checked during the current Word session.
Ignore Rule	Leaves all occurrences of the highlighted grammar error unchanged throughout the document and continues checking the document. Word ignores the grammar rule in this document and in all documents whose spelling and grammar is checked during the current Word session.
Next Sentence	Transfers to the document the corrections you've typed within the Spelling and Grammar dialog box and continues checking the document. This enables you to correct grammatical errors without having to switch between the Spelling and Grammar dialog box and the document window.
Add to Dictionary	Adds the selected word in the "Not in dictionary" text box to the custom dictionary. The custom dictionary contains the words you specify.
Change	Changes the highlighted error to the word you select in the Suggestions box.
Change All	Changes all occurrences of the highlighted error to the word you select in the Suggestions box and continues checking the document.
Explain	Provides more information about the grammar error.
AutoCorrect	Adds the spelling error and its correction to the AutoCorrect list so that Word corrects it automatically the next time you type it.
Undo	Undoes the last spelling or grammar action you performed.
Options	Opens the Spelling and Grammar options dialog box. Use this dialog box to open a different custom dictionary or to change the rules that Word uses to check spelling and grammar.

In this exercise, you'll check the spelling in the document and add common terms that are not already in the online dictionary. Then you will find, review, and correct a grammar error.

USE the *SpellCheck* document in the practice file folder for this topic. This practice file is located in the *My Documents\Microsoft Press\Word 2003 SBS\EditingProof\CheckingSpell* folder and can also be accessed by clicking *Start/All Programs/Microsoft Press/Word 2003 Step by Step*.
OPEN the *SpellCheck* document.

1 Right-click *bot*, the first word with a red wavy underline.

The shortcut menu lists possible correct spellings for this word, as well as actions you might want to carry out.

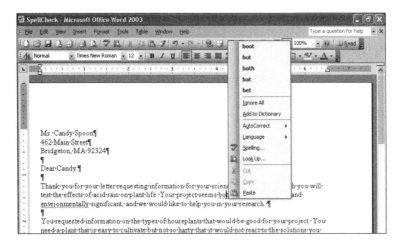

2 On the shortcut menu, click **both**.

Word removes the red wavy underline and inserts the correction.

Spelling and Grammar

3 Press Ctrl+Home to move to the beginning of the document, and on the Standard toolbar, click the **Spelling and Grammar** button.

The Spelling and Grammar dialog box appears, highlighting *envrionmentally*, the first word that Word does not recognize.

Troubleshooting   If the spelling and grammar checker doesn't find the errors in this document, you need to reset the spelling and grammar checker. On the Tools menu, click Options, click the Spelling & Grammar tab, click Recheck Document, and then click Yes to recheck words and grammar that were previously checked or that you chose to ignore.

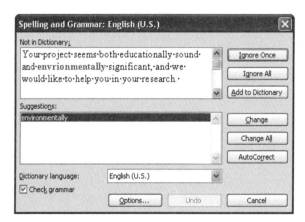

4 With *environmentally* selected in the **Suggestions** box, click **AutoCorrect**.

Word adds the misspelling and its correction to the AutoCorrect list, so the next time you type *envrionmentally* by mistake, the spelling will be corrected for you as you type. Word then flags *harty* as the next possible misspelling.

5 With the word *hearty* selected in the **Suggestions** box, click **Change All**.

Word changes this and a subsequent occurrence of *harty* to *hearty*. It then flags *crassula* as a word that it doesn't recognize. *Crassula*, a type of plant, is spelled correctly. By adding words like this one to the custom dictionary, you can prevent Word from continuing to flag them.

6 Click **Add to Dictionary**.

7 Click **Ignore All** for each of the three Latin plant names.

Word then flags a possible grammar error and indicates that this text could be a sentence fragment, meaning, in this case, that the sentence is missing a verb.

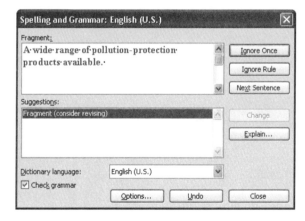

8 In the **Fragment** box, click before the word *available*, type are, press [Space],
and then click **Change**.

Word displays a message, indicating that it has finished checking the spelling
and grammar of the document.

9 Click **OK** to close the message box.

Save

10 On the Standard toolbar, click the **Save** button.

Word saves your changes to the document.

CLOSE the *SpellCheck* document, and if you are not continuing on to the next chapter, quit Word.

Key Points

- You can undo and redo a single action or the last several actions you
performed, by using the Undo and Redo buttons.

- You can cut or copy text and paste it elsewhere. Cut and copied text is stored
on the Office Clipboard.

- You can create text for repeated use with Word's AutoCorrect and AutoText
features. You can also insert fields that display the date and time.

- You can use the Thesaurus to look up alternative words or synonyms for a
selected word, and use the Research service to access specialized reference
materials and online resources.

- You can outline a document and use the outline to rearrange the document.

- You can find each occurrence of a word or phrase and replace it with another.

- You can correct individual spelling and grammar errors as you type, or you can
check an entire document for errors.

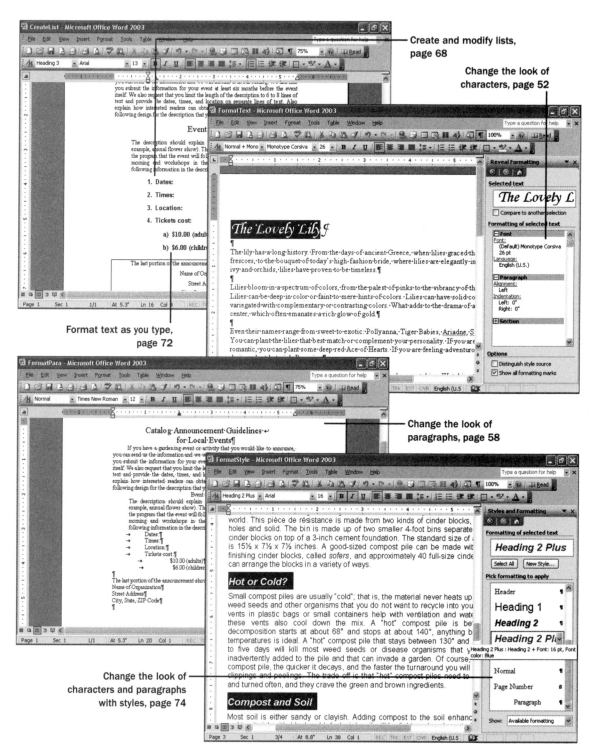

Create and modify lists, page 68

Change the look of characters, page 52

Format text as you type, page 72

Change the look of paragraphs, page 58

Change the look of characters and paragraphs with styles, page 74

Chapter 3 at a Glance

3 Changing the Appearance of Text

In this chapter you will learn to:

✔ Change the look of characters.

✔ Change the look of paragraphs.

✔ Create and modify lists.

✔ Format text as you type.

✔ Change the look of characters and paragraphs with styles.

The way your documents look helps them convey their message. You want the documents you create with Microsoft Office Word 2003 to look professional—well designed and polished—and you want the appearance of your text to reflect its contents. The format of your paragraphs and pages influences the appeal of your documents and helps draw the reader's attention to important information. To enhance the appearance of your documents, you can format the text so that key points stand out and your arguments are easy to grasp.

In this chapter, you'll improve the appearance of the text in a document by changing text characteristics. You'll also change the appearance of the paragraphs in a document by indenting them and changing their alignment, and by setting tab stops for lines within paragraphs. You'll also create and modify bulleted and numbered lists. Finally, you'll see how to use Word features that format text as you type and that apply sets of formatting with a few mouse clicks.

See Also Do you need only a quick refresher on the topics in this chapter? See the Quick Reference entries on pages xxxiv–xxxviii.

Important Before you can use the practice files in this chapter, you need to install them from the book's companion CD to their default location. See "Using the Book's CD-ROM" on page xiii for more information.

Changing the Look of Characters

The text you type in a document is displayed in a particular font. A *font* is a complete set of characters that all have the same design. The fonts that are available vary from one computer to another. Common fonts include Times New Roman, Courier, and Arial.

You can vary a font's basic design by changing the following *attributes*:

- Almost every font comes in a range of *font sizes*. The font size is measured in *points*, from the top of letters that have parts that stick up (ascenders), such as *b*, to the bottom of letters that have parts that drop down (descenders), such as *p*. Each point is equal to about 1/72 of an inch.

- Almost every font comes in a range of *font styles*. The most common are regular (or plain), italic, bold, and bold italic.

- Fonts can be enhanced by applying *font effects*, such as underlining, small capital letters, or shadows.

- A range of *font colors* is available in a standard palette, but you can also specify custom colors.

- You can alter *character spacing* by pushing characters apart or squeezing them together to achieve a desired effect.

After you have selected an appropriate font for each element of a document, you can use these sets of attributes to achieve different effects. Although some attributes might cancel each other out, they are usually cumulative. For example, The Garden Company might use a bold font in various sizes and various shades of green to make different heading levels stand out in a newsletter. Collectively, the font and the attributes used to vary its look are called *character formatting*.

Tip The way you use attributes in a document can influence its visual impact on your readers. Used judiciously, attributes can make a plain document look attractive and professional, but excessive use can make it look amateurish and detract from the message. For example, using too many different fonts within the same document is the mark of inexperience, so the rule of thumb is to not use more than two or three. Also, because lowercase letters tend to recede, using all uppercase (capitals) letters can be useful for titles and headings or for certain kinds of emphasis. However, large blocks of uppercase letters are tiring to the eye. (Where do the terms *uppercase* and *lowercase* come from? Until the advent of computers, individual letter blocks were assembled to form the words that would appear on a printed page. The blocks were stored alphabetically in cases, with the capital letters in the upper case and the small letters in the lower case.)

When you are formatting a document, you can open the Reveal Formatting task pane to display the formatting of selected text, such as its font and font effects. In this task pane you can display, change, or clear the formatting for the selected text. You can also use the Reveal Formatting task pane to select text based on formatting, which enables you to compare the formatting used in the selected text with formatting used in other parts of the document.

In this exercise, you will format the text in a document by changing its font, font size, font color, and character spacing.

BE SURE TO start Word before beginning this exercise.
USE the *FormatText* document in the practice file folder for this topic. This practice file is located in the *My Documents\Microsoft Press\Word 2003 SBS\ChangingText\ChangingChar* folder and can also be accessed by clicking *Start/All Programs/Microsoft Press/Word 2003 Step by Step*.
OPEN the *FormatText* document.

1 Select *The Lovely Lily*, the title at the top of the document.

Font

2 On the Formatting toolbar, click the down arrow to the right of the **Font** box, scroll the list of available fonts, and click **Monotype Corsiva**.

Troubleshooting If Monotype Corsiva is not available, select a similar script-style font, such as Brush Script MT.

The title at the top of the document now appears in the new font.

Font Size

3 On the Formatting toolbar, click the down arrow to the right of the **Font Size** box, and click **26** in the list.

The size of the title text increases to 26 points.

4 On the **Format** menu, click **Reveal Formatting**.

The Reveal Formatting task pane appears, displaying the formatting of the selected text.

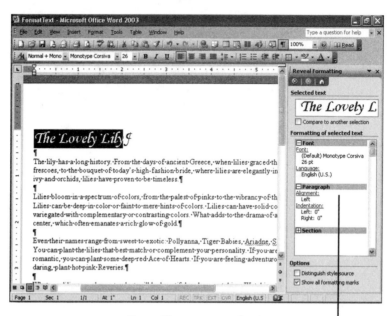

Formatting summary for the selected text

5 In the **Font** area of the **Reveal Formatting** task pane, click the **Font** link (the blue underlined word) to display the **Font** dialog box.

6 In the **Effects** area of the Font dialog box, select the **Outline** check box.

In the Preview box, the text changes to show how it will look with this effect applied.

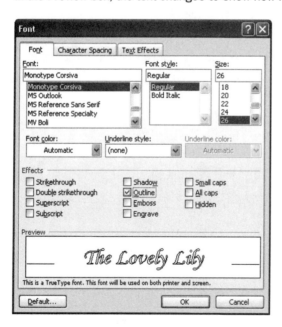

7 Click the **Character Spacing** tab.

8 Click the down arrow to the right of the **Spacing** box, and click **Expanded**.

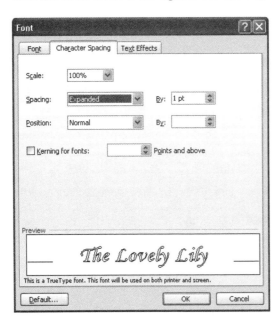

9 Click the up arrow to the right of the adjacent **By** box until the spacing is expanded by **2 pt** (points), and then click **OK**.

The selected text appears with an outline effect and with the spacing between the characters expanded by 2 points. Both of these effects are now listed in the Font area of the Reveal Formatting task pane.

10 At the top of the **Reveal Formatting** task pane, point to the **Selected text** box, and when a down arrow appears, click the arrow, and then click **Clear Formatting**.

The formatting of the selected text is removed.

Undo

11 On the Standard toolbar, click the **Undo** button.

The formatting of the selected text is restored.

12 Select the word *pinks* in the first sentence of the second paragraph.

Font Color

13 On the Formatting toolbar, click the down arrow to the right of the **Font Color** button, and then on the color palette, click the **Pink** box in the first column of the fourth row.

The color of the selected word is now pink. (You'll need to deselect it in order to see the color.) Its formatting is listed in the Font area of the Reveal Formatting task pane.

Highlight

Tip To apply the most recently selected color to other text, select the word or phrase, and then click the Font Color button (not the down arrow). The color that appears on the Font Color button is applied to the selected text.

14 Select the phrase *rich glow of gold* at the end of the second paragraph, click the down arrow to the right of the **Highlight** button on the Formatting toolbar, and then on the color palette, click the **Yellow** box in the first column of the first row.

The highlighted phrase now stands out from the rest of the text.

Tip You don't have to select the text before choosing a highlighting color. If you select a highlighting color from the color palette without first selecting text, the mouse pointer becomes a highlighter, and you can drag across text to highlight it. Click the Highlight button to turn off the highlighter.

15 Select the text *Pollyanna, Tiger Babies, Ariadne, Scheharazade* in the third paragraph.

Troubleshooting If the Reveal Formatting task pane overlays some of the text in the document, you can either scroll the horizontal scroll bar or make the task pane narrower. Point to the left border of the task pane, and when the pointer changes to a double arrow, drag the border toward the right so that more of the document's text is visible.

16 On the **Format** menu, click **Font** to open the **Font** dialog box, select the **Small caps** check box, and click **OK**.

The lowercase letters in the names of the lilies now appear in small capital letters, making those names easy to find in the text.

17 In the same paragraph, select *Ace of Hearts*, hold down the Ctrl key, and double-click *Reveries* in the last line of the paragraph to add that word to the selection.

18 Press the F4 key.

These two lily names now appear in small caps. When you press F4, your last editing or formatting action is applied to the selected text.

19 In the **Reveal Formatting** task pane, point to the **Selected text** box, click the down arrow, and then click **Select All Text With Similar Formatting**.

All the flower names that have been formatted in small caps are selected.

B
Bold

20 On the Formatting toolbar, click the **Bold** button.

The flower names are now both small caps and bold.

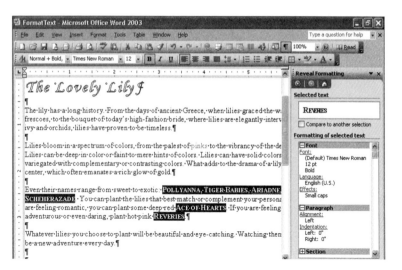

Close

21 In the **Reveal Formatting** task pane, click the **Close** button.

The Reveal Formatting task pane closes.

22 On the Standard toolbar, click the **Save** button.

Save

Word saves your changes to the document.

CLOSE the *FormatText* document.

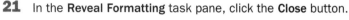

Animating Text

If someone will be reading your document on a computer, you can apply effects that will make your text vibrant and visually alive. For example, you can add flashing lights or a marquee that will draw your reader's attention to specific words and phrases. To create these special effects, you apply an animation effect to selected text.

To apply an animation effect:

1 Select the text that you want to animate.

2 On the **Format** menu, click **Font**.

The Font dialog box appears.

3 Click the **Text Effects** tab.

4 In the **Animations** box, select the animation effect you want to apply to the selected text.

5 Click **OK**.

Changing the Look of Paragraphs

Microsoft Office Specialist

You can enhance the appearance of a paragraph by changing the way text is aligned, modifying the spacing between paragraphs, and adding borders and shading around text. In Word, a *paragraph* is any amount of text that ends when you press the ⌨ Enter ⌨ key. A paragraph can include a single sentence consisting of one or more words, or several sentences.

You control the width of paragraphs by setting the left and right margins, and you control the length of pages by setting the top and bottom margins. The margin size controls the amount of white space that surrounds your text. You can use the options in the Page Setup dialog box to control the margins of the entire document and of specific sections of the document.

See Also   For more information about sections, see "Previewing and Printing a Document" in Chapter 4.

After you've set up a document's margins, you can control the position of the text within the margins. In Word, you can align lines of text in different locations along the horizontal ruler using tab stops. You can also indent paragraphs, controlling where the first line of text begins, where the second and subsequent lines begin, and where paragraph text wraps at the right margin.

Finding and Replacing Formatting

In addition to searching for words and phrases, you can use the Find and Replace dialog box to search for a specific format and replace it with a different format.

To search for a specific format and replace it with a different format:

1   On the **Edit** menu, click **Replace**.

The Find and Replace dialog box appears, displaying the Replace tab.

2   Click the **More** button to expand the dialog box, click the **Format** button, and then click **Font** or **Paragraph**.

The Find Font or Find Paragraph dialog box appears. (You can also click Style to search for paragraph styles or character styles.)

3   In the dialog box, click the format you want to find, and then click **OK**.

4   Click the **Replace With** text box, click **Format**, click **Font** or **Paragraph**, click the format you want to use, and then click **OK**.

5   Click **Find Next** to search for the next occurrence of the format, and then click **Replace** to replace that one instance or **Replace All** to replace every instance.

While you are adjusting the appearance of paragraphs in a document, it is a good idea to work in Print Layout view, which shows two rulers: the horizontal ruler at the top and the vertical ruler along the left side of the document window.

You can use Word's horizontal ruler to set *tab stops*. Tab stops are locations across the page that you can use to align text. By default, left-aligned tab stops are set every half-inch, as indicated by gray marks below the ruler. To set a tab stop using the ruler, you click the Tab button located at the left end of the ruler until the type of tab stop you want appears. This table shows the Tab button options.

Tab	Symbol	Action
Left Tab	**L**	Aligns the left end of the text with the stop.
Center tab	**⊥**	Aligns the center of the text with the stop.
Right Tab	**⅃**	Aligns the right end of the text with the stop.
Decimal Tab	**⊥·**	Aligns the decimal point in the text with the stop.
Bar Tab	**I**	Draws a vertical bar the length of the paragraph containing the insertion point.

Custom tab stop   Default tab stop   Horizontal ruler

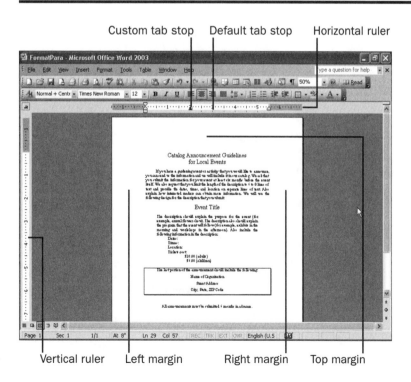

Vertical ruler   Left margin   Right margin   Top margin

After selecting the type of tab stop, you click the ruler where you want to set the tab stop. Word then removes any default tab stops to the left of the one you set. To remove a tab stop, you drag it down and away from the ruler.

To move the text to the right of the insertion point to the next tab stop, you press the [Tab] key. The text is then aligned on the tab stop according to its type. For example, if you set a center tab stop, pressing [Tab] moves the text so that its center is aligned with the tab stop.

Tip When you want to fine-tune the position of tab stops, you can click Tabs on the Format menu to display the Tabs dialog box. You might also open this dialog box if you want to use *tab leaders*—visible marks such as dots or dashes connecting the text before the tab with the text after it. For example, tab leaders are useful in a table of contents to carry the eye from the text to the page number.

In addition to tab stops, the horizontal ruler also displays *indent markers* that use to control how text wraps on the left or right side of a document. You use these markers to indent text from the left or right margins as shown in this table.

Indent	Symbol	Action
First Line Indent	▽	Begins a paragraph's first line of text at this marker.
Hanging Indent	△	Begins a paragraph's second and subsequent lines of text at this marker.
Left Indent	▢	Indents the text to this marker.
Right Indent	△	Wraps the text when it reaches this marker.

You can also position text within the document's margin using the alignment buttons on the Formatting toolbar, as shown in this table.

Alignment	Button	Action
Align Left	▤	Aligns each line of the paragraph at the left margin, with a ragged right edge.
Align Right	▤	Aligns each line of the paragraph at the right margin, with a ragged left edge.
Center	▤	Aligns the center of each line in the paragraph between the left and right margins, with ragged left and right edges.
Justify	▤	Stretches each line between the margins, creating even left and right edges.

To add space between paragraphs, you can press the [Enter] key to insert a blank line, or for more precise control, you can adjust the spacing before and after paragraphs. For example, instead of indicating a new paragraph by indenting the first line, you could add 12 points of blank space before a new paragraph. You use the Paragraph dialog box to adjust the paragraph spacing.

You also use the Paragraph dialog box to adjust line spacing. You can select Single, 1.5 lines, or Double spacing; or you can enter a specific spacing in points.

To set off a paragraph from the rest of the document, you can add borders and shading. For example, if The Garden Company is sending a letter to customers advertising a spring sale, they might put a border around the paragraph they want customers to pay the most attention to. Alternatively, they might shade the background of the paragraph to create a subtler effect.

Collectively, the settings used to vary the look of paragraphs are called *paragraph formatting*. After you indent, align, space, border, or shade one paragraph, you can press [Enter] to apply the same formatting to the next paragraph that you type. To apply the formatting to an existing paragraph, you can use the Format Painter button to quickly copy the formatting of one paragraph to another.

In this exercise, you'll set margins, change text alignment, insert and modify tab stops, modify line spacing, and add borders and shading around text to change the appearance of the paragraphs in the document.

USE the *FormatPara* document in the practice file folder for this topic. This practice file is located in the *My Documents\Microsoft Press\Word 2003 SBS\ChangingText\ChangingPara* folder and can also be accessed by clicking *Start/All Programs/Microsoft Press/Word 2003 Step by Step*.
OPEN the *FormatPara* document.

Print Layout
View

1 In the lower-left corner of the document window, click the **Print Layout View** button. Then zoom the page to **75%**.

You can now see how the text column is aligned between the left and right margins. In addition to the horizontal ruler at the top of the document window, a vertical ruler appears on the left side of the document window.

2 On the **File** menu, click **Page Setup**.

The Page Setup dialog box appears, displaying the Margins tab with the value in the Top text box selected in the Margins area,

3 Type 1.5". Then select the value in the **Bottom** text box, and type 1.5".

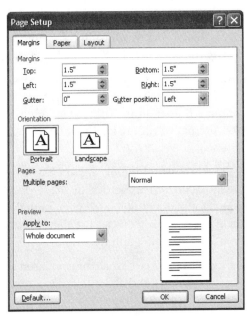

4 Click **OK** to close the **Page Setup** dialog box.

The amount of blank space at the top and bottom of each page increases from 1 inch to 1.5 inches.

Tip The standard size of a page is 8.5 inches by 11 inches. With margins of 1.5 inches on each side, you are left with a work area that is 5.5 inches wide.

Center

5 Click immediately to the left of the word *for* in the title, hold down the [Shift] key, press the [Enter] key, and then on the Formatting toolbar, click the **Center** button.

You have broken the title so that it wraps to a second line without starting a new paragraph. Word indicates this *text wrapping break* or *line break* with a bent arrow and centers the two lines of the title, making it appear more balanced.

Tip When you apply paragraph formatting to a line of text that ends with a line break, the formatting is applied to the entire paragraph, not just that line.

Line break

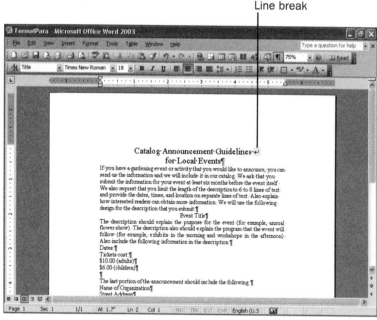

6 Click anywhere in the first paragraph, and then on the Formatting toolbar, click the **Justify** button.

The edges of the paragraph are now flush against both the left and right margins.

7 On the horizontal ruler, drag the **First Line Indent** marker to the 0.5-inch mark.

The first line of text is indented a half inch from the left margin.

8 Click anywhere in the paragraph that starts *The description should explain*, and on the horizontal ruler, drag the **Left Indent** marker to the 0.5-inch mark.

The First Line Indent and Hanging Indent markers move with the Left Indent marker, and the entire paragraph is now indented a half inch from the left margin.

9 Drag the **Right Indent** marker to the 5-inch mark.

The paragraph is now indented from the right margin as well.

Tip Left and right margin indents are often used to draw attention to special paragraphs, such as quotations.

Left indent   First-line indent   Right indent

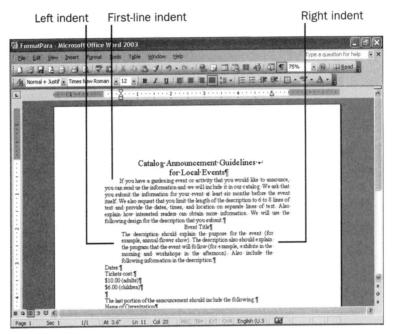

Left Tab

10 Scroll down the page, select the *Dates:* and *Tickets cost:* paragraphs, make sure the **Left Tab** button is active, and click the ruler at the 1-inch mark to set a left tab stop.

11 Click to the left of the word *Dates:* to position the insertion point there, and then press the Tab key.

Word left-aligns the text at the new tab stop.

12 Press End to move the insertion point to the end of the line, and press Enter to create a new paragraph. Press Tab, and then type **Times:**.

13 Press Enter to create a new paragraph, press Tab, type **Location:**, press the → key to move the insertion point to the beginning of the next paragraph, and then press Tab.

Decimal Tab

14 Drag through any part of the two paragraphs that start with *$10.00* and *$6.00*, click the **Tab** button three times to activate the **Decimal Tab** button, and then click the ruler at the 2.5-inch mark to set a decimal tab.

Tip When applying paragraph formatting, you don't have to select the entire paragraph.

15 Click to the left of *$10.00*, press [Tab], click to the left of *$6.00*, and press [Tab] again.

The dollar amounts are now aligned on their decimal points.

16 Drag again through any part of the two paragraphs with dollar amounts, and on the horizontal ruler, drag the decimal tab stop from the 2.5-inch mark to the 2.0-inch mark. Then press the [Home] key to see the results.

Left-aligned tabs

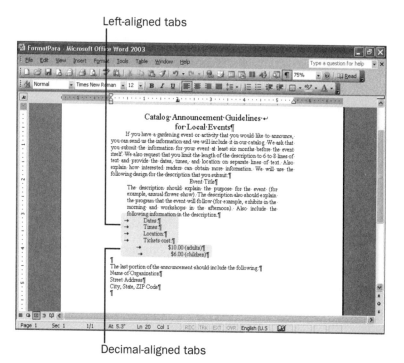

Decimal-aligned tabs

17 Press [Ctrl]+[Home] to move the insertion point to the top of the document, and on the **Format** menu, click **Paragraph**.

The Paragraph dialog box appears.

Tip When you want to make several adjustments to the alignment, indentation, and spacing of selected paragraphs, it is sometimes quicker to use the Paragraph dialog box than to click buttons and drag markers.

18 In the **Spacing** area, click the up arrow to the right of the **After** text box until the setting is **12 pt**.

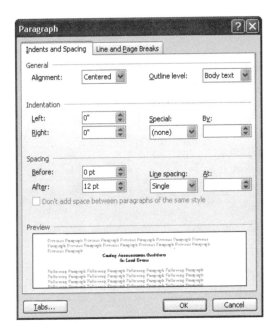

19 Click **OK** to close the **Paragraph** dialog box.

The paragraph below the title moves down, setting the title off from the rest of the document.

Format Painter

20 On the Standard toolbar, click the **Format Painter** button, point to the *Event Title* paragraph, and click to copy the formatting from the title paragraph.

Word changes the font size of the paragraph to 18 points and adds space between the title paragraph and the following one.

21 On the **Format** menu, click **Paragraph**, and in the **Spacing** area of the **Paragraph** dialog box, click the up arrow to the right of the **Before** text box until the setting is **12 pt**. Then click **OK**.

Word adds space between the *Event Title* paragraph and the one before it.

Center

22 Scroll to the bottom of the document, drag through any part of the last four paragraphs, and then on the Formatting toolbar, click the **Center** button.

Word centers the paragraphs.

23 On the **Format** menu, click **Paragraph**, click the down arrow to the right of the **Line Spacing** text box, click **1.5 lines**, and click **OK**.

24 On the **Format** menu, click **Borders and Shading**.

The Borders and Shading dialog box appears, displaying the Borders tab.

25 In the **Setting** area, click the **Shadow** icon to select that border style.

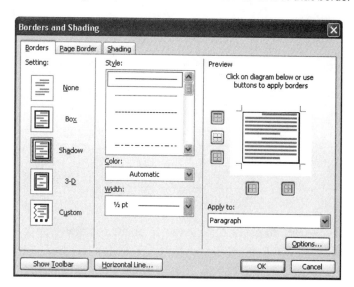

Tip You can change the settings in the Style, Color, and Width boxes to create the kind of border you want. If you want only one, two, or three sides of the paragraph to have a border, click the buttons surrounding the image in the Preview area.

26 Click the **Shading** tab, click the **Light Yellow** box in the third column of the last row of the color palette, and then click **OK**.

A border with a shadow surrounds the text, and the background color is light yellow.

27 Move the pointer to the center of the page about two lines below the yellow shaded box.

The pointer's shape changes to indicate that double-clicking will center whatever text you type next. You can use this *Click and Type* feature to create appropriately aligned text wihtout pressing the [Enter] key.

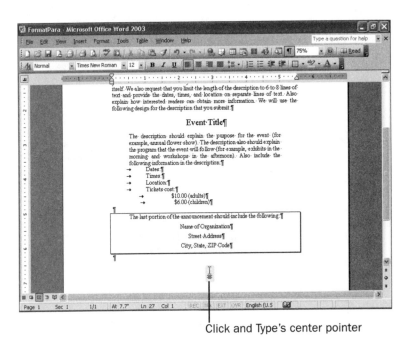

Click and Type's center pointer

28 Double-click to position the insertion point, and then type All announcements must be submitted 6 months in advance.

The newly inserted text appears centered in the document.

¶
Show/Hide ¶

29 On the Formatting toolbar, click the **Show/Hide** ¶ button to hide the formatting marks.

Word hides the non-printing characters.

Save

30 On the Standard toolbar, click the **Save** button.

Word saves your changes to the document.

CLOSE the *FormatPara* document.

Creating and Modifying Lists

Microsoft Office Specialist

To organize lists in a document, such as lists of events, names, numbers, or procedures, you can format the information in a bulleted or numbered list. A *bullet* is a small graphic, such as a dot, that introduces an item in a list. Where the order of items is not important, use bullets. Use numbers instead of bullets when you want to emphasize sequence, as in a series of steps. If you move, insert, or delete items in a numbered list, Word renumbers the list for you. If the items in a list are out of order, alphabetically or numerically, you can sort the items in ascending or descending order using the Sort command on the Table menu.

For emphasis, you can change any bullet or number style to one of Word's predefined formats. For example, you can switch round bullets to check boxes, or change the letters in Roman numerals from uppercase to lowercase. You can also customize the list style or insert a picture as a bullet. Use the Bullets and Numbering dialog box to modify, format, and customize your list.

Word makes it easy to start a bulleted or numbered list, like this:

- To create a bulleted list, type * (an asterisk) at the beginning of a paragraph, and then press [Space] or [Tab].

- To create a numbered list, type 1. (the numeral 1 followed by a period) at the beginning of a paragraph, and then press [Space] or [Tab].

Then type the first item in the list and press [Enter]. The next bullet or number in the list appears, and Word changes the formatting to a list. You can type the next item in the list or press [Enter] or [Backspace] to end the list.

You can change a bulleted or numbered list into an outline consisting of main headings and subheadings. To create an outline from scratch, type I. at the beginning of a line, press [Tab], type a main heading, and then press [Enter]. You can type another main heading or press [Tab] to add a subheading under the main heading.

See Also For another way to create outlines, see "Using an Outline to Rearrange Paragraphs" in Chapter 2.

In this exercise, you will create a bulleted and numbered list, modify them by adjusting their indents, and then apply outline numbering.

USE the *CreateList* document in the practice file folder for this topic. This practice file is located in the *My Documents\Microsoft Press\Word 2003 SBS\ChangingText\CreatingList* folder and can also be accessed by clicking *Start/All Programs/Microsoft Press/Word 2003 Step by Step*.
OPEN the *CreateList* document.

1 Scroll down the document, and drag through any part of the four paragraphs aligned with *Dates:*.

2 On the Formatting toolbar, click the **Numbering** button.

Numbering

The selected paragraphs are reformatted as a numbered list.

3 On the **Format** menu, click **Bullets and Numbering**.

The Bullets and Numbering dialog box appears, displaying the Numbered tab.

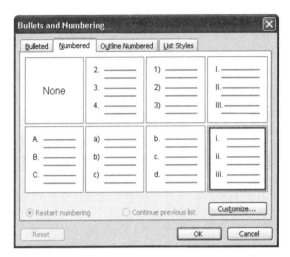

4 Click the **A. B. C.** box in the first column of the second row, and click **OK**.

The numbers change to capital letters.

5 On the **Table** menu, click **Sort**.

The Sort Text dialog box appears.

6 With the **Ascending** option selected, click **OK**.

The list changes to reflect the new sort order. Because the prices of tickets are not included in the sorting, the list now makes no sense.

Undo

7 On the Standard toolbar, click the **Undo** button.

The list returns to its unsorted state.

8 Drag through any part of the two paragraphs that start with *$10.00* and *$6.00*.

9 On the Formatting toolbar, click the **Bullets** button.

Bullets

The selected paragraphs appear as a bulleted list.

10 On the Formatting toolbar, click the **Decrease Indent** button.

Decrease
Indent

The bulleted list merges with the numbered list because the two lists are now indented at the same level.

11 On the Formatting toolbar, click the **Increase Indent** button.

Increase
Indent

The selected items move back to the right and become a bulleted list again.

12 On the **Format** menu, click **Bullets and Numbering**.

The Bullets and Numbering dialog box appears, displaying the Bulleted tab.

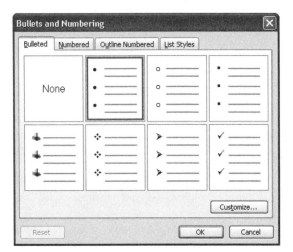

13 Click the color bullet box in the first column of the second row, and then click **OK**.

The bullet character changes from circles to colors.

14 Drag through any part of all the paragraphs in the numbered and bulleted lists.

15 On the **Format** menu, click **Bullets and Numbering**, and then click the **Outline Numbered** tab.

16 Click the box in the third column of the second row, click **OK**, and then press [Home].

The lettered list changes from letters to numbers and the bulleted list changes to letters.

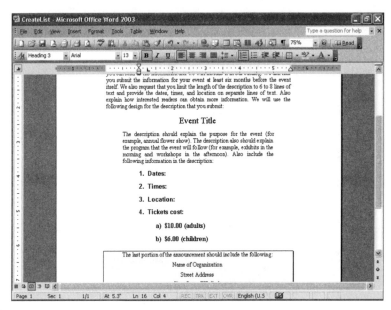

Save

17 On the Standard toolbar, click the **Save** button.

Word saves your changes to the document.

CLOSE the *CreateList* document.

Formatting Text as You Type

Word's list formatting capabilities are just one example of its ability to intuit how you are going to want to format an element based on what you type. For example, instead of manually creating a line by typing underscores (_) across the length of a page, you can type three consecutive hyphens (-) and press [Enter] to have Word's AutoFormat feature draw a single line across the page. Or you can type three consecutive equal signs (=) and press [Enter] to have Word draw a double line.

In this exercise, you will add a double border using an AutoFormat shortcut. You'll also inspect the AutoFormat As You Type tab of the AutoCorrect dialog box to see what items Word can automatically format for you.

USE the *FormatAuto* document in the practice file folder for this topic. This practice file is located in the *My Documents\Microsoft Press\Word 2003 SBS\ChangingText\AutoFormatting* folder and can also be accessed by clicking *Start/All Programs/Microsoft Press/Word 2003 Step by Step*.
OPEN the *FormatAuto* document.

1 Press [Ctrl]+[End] to move the insertion point to the end of the document, and then press [Enter].

AutoCorrect
Options

2   Press ⦂ three times, and press Enter.

Word draws a double line across the page and displays the AutoCorrect Options button.

Tip   Clicking the AutoCorrect Options button displays a menu of options related to the line you just drew. You can remove the line, disable (turn off) the AutoCorrect border lines options, or open the AutoCorrect dialog box, where you can make further modifications to this feature.

3   Type: Color:, and press Enter.

4   Type 1., and press Tab. Then type Palest pink to deepest red, and press Enter.

Word assumes you want to continue the list and indents both list items.

5   Type Solid or variegated, and press Enter twice.

Word continues the list the first time you press Enter, but ends the list and creates a normal paragraph when you press Enter the second time.

6   Type Names:, and press Enter.

7   On the **Tools** menu, click **AutoCorrect Options**, and then click the **AutoFormat As You Type** tab.

> **Tip** You can automatically format a document as you type using the options in the AutoFormat As You Type tab in the AutoCorrect dialog box, or you can format a document after you type using the AutoFormat command on the Format menu. In the AutoFormat dialog box, select the "AutoFormat now" option or the "AutoFormat and review each change" option, and then click OK.

8 In the **Apply as you type** area, clear the **Automatic numbered lists** check box, and click **OK**.

9 Type **1.**, press the [Tab] key, type **Pollyanna**, and press [Enter].

Instead of setting up the numbered list, Word starts a normal paragraph.

10 On the **Tools** menu, click **AutoCorrect Options**, and click the **AutoFormat As You Type** tab.

11 In the **Apply as you type** area, select the **Automatic numbered lists** check box, and click **OK**.

12 Press the [Backspace] key to move back to the previous paragraph, and then press [Enter] again.

Word assumes you want to continue the list and indents both list items.

13 Click the **AutoCorrect Options** button to view the commands available, and then click away from the menu to close it without making a selection.

CLOSE the *FormatAuto* document without saving your changes.

Changing the Look of Characters and Paragraphs with Styles

Microsoft Office Specialist

As you change the appearance of the text in your documents, you might find that you have created a look, or style, of your own. In Word, a *style* is a collection of character and paragraph formatting that can be saved. Then instead of applying each format individually, you can apply all of them at once by using a style.

Styles come in two varieties:

■ You use *character styles* to format selected characters. You can apply character styles to a single letter, a word, a paragraph, or the entire document. This type of style consists of collections of attributes. For example, a character style might specify that the selected text should be 18-point, bold, underlined, and red.

■ You use *paragraph styles* to format entire paragraphs. This type of style consists of indents, alignment, paragraph and line spacing, bullets or numbering, and tabs as well as character attributes to be applied to the entire paragraph. For example, a paragraph style might specify that the paragraph containing the insertion point should be centered, with a border and a hanging indent, as well as 18-point, bold, underlined, and red.

Styles are stored in *templates*, and Word's default template is called the *Normal template*. Unless you specify otherwise, the documents you create are all based on the Normal template, which contains a set of predefined styles. The most basic of these predefined styles, *Normal style*, is used for all regular paragraphs, formatting them as 12-point, regular Times New Roman text that is left-aligned and single-spaced, with no extra space above and below it.

All the text you type in documents based on the Normal template uses the Normal style until you apply another style. For example, you might apply the predefined Heading 1 style to text you want to serve as a document's title. To apply another style, you can click the down arrow to the right of the Style box on the Formatting toolbar and make a selection from the drop-down list, or you can use the Styles and Formatting task pane.

Tip   If a wavy blue line appears under a word or phrase as you type, Word detects inconsistent formatting. To remove the wavy blue line without making any change, right-click the word or phrase, and then click Ignore Once to bypass that instance of the inconsistency, or Ignore All to bypass that and all upcoming instances of the inconsistency. To turn off the formatting options, click Options on the Tools menu, click the Edit tab, clear the "Keep track of formatting" check box, clear the "Mark formatting inconsistencies" check box, and click OK.

When Word's predefined styles don't meet your needs, you can create new ones in several ways:

■   You can modify an existing style. You can redefine the style for just this document or for all documents based on this template. The formatting of any text to which you have already applied the style will be updated to reflect the new definition.

■   You can create a style by example. You can format text the way you want it and then create a style that reflects the look of the text.

■   You can define a style from scratch. You can click New Style in the Style and Formatting task pane and then use the New Style dialog box to specify the character formatting and paragraph formatting for the style.

Tip   If you want to define a style for a bulleted or numbered list, click Bullets and Numbering on the Format menu. Then click the List Styles tab, click Add, define the style, and click OK.

In this exercise, you will apply, modify, and delete a style using the Styles and Formatting task pane.

USE the *FormatStyle* document in the practice file folder for this topic. This practice file is located in the *My Documents\Microsoft Press\Word 2003 SBS\ChangingText\ChangingStyle* folder and can also be accessed by clicking *Start/All Programs/Microsoft Press/Word 2003 Step by Step*.
OPEN the *FormatStyle* document.

1   If necessary, change the **Zoom** setting to **100%**, and then select the *Why Compost?* paragraph.

2   On the **Format** menu, click **Styles and Formatting**.

The Styles and Formatting task pane appears.

Available styles

3   In the **Styles and Formatting** task pane, point to the **Formatting of selected text** box.

A ScreenTip appears, listing the formatting of the style applied to the selected text. In this case, the style is Body Text.

4   Scroll down the **Pick formatting to apply** list, and click the **Heading 2** style.

The selected text changes to reflect the formatting assigned to the Heading 2 style.

5   Scroll down the document, and select the *What Is a Compost Pile?* paragraph. Then scroll until you can see *How Do You Make a Compost Pile?*, hold down the [Ctrl] key, and select that paragraph. Then add the *Hot or Cold?* and *Compost and Soil* paragraphs to the selection.

6 In the **Styles and Formatting** task pane, click the **Heading 2** style to apply the style to the selected paragraphs.

7 Scroll to the top of the document, click anywhere in the *Why Compost?* paragraph, and in the **Styles and Formatting** task pane, click **Select All**.

Word selects all the text formatted with the style of the selected text, which is Heading 2.

8 In the **Styles and Formatting** task pane, click **New Style**.

The New Style dialog box appears.

9 In the **Name** text box, type Heading 2 Plus to create a new style of that name.

10 In the **Formatting** area, click the down arrow to the right of the **Font Size** box, and click **16**. Then click the down arrow to the right of the **Font Color** box, and click the **Blue** box in the sixth column of the second row.

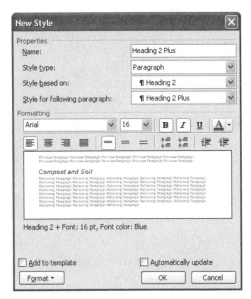

11 Click **OK** to close the **New Style** dialog box.

The Heading 2 Plus style appears in the Styles and Formatting task pane.

12 In the **Styles and Formatting** task pane, click the **Heading 2 Plus** style.

Word applies the new style to all the selected paragraphs. A ScreenTip tells you the main characteristics of this style.

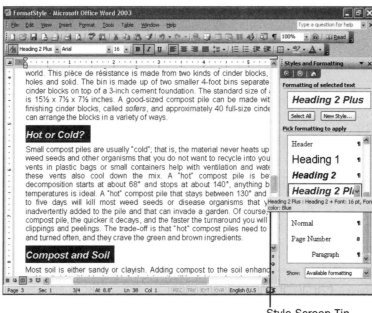

Style Screen Tip

13 In the **Styles and Formatting** task pane, point to the **Heading 2 Plus** style, click the down arrow that appears to its right, and click **Modify**.

The Modify Style dialog box appears.

Italic

14 In the **Formatting** area, click the **Italic** button to deselect that attribute, and click **OK**.

The Heading 2 Plus style is updated, along with all text to which the style is applied.

15 In the **Styles and Formatting** task pane, click the **Heading 2 style**.

The selected text changes to reflect that style.

16 In the **Styles and Formatting** task pane, point to the **Heading 2 Plus** style, click the down arrow that appears to its right, and click **Delete**.

A message asks whether you want to delete the style.

17 Click **Yes** to delete the **Heading 2 Plus** style.

18 At the bottom of the **Styles and Formatting** task pane, click the down arrow to the right of the **Show** text box, and then click **Formatting in use**.

The task pane now lists only the styles actually used in the document.

19   Close the **Styles and Formatting** task pane.

Save

20   On the Standard toolbar, click the **Save** button.

Word saves your changes to the document.

CLOSE the *FormatStyle* document, and if you are not continuing to the next chapter, quit Word.

Key Points

- ■ You can change the look of characters by changing the font, size, style, and effect.

- ■ You can change the look of paragraphs by varying their indentation, spacing, and alignment and by setting tab stops.

- ■ You can create and modify bulleted and numbered lists by using the buttons on the Formatting toolbar and the Bullets and Numbering dialog box.

- ■ You can use the AutoFormat feature to automatically format text as you type.

- ■ You can apply character styles and paragraph styles to selected text to change several formats at once.

- ■ You can use the Reveal Formatting task pane to display, change, or clear the formatting for the selected text. You can also use this task pane to select text with the same formatting throughout a document.

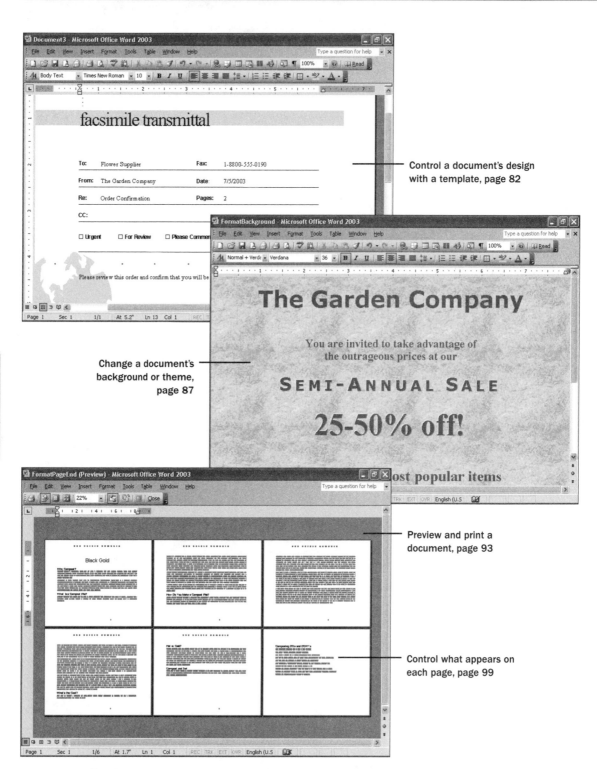

Control a document's design
with a template, page 82

Change a document's
background or theme,
page 87

Preview and print a
document, page 93

Control what appears on
each page, page 99

Chapter 4 at a Glance

4 Arranging and Printing Documents

In this chapter you will learn to:

✔ Control a document's design with a template.

✔ Change a document's background.

✔ Change a document's theme.

✔ Preview and print a document.

✔ Control what appears on each page.

Microsoft Office Word 2003 comes with formatting tools, such as templates and themes, that you can use to ensure the consistent presentation of entire documents. You can create documents based on one of Word's predefined business or personal templates, and you can also create your own templates. To ensure a consistent and polished look for a document, you can specify a background for its pages and a theme for its major elements. You can control how text will appear in a printed document by specifying page and section breaks, and you can use headers and footers to hold information that appears on every page. When your document is complete, you can preview it and make adjustments to its layout before printing or distributing it.

In this chapter, you'll create a new template by modifying one of Word's templates. Then you will use the new template to create a fax cover page. You will also enhance the appearance of printed and online documents with watermarks and background formatting. After previewing how a document will look when printed, you'll adjust its margins and page orientation before printing it. Finally, you'll insert page and section breaks in a multi-page document, ensure that the page breaks do not leave single words or phrases at the top or bottom of a page, and add text that will appear at the top and bottom of every page.

See Also Do you need only a quick refresher on the topics in this chapter? See the Quick Reference entries on pages xxxviii–xli.

 Important Before you can use the practice files in this chapter, you need to install them from the book's companion CD to their default location. See "Using the Book's CD-ROM" on page xiii for more information.

Control a Document's Design with a Template

Microsoft Office Specialist

The accuracy of the information in a document is essential, but the document's appearance is also important for effective communication. To help create visually appealing documents, you can use one of Word's professionally designed templates. A *template* is a file that stores text, character and paragraph styles, page formatting, and *macros* for use as a pattern in creating other documents.

See Also For information about macros, see "Creating a Macro to Automate a Task" in Chapter 13.

Unless you specify otherwise, all new documents are based on the Normal template, which contains a minimum number of fairly plain styles, including the Normal style used for regular text paragraphs. Word also comes with templates for a variety of business and personal documents, including publications, reports, letters, faxes, memos, and Web pages.

To create a document based on one of Word's predefined templates, you select the location of the template in the New Document task pane and then select the template you want from the list presented. Some templates are installed on your computer during the program's installation; others are available on the Office Online Web site.

Tip Word supports *workgroup templates*, which are templates stored in a central location for use by workgroup members over a network. You can designate this location on the File Locations tab of the Options dialog box, which you open by clicking Options on the Tools menu. Then you can locate these templates by clicking the "On my Web sites" link in the Templates area of the New Document task pane.

A document based on a Word template often displays formatted placeholders surrounded by square brackets—for example, *[Click here and type name]*. You replace a placeholder with your own text by clicking it and then typing the replacement. If you don't need a placeholder, you simply delete it. After you have entered all the text you need for the document, you save it in the usual way. The changes you have made affect the document, not the template it is based on, which remains available to help create other documents.

If you want to modify one of Word's templates—for example, to add your own name and address—you can create a document based on the template you want to modify, make your changes, and then save the document as a template with a different name. The next time you need this template, you can use your modified version instead of the one provided by Word.

After you have created a document, you can change its look by attaching a different template. To attach a template to an existing document, you click Templates and Add-Ins on the Tools menu, click Attach, and then navigate to and open the template. If the two templates have styles with the same names, you can specify whether or not the formatting defined by the new template's styles should replace the formatting defined by the old template's styles, by selecting the "Automatically update document styles" option.

In this exercise, you will create a new template based on a predefined Word template. Then you'll create a fax cover page using the new template.

BE SURE TO start Word before beginning this exercise.

1 Click the arrow to the right of the title bar of the **Getting Started** task pane, and click **New Document**.

If the task pane is not open, you can open it by clicking Task Pane on the View menu.

2 In the **Templates** area of the **New Document** task pane, click **On my computer**.

Word opens the Templates dialog box.

3 Click the **Letters & Faxes** tab, and then click (don't double-click) the **Contemporary Fax** icon.

The template appears in the Preview box.

Templates are organized by type on separate tabs.

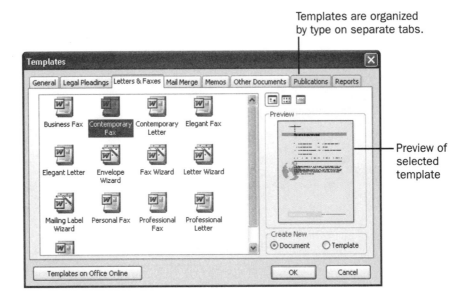

Preview of selected template

4 Click **OK**.

Word creates a new document based on the selected template, with placeholders for text you need to supply.

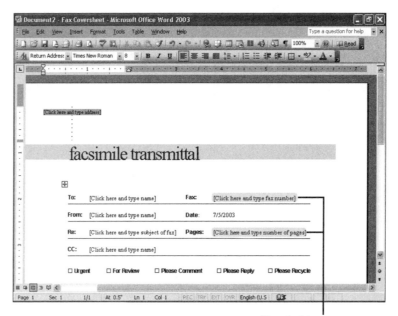

Placeholders

5 At the top of the page, click the *[Click here and type address]* placeholder, type **The Garden Company**, and then press the Enter key.

6 Type **1234 Oak Street**, press Enter, and then type **Seattle, WA 10101** to enter the address.

7 In the *From* line, click the *[Click here and type name]* placeholder, and type **The Garden Company**.

8 On the **File** menu, click **Save As**.

The Save As dialog box appears.

9 In the **File name** box, type **FaxTemplate**.

10 Click the down arrow to the right of the **Save as type** text box (not the **File name** text box), and click **Document Template**.

11 Check that the Templates folder appears in the **Save in** text box as the folder in which your new template will be saved.

Troubleshooting   By default, Word expects templates to be stored in your Templates folder. (The folder's location is C:\Documents and Settings*your name* \\Application Data\\Microsoft\\Templates.) If you do not store the templates you create in this folder, Word will not display them in the Templates dialog box with Word's predefined templates.

12 Click **Save**.

Word saves the template.

13 Click the **Close Window** button to close the document window.

The FaxTemplate document closes.

×
Close Window

14 On the **File** menu, click **New**.

The New Document task pane appears.

15 In the **Templates** area of the **New Document** task pane, click **On my computer**.

The Templates dialog box appears.

16 Click the **General** tab, click the **FaxTemplate** icon, and click **OK**.

The Garden Company's new fax template appears in the document window.

17 In the *To* line, click the *[Click here and type name]* placeholder, and type Flower Supplier.

18 In the *Fax* line, click the *[Click here and type fax number]* placeholder, and type 1-800-555-0190.

19 In the *Re* line, click the *[Click here and type subject of fax]* placeholder, and type Order Confirmation.

20 In the *Pages* line, click the *[Click here and type number of pages]* placeholder, and type 2.

21 In the *CC* line, click the *[Click here and type name]* placeholder, and press the [Del] key.

22 Scroll down, select the paragraph that starts with *Notes: Select this text and delete*, and press [Del].

The instructional text is deleted.

23 Type Please review this order and confirm that you will be able to deliver on time. and press [Enter].

The fax cover page is complete. Notice that Word has inserted today's date in the *Date* line.

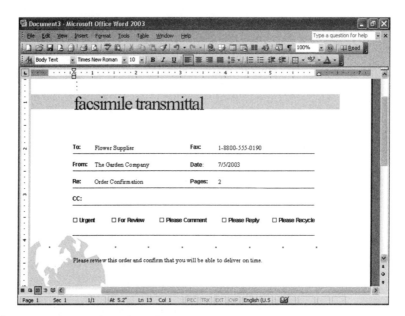

Save

24 On the Standard toolbar, click the **Save** button.

The Save As dialog box appears.

Troubleshooting Because you are working on a document, the setting in the "Save as type" text box should be Word Document. If it isn't, click the down arrow to the right of the text box, and click Word Document.

25 In the **File name** box, type FaxCover.

26 If My Documents is not displayed in the **Save in** text box, click the **My Documents** icon on the Places bar.

27 Double-click the *Microsoft Press* folder, double-click the *Word 2003 SBS* folder, double-click the *ArrangingDoc* folder, double-click the *ChangingTemplate* folder, and then click **Save**.

The document based on the template is saved in the designated folder.

CLOSE the *FaxCover* document.

Applying a New Template to an Existing Document

A quick and easy way to change the look of an existing document is to apply a new template to it. For this to work smoothly, the new template must use the same paragraph and character style names as the existing template. For example, if the existing template uses the name Heading 1 for top-level headings, the new template must also use the name

Heading 1. If the style names do not match, you can still apply a new template to a document and then use the Replace command on the Edit menu to find all instances of each particular style and replace them with one of the new template's corresponding styles.

To apply a new template to an open document:

1 On the **Tools** menu, click **Templates and Add-Ins**.

The Templates and Add-ins dialog box appears.

2 Click **Attach**, and then either double-click the template you want to apply, or browse to the location of the template you want and double-click it.

3 Make sure **Automatically update document styles** is selected, and then click **OK**.

The new template is attached and the styles used in the document change according to the new template.

To replace all instances of one style with another style:

1 On the **Edit** menu, click **Replace**.

The Find and Replace dialog box appears.

2 On the **Replace** tab, click the **Find what** box, and if the **Search Options** area isn't visible, click the **More** button.

3 Click the **Format** button, and then click **Style** to open the **Find Style** dialog box.

4 Click a style in the **Find what style** list, and then click **OK**.

5 Click the **Replace with** box, click **Format**, click **Style**, make a selection in the **Replace With Style** box, and click **OK**.

6 Click **Replace All**.

7 Repeat steps 2 through 6 for each style that needs replacing.

Changing a Document's Background

Microsoft
Office
Specialist

If you are creating a document that will be published on the Internet and viewed in a Web browser, you can make your document stand out by adding a background color or pattern. This type of background is displayed only in Web Layout view and is not designed to be printed.

There might be times when you want words or a graphic to appear faintly behind the text of a printed or online document. For example, the owner of The Garden Company might want the word *CONFIDENTIAL* to appear faintly behind the text in a contract, or an image of a plant to appear faintly behind the text in a press release. These faint background images are called *watermarks*. Watermarks are visible in a document but because they are faint, they don't interfere with the readers' ability to view the document's main text.

In this exercise, you will apply a background color and pattern, and then you'll add a text watermark.

USE the *FormatBackground* document in the practice file folder for this topic. This practice file is located in the *My Documents\Microsoft Press\Word 2003 SBS\ArrangingDoc\ChangingBack* folder and can also be accessed by clicking *Start/All Programs/Microsoft Press/Word 2003 Step by Step*.
OPEN the *FormatBackground* document.

Web Layout
View

1 In the lower-left corner of the document window, click the **Web Layout View** button.

2 On the **Format** menu, point to **Background**, and then in the fourth column of the fifth row of the color palette, click the **Light Green** box.

The background of the document changes to the selected color.

3 On the **Format** menu, point to **Background**, and then below the color palette, click **Fill Effects**.

The Fill Effects dialog box appears.

4 Click the **Texture** tab.

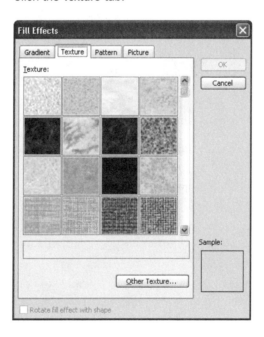

5 Click the effect in the fourth column of the first row, and click **OK**.

The background changes to display the effect.

6 In the lower-left corner of the window, click the **Print Layout View** button.

Because the background texture was applied in Web Layout view, the background does not appear in this view.

7 On the **Format** menu, point to **Background**, and then click **Printed Watermark**.

The Printed Watermark dialog box appears.

8 Select the **Text watermark** option.

9 Click the down arrow to the right of the **Text** box, scroll down the list, and click **URGENT**.

10 Click the down arrow to the right of the **Color** box, and click the **Bright Green** box in the fourth column of the fourth row.

11   Click **OK**.

12   Click the down arrow to the right of the **Zoom** box, and click **Whole Page**.

The document displays the watermark with the style you specified.

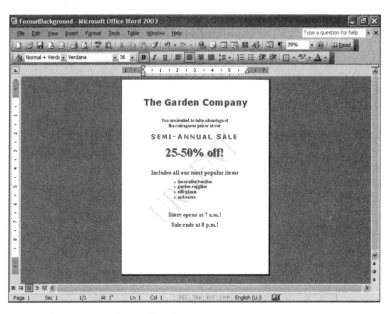

13   On the Standard toolbar, click the **Save** button.

Word saves your changes to the document.

CLOSE the *FormatBackground* document.

Using a Picture as a Watermark

When you want to dress up the pages of your document without distracting attention from the main text, you might want to consider adding a graphic watermark.

To add a graphic watermark to every page of a document:

1   If you are not in Print Layout view, in the lower-left corner of the window, click the **Print Layout View** button.

2   On the **Format** menu, point to **Background**, and click **Printed Watermark**.

The Printed Watermark dialog box appears.

3   Select the **Picture watermark** option, and then click the **Select Picture** button.

The Insert Picture dialog box appears.

4   Double-click the picture you want to insert as a watermark. (You might have to browse to find it.)

5   Click the down arrow to the right of the **Scale** box, and choose how big or small you want the watermark picture to appear in the document.

6   For a more vibrant picture, clear the **Washout** check box.

7   Click **OK**.

Changing a Document's Theme

Microsoft Office Specialist

You can change the entire look of a document by applying one of Word's pre-defined themes. A *theme* is a unified look that incorporates heading styles, text styles formatted with font effects, lists with specially designed bullet characters, background colors, fill effects, and images. Each theme provides color schemes and graphical design elements that project a specific image or tone. For example, the Axis theme uses a background that looks like parchment paper with text design elements that match. You might want to use a theme when designing Web pages, reports, and presentations.

In this exercise, you'll apply a theme to an existing document and then display the theme styles in the Styles and Formatting task pane.

USE the *FormatTheme* document in the practice file folder for this topic. This practice file is located in the *My Documents\Microsoft Press\Word 2003 SBS\ArrangingDoc\ChangingTheme* folder and can also be accessed by clicking *Start/All Programs/Microsoft Press/Word 2003 Step by Step.*

OPEN the *FormatTheme* document.

1 On the **Format** menu, click **Theme**.

The Theme dialog box appears.

2 Scroll the **Choose a Theme** list until the Layers theme appears, and then click **Layers**.

Troubleshooting Some themes don't appear in the Theme dialog box until you install them. Word will display a message if you need to install the selected theme.

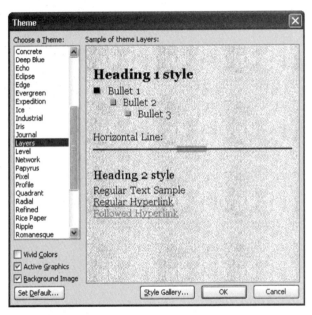

3 Click **OK** to apply the Layers theme to the document.

4 Select the *Why Compost?* heading.

5 On the **Format** menu, click **Styles and Formatting**.

The Styles and Formatting task pane appears, displaying the styles used in the Layers theme.

6 Scroll down the **Pick formatting to apply** list, and point to Heading 2 to see the formatting of the style.

7 Close the **Styles and Formatting** task pane.

Save

8 On the Standard toolbar, click the **Save** button.

Word saves your changes to the document.

CLOSE the *FormatTheme* document.

Previewing and Printing a Document

*Microsoft
Office
Specialist*

Before printing a document, you should verify that it looks the way you want. You save time, money, and paper by avoiding duplicate printing. Print Preview shows you exactly how your text will be printed on each page. This is essential for multi-page documents, but is helpful even for one-page documents. The Print Preview toolbar provides the tools that you need to check the presentation of each page. You can see the layout, and you can even change the text from this view.

The way a page is laid out in a printed document is called the page *orientation*. The default orientation in Word is *portrait*. With this orientation, the page is taller than it is wide. You can also set the orientation to *landscape*, in which the page is wider than it is tall.

Print Preview toolbar   Portrait orientation

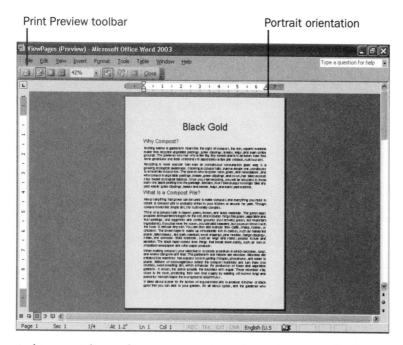

A document has only one page orientation unless you divide your document into sections. Then each section can have its own page orientation.

See Also   For more information about sections, see "Controlling What Appears on Each Page" later in this chapter.

You can change the margins of a document to fit more or less information on a page or to control where the information appears. You define the size of the top, bottom, left, and right margins on the Margins tab of the Page Setup dialog box.

When you are satisfied with the way a document looks in Print Preview, you can print it by clicking the Print button on the Standard toolbar or on the Print Preview toolbar. Word then uses the settings specified in the Print dialog box and your computer's default printer. To view or change the print settings, click Print on the File menu to open the Print dialog box. You can then specify which printer to use, what to print, and how many copies, and make other changes to the settings.

In this exercise, you will preview a document, adjust the top margin, change the orientation, and select a new printer before sending the document to be printed.

BE SURE TO install a printer and turn it on before starting this exercise.
USE the *ViewPages* document in the practice file folder for this topic. This practice file is located in the *My Documents\Microsoft Press\Word 2003 SBS\ArrangingDoc\PreviewingDoc* folder and can also be accessed by clicking *Start/All Programs/Microsoft Press/Word 2003 Step by Step.*
OPEN the *ViewPages* document.

Print Preview

1   On the Standard toolbar, click the **Print Preview** button.

The Print Preview window appears.

Multiple Pages

2   On the Print Preview toolbar, click the **Multiple Pages** button, and then click the page box in the third column of the second row.

You have told Word to display up to six pages (2 x 3 Pages), and all four pages of the document are now visible.

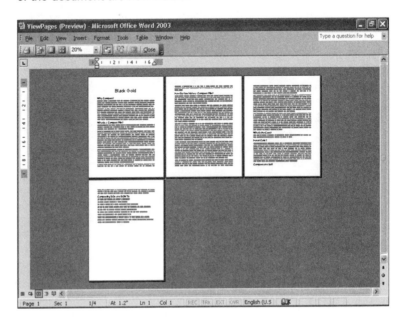

3 On the **File** menu, click **Page Setup**.

The Page Setup dialog box appears, displaying the Margins tab.

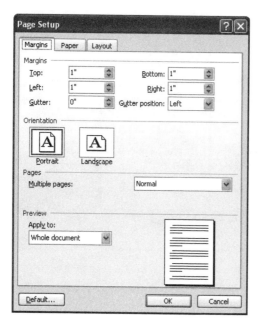

4 In the **Margins** area, replace the value in the **Top** box by typing **1.5"**. Then replace the values in the **Bottom**, **Left**, and **Right** boxes with **1.5"**, and click **OK**.

The width of the margins increases, and the text rewraps to fill an extra page. Page 5 is now visible in Print Preview.

Tip With margins of 1.5 inches on all sides, you are left with a work area that is 5.5 inches by 8 inches.

5 On the Print Preview toolbar, click the **Close** button to close the Print Preview window.

6 On the **File** menu, click **Page Setup** to open the Page Setup dialog box

7 In the **Orientation** area of the **Margins** tab, click the **Landscape** icon, and click **OK**.

8 On the Standard toolbar, click the **Print Preview** button.

The pages of the document are now wider than they are tall.

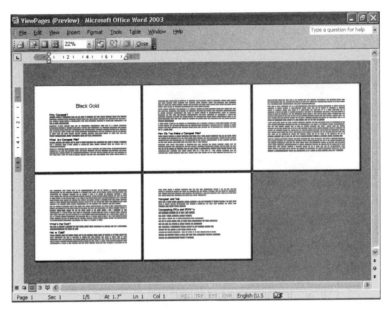

9   Point to the top of the white section of the vertical ruler, and when the pointer changes to a two-headed arrow and you see the **Top Margin** ScreenTip, drag the pointer up about a half inch.

10   Repeat step 9 to decrease the bottom margin on the vertical ruler and the left and right margins on the horizontal ruler about a half inch.

Troubleshooting   Be careful not to change the left or right indent; you want to adjust the margin using the two-headed arrow.

The document is now four pages long again.

Tip   You can fine-tune your page settings on the Margins tab of the Page Setup dialog box.

11   Point to the top of the first page of the document, where the pointer becomes a magnifying glass, and click.

The Zoom percentage changes to 100%.

12   Click near the top of the document again.

The Zoom percentage changes back to showing all the pages of the document.

13 On the Print Preview toolbar, click the **Close Preview** button.

14 On the **File** menu, click **Print**.

The Print dialog box appears.

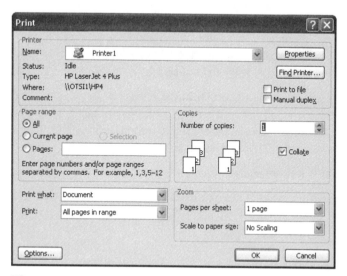

Print

Tip If you want to use the current Print dialog box settings, you can click the Print button on either the Print Preview or Standard toolbar to print the document without first viewing the settings.

15 If you have more than one printer available to you and you want to switch printers, click the down arrow to the right of the **Name** box, and click the printer you want in the drop-down list.

16 In the **Page Range** area, click the **Current Page** option.

17 In the **Copies** area, change the **Number of copies** setting to **2**, and then click **OK**.

Word prints two copies of the first page of the document on the printer you have designated.

CLOSE the *ViewPages* document without saving it.

Printing Envelopes and Labels

You can print envelopes and labels using addresses that you have entered in a document. To do this, you select the text you want for the envelope or label, point to Letters and Mailings on the Tools menu, and then click Envelopes and Labels to open the Envelopes and Labels dialog box. You can edit the addresses directly in this dialog box, and you can choose to print the envelope and label text in the font and font size that match those used in the document. You can choose the type of envelope or label that you need.

You can include a return address on the envelope. To provide a return address, Word uses the information that you entered when you installed Word. You can change that information on the User Information tab in the Options dialog box, which you open by clicking Options on the Tools menu.

To print an envelope using information in a document:

1   Select the lines of the address. (Do not select any blank lines below the address.)

2   On the **Tools** menu, point to **Letters and Mailings**, and then click **Envelopes and Labels**.

     The Envelopes and Labels dialog box appears with the address selected in the "Delivery address" box.

3   If you are using preprinted envelopes and don't want Word to print a return address, select the **Omit** check box.

4   Size 10 is the default envelope size. If you want to select a different envelope size, click **Options**, make your selection, and click **OK**.

5   Insert an envelope in the printer according to your printer manufacturer's directions, and click **Print**.

To print a label using information in a document:

1   Select the lines of the address. (Do not select any blank lines below the address.)

2   On the **Tools** menu, point to **Letters and Mailings**, click **Envelopes and Labels** to display the Envelopes and Labels dialog box, and then click the **Labels** tab.

3   In the **Print** area, select the **Single label** option.

     Row 1 and Column 1 appear under the "Single label" option.

4   Click **Print**.

Controlling What Appears on Each Page

Microsoft Office Specialist

When you create a document that contains more than one page, Word paginates your document by inserting soft page breaks. A *soft page break* produces separate pages in Print Layout view, and appears as a dotted line across the page in Normal view.

If you want to control how pages break, you can insert manual page breaks. A *manual page break* produces separate pages in Print Layout view, and appears as a dotted line across the page with the words *Page Break* in the middle in Normal view.

Tip   Word repaginates a document as you make changes to it. In other words, as you insert, delete, and move text, Word changes where it inserts soft page breaks. Word does not change the location of manual page breaks; you must do that yourself.

Regardless of whether you keep Word's soft page breaks or insert your own manual page breaks, you should make sure that these page breaks do not leave widows and orphans—individual lines that don't stay with their paragraphs. Word defines a *widow* as the last line of a paragraph printed by itself at the top of a page and an *orphan* as the first line of a paragraph printed by itself at the bottom of a page. Leaving one line at the top or bottom of a page can interrupt the flow of long documents. To eliminate widows and orphans and to control where Word inserts page breaks, you can use the following options on the Line and Page Breaks tab of the Paragraph dialog box:

- The "Widow/Orphan control" option prevents Word from printing the last line of a paragraph by itself at the top of a page (widow) or the first line of a paragraph by itself at the bottom of a page (orphan).

- The "Keep lines together" option prevents a page break within a paragraph.

- The "Keep with next" option prevents a page break between the selected paragraph and the following paragraph.

- The "Page break before" option inserts a page break before the selected paragraph.

Tip   You can apply the options in the Paragraph dialog box to individual paragraphs, or you can incorporate them into paragraph styles.

In addition to page breaks, you can insert section breaks in your documents. A *section break* identifies a part of the document to which you can apply page settings, such as orientation or margins, that are different from those of the rest of the document.

Dividing a document into sections is especially helpful when you are creating long documents that include elements such as tables that need to be turned sideways or skinny lists that look better when formatted in multiple columns. Several types of section breaks are available:

- The "Next page" option starts the following text on the next page.

- The "Continuous" option creates a section break without affecting page breaks.

- The "Even page" option forces a break to the next even-numbered page.

- The "Odd page" option forces a break to the next odd-numbered page.

A section break is not displayed in Print Layout view. In Normal view, a section break appears as a double-dotted line across the page with the words *Section Break* and the type of section break in the middle.

If you have a multi-page document, you might want to insert page numbers. You can do this by using the Page Numbers command on the Insert menu. By default, page numbers appear in the lower-right corner of each page, but you can change their position and alignment by using the Position and Alignment options in the Page Numbers dialog box. For example, you can display page numbers at the top or bottom of a page, and centered or in a corner.

You can also display page numbers and other information on every page of your document by creating *headers* and *footers*—regions at the top and bottom of a page that can be created and formatted independently. If your document contains section breaks, you can have different headers and footers for each section. To create a header or footer, you click the Header and Footer command on the View menu. Word then switches to Print Layout view, outlines the header and footer areas with dotted borders, and displays the Header and Footer toolbar. You can enter information in the header and footer areas the same way you enter ordinary text, and you can use the buttons on the toolbar to enter and format items such as page numbers and to move from one header or footer to another.

In this exercise, you will insert page and section breaks, ensure that page breaks do not leave widows and orphans, and add a header and a footer to a document.

USE the *FormatPage* document in the practice file folder for this topic. This practice file is located in the *My Documents\Microsoft Press\Word 2003 SBS\ArrangingDoc\ControllingPage* folder and can also be accessed by clicking *Start/All Programs/Microsoft Press/Word 2003 Step by Step.*
OPEN the *FormatPage* document.

1 If necessary, switch to Print Layout view, and set your zoom level to **100%**.

2 Scroll through the document, noticing any widows or orphans.

3 On the **Edit** menu, click **Select All**.

4 On the **Format** menu, click **Paragraph** to display the **Paragraph** dialog box, and then click the **Line and Page Breaks** tab.

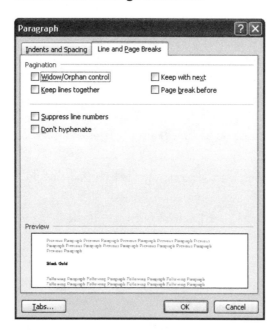

5 Select the **Widow/Orphan control** check box, select the **Keep lines together** check box, and then click **OK**.

Now all the lines of text in each paragraph appear on the same page.

6 Scroll the document, and click to the left of the *Hot or Cold?* heading.

7 On the **Insert** menu, click **Break**.

The Break dialog box appears.

8 In the **Break types** area, verify that the **Page break** option is selected, and then click **OK**.

9 Switch to Normal view, and scroll upward.

A dotted line with the words *Page Break* indicates the location of a manual page break.

10 Scroll down the document, and click to the left of the *Composting DOs and DON'Ts* heading.

11 On the **Insert** menu, click **Break** to open the Break dialog box, select the **Next page** option in the **Section break types** area, and click **OK**.

A double dotted line with the words *Section Break (Next Page)* appears.

12 Press ⌃Ctrl+Home to move the insertion point to the beginning of the document, and then on the **View** menu, click **Header and Footer**.

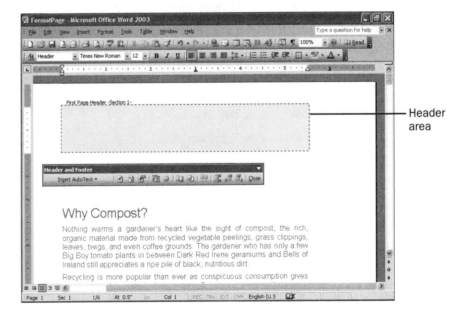

Header area

Word switches to Print Layout view, outlines the header area at the top of the page, positions the insertion point in the header, and displays the Header and Footer toolbar.

Center

13 Type The Garden Company, and on the Formatting toolbar, click the **Center** button. Then select the text, click **Font** on the **Format** menu, change the font to **Verdana**, change the size to **14**, and make the text bold and green.

14 Click the **Character Spacing** tab, change the spacing so that it is expanded by **10 pt**, and click **OK**.

Show Next

15 On the Header and Footer toolbar, click the **Show Next** button.

Word moves to the page after the section break you inserted earlier. By default, the header for this section is the same as the previous one.

Link to
Previous

16 On the Header and Footer toolbar, click the **Link to Previous** button to toggle it off.

You can now use a different header for this section of the document or leave the header blank.

17 Select The Garden Company, and press ⌈Del⌋.

The company name is deleted from the header.

Switch
Between
Header and
Footer

18 Click the **Switch Between Header and Footer** button to switch to the footer text box.

The insertion point is now positioned in the footer.

Show Previous

19 On the Header and Footer toolbar, click the **Link to Previous** button to toggle it off, and then click the **Show Previous** button.

Word displays the footer for the previous section.

Insert Page
Number

20 Press the ⌈Tab⌋ key twice to move the insertion point to the right tab stop, click the **Insert Page Number** button on the Header and Footer toolbar, select the number, and make it bold and green.

The first five pages in the first section of the document are now numbered, but the sixth page isn't.

Tip   On the Header and Footer toolbar are buttons you can click to insert the data and time, as well as page numbers and the number of pages in the document. You can also click the Insert AutoText button to drop down a list of other items that can be inserted. These items all insert fields that Word then substitutes with the requested information. You can also insert a field directly in a document by clicking Field on the Insert menu and then clicking an option in the "Field names" list.

Close

21 On the Header and Footer toolbar, click the **Close** button.

22 Switch to Print Layout view, and scroll through the document to see your formatting.

Save

23 On the Standard toolbar, click the **Save** button.

Word saves your changes to the document.

CLOSE the *FormatPage* document, and if you are not continuing on to the next chapter, quit Word.

Formatting Page Numbers

When you insert page numbers in headers or footers, you can format them directly using buttons on the Formatting toolbar as long as the header and footer areas are active. If you want to change the formatting later you can change it by by clicking Page Numbers on the Insert menu and making changes in the Page Numbers dialog box.

To format existing page numbers:

1 On the **Insert** menu, click **Page Numbers**.

The Page Numbers dialog box appears.

2 Click the **Format** button.

The Page Number Format dialog box appears.

3 Click the down arrow to the right of the **Number Format** box, and click the number format you want.

4 Select any other options you want to apply, and then click **OK**.

5 Click the down arrow to the right of the **Position** box, and click the location where you want the page numbers to appear.

6 Click the down arrow to the right of the **Alignment** box, and click the alignment setting you want.

7 Click **OK** to close the Page Numbers dialog box.

Key Points

- You can create a document based on one of Word's predefined templates. You can also create your own templates by modifying an existing template or saving a formatted document as a template.

- You can apply a background color or pattern to a document that will be viewed onscreen, and you can add a text or picture watermark to a print document.

- By applying a theme, you can give a document a unified look that incorporates heading and text styles, lists with specially designed bullet characters, background colors and fill effects, and images.

- You can see how a document will look when printed by using Print Preview, and you can adjust margins and page orientation. You can then print the document with the default print settings or specific settings.

- You can control how each page in your document looks by applying different margins and formatting to different sections, specifying which elements should be kept together on a page, and adding information in headers and footers.

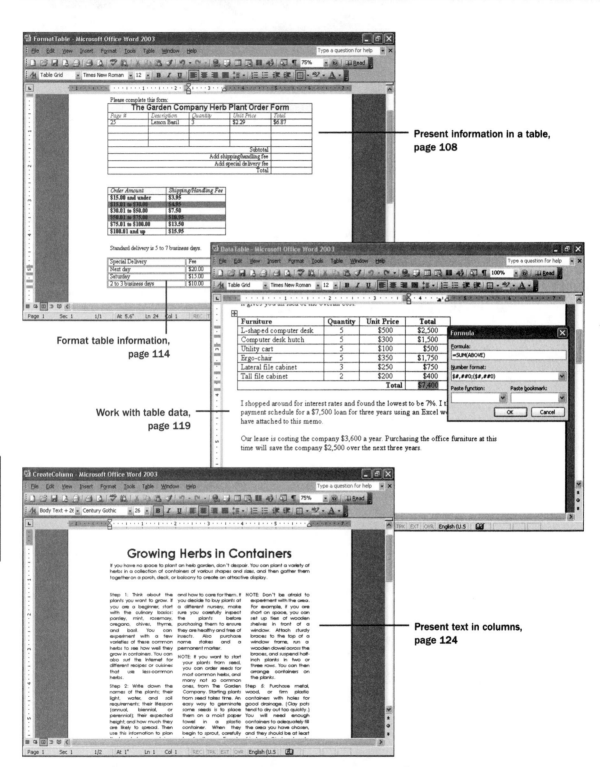

Present information in a table,
page 108

Format table information,
page 114

Work with table data,
page 119

Present text in columns,
page 124

Chapter 5 at a Glance

5 Presenting Information in Tables and Columns

In this chapter you will learn to:

✔ Present information in a table.

✔ Format table information.

✔ Work with table data.

✔ Present text in columns.

You can use a table to make information in a document concise, consistent, and easy to read. A table organizes information neatly into rows and columns. The intersection of a row and column is called a *cell*. With Microsoft Office Word 2003, you can create a uniform table with standard-sized cells, draw a custom table with various-sized cells, or you can create a table from existing text. After you create your table, you can enter text, numbers, and graphics into cells. At any time, you can change the table's size; insert and delete columns, rows, and cells; and format individual entries or the entire table. To help readers interpret the information in your table, you can sort the information in a logical order. To perform standard mathematical calculations on numbers in a table—for example, to total the values in a column or row—you can use the Formula command on the Table menu. To perform more complex calculations or statistical analysis, you can create a Microsoft Excel worksheet and insert it into your document.

To group and organize information in a document, you can use columns of text. Dividing text into columns is useful when you are creating a newsletter or brochure. In Word, you can define the number of columns you want on a page and then allow text to flow from the bottom of one column to the top of the next, as in newspapers. You can also manually end one column and move subsequent text to the next column.

In this chapter, you will create and format tables, and work with table data. You will also format text that currently appears in one column into four columns.

See Also   Do you need only a quick refresher on the topics in this chapter? See the Quick Reference entries on pages xli–xlii.

Important Before you can use the practice files in this chapter, you need to install them from the book's companion CD to their default location. See "Using the Book's CD-ROM" on page xiii for more information.

Presenting Information in a Table

Microsoft
Office
Specialist

To add a simple table to a document, you can use the Insert Table button on the Standard toolbar and then select the number of rows and columns you want from the grid that appears. If you want to set the size of the table along with other options, such as table formatting, you use the Insert command on the Table menu to open the Insert Table dialog box. You can also convert existing plain text into a table.

After you create a table, you can type text or numbers into cells and press the [Tab] key to move the insertion point from cell to cell. If the insertion point is positioned in the rightmost cell in the last row of the table, pressing [Tab] adds another row to the bottom of the table. In addition to the [Tab] key, you can use the arrow keys or you can simply click a cell to position the insertion point there.

You can modify a table's structure at any time. To change the structure, you often need to select the entire table or specific rows or columns, using the following methods:

■ To select the entire table, click the Select Table button that appears above and to the left of the first cell in the table whenever you point to the table. Or on the Table menu, point to Select, and then click Table.

■ To select a column or row, point to the top border of the column or the left border of the row, and when the pointer changes to an arrow, click once.

■ To select a cell, triple-click the cell.

■ To select multiple cells, click the first cell, hold down the [Shift] key, and press the arrow keys to select adjacent cells in a column or row.

Tip The document must be in Print Layout view for you to use the Select Table button at the upper-left of the table or the table resize handle at the lower right of the table.

After you've learned the fundamentals of working with tables, you can efficiently organize large amounts and various types of information. The basic methods for manipulating tables are as follows:

■ Insert a row or column. Click anywhere in a row or column adjacent to where you want to make the insertion. Then on the Table menu, point to Insert, and click Rows Above, Rows Below, Columns to the Right, or Columns to the Left. If you select more than one row or column and use an Insert command, Word inserts that number of rows or columns in the table.

- Delete a row or column. Click anywhere in the row or column, and on the Table menu, point to Delete, and then click Rows or Columns.

- Size an entire table. To size a table quickly, drag the table resize handle in the lower-right corner of the table in Print Layout view.

- Size a single column or row. Change the width of a column or row by pointing to its right or bottom border and dragging it.

- Merge cells. Create cells that span columns by selecting the cells you want to merge and clicking Merge Cells on the Table menu. For example, to center a title in the first row of a table, you can create one merged cell that spans the table's width.

- Split cells. If you need to divide a merged cell into its component cells, split it by clicking Split Cells on the Table menu.

- Move a table. Select the table, and drag it to a new location. Or use the Cut and Paste commands to move the table.

- Sort information. Use the Sort command on the Table menu to sort the rows in ascending or descending order by the data in any column. For example, you can sort a table that has the column headings Name, Address, ZIP Code, and Phone Number on any one of those columns to arrange the information in alphabetical or numerical order.

In this exercise, you will work with three tables. First you'll create a table, enter text, add rows, and merge cells. Then you'll create a second table by converting existing tabbed text. Finally, you'll sort information in a third table.

BE SURE TO start Word before beginning this exercise.
USE the *CreateTable* document in the practice file folder for this topic. This practice file is located in the *My Documents\Microsoft Press\Word 2003 SBS\PresentingInfo\PresentingTable* folder and can also be accessed by clicking *Start/All Programs/Microsoft Press/Word 2003 Step by Step*.
OPEN the *CreateTable* document.

1 Press the ⬇ key to position the insertion point in the blank line below the *Please complete this form* paragraph.

2 On the **Table** menu, point to **Insert**, and then click **Table**.

The Insert Table dialog box appears.

3 Be sure that the **Number of columns** box displays **5**, click the **Number of rows** up arrow to display **5**, and then click **OK**.

A blank table with five columns and five rows appears. The insertion point is located in the first cell.

4 In the selection area, point to the first row, and click to select the row.

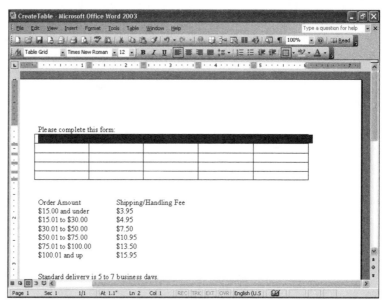

5 On the **Table** menu, click **Merge Cells** to combine the cells in the first row into one cell.

6 Type The Garden Company Herb Plant Order Form.

The text appears in the first row.

7 Click the first cell in the second row, type Page #, and press [Tab].

8 Type Description, and press [Tab]. Then, pressing [Tab] after each entry to move the insertion point to the next column, type Quantity ([Tab]), Unit Price ([Tab]), and Total ([Tab]).

The insertion point is now in the first column of the third row.

9 Type 25, press [Tab], and then type Lemon basil ([Tab]), 3 ([Tab]), $2.29, ([Tab]), and $6.87.

10 In the selection area, point to the fourth row, hold down the mouse button, and drag downward to select the last two rows.

11 On the **Table** menu, point to **Insert**, and then click **Rows Below**.

Word adds two new rows and selects them.

12 In the last row, click the first cell, hold down [Shift], and then press [→] four times to select the first four cells in the row.

13 On the **Table** menu, click **Merge Cells**.

Word combines the selected cells in the last row into one cell.

14 Type Subtotal, and press [Tab] twice.

Word adds a new row to the bottom of the table. Note that the new row has the same structure as the preceding row.

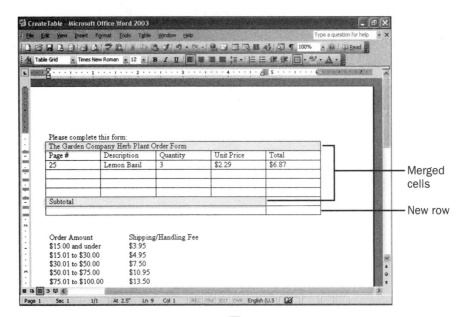

15 Type Add shipping/handling fee, press [Tab] twice to add a new row, and then type Add special delivery fee.

16 Press [Tab] twice to add a new row, and then type Total.

17 Below the table, select the paragraphs that begin with *Order Amount* and end with *$15.95*.

18 On the **Table** menu, point to **Convert**, and then click **Text to Table**.

The Convert Text to Table dialog box appears.

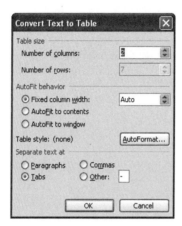

19 Make sure that the **Number of columns** box displays **2**, and then click **OK**.

The selected text appears in a table with two columns and seven rows.

20 Click the table to deselect the cells, and point to the right border of the table. When the pointer changes to two opposing arrows, double-click the right border to make the right column just wide enough to hold its longest line of text.

21 Scroll down, click anywhere in the special delivery table, and on the **Table** menu, click **Sort**.

The Sort dialog box appears.

22 Click the down arrow to the right of the **Sort by** box, and click **Fee**.

23 Select the **Descending** option. Then make sure the **Header row** option in the **My list has** area is selected, and click **OK**.

Word sorts the table in descending order based on the Fee column.

24 Point to the selected special delivery table.

Word displays a Select Table button and a table resize handle.

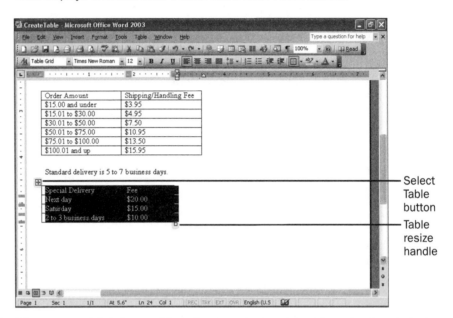

Select Table button

Table resize handle

25 With the special delivery table still selected, drag the table resize handle in the lower-right corner to the right, releasing the mouse button when the right edges of the special delivery and shipping and handling fees tables are aligned.

Tip To make finer adjustments, hold down the Alt key while you drag, but be careful not to click the mouse button. Alt+click opens the Research task pane.

26 On the Standard toolbar, click the **Save** button.

Save

Word saves your changes to the document.

CLOSE the *CreateTable* document.

Formatting Table Information

Microsoft Office Specialist

To enhance the appearance of a table, you can format its text by using the buttons on the Formatting toolbar, just as you would to format any text in a Word document. You can apply character formatting such as font styles and font effects, and you can apply paragraph formatting such as alignment and indenting.

You can also format the table's structure by adding borders and shading. Clicking the Borders and Shading command on the Format menu opens the Borders and Shading dialog box, where you can specify options to best delineate the relationships within your table.

To quickly apply predefined sets of formatting to a table, you can choose a *table autoformat*. Clicking the Table AutoFormat command on the Table menu displays the Table AutoFormat dialog box, which offers formats that include a variety of borders, colors, and attributes to give your tables a professional look.

Working with Table Properties

You can control many aspects of a table by clicking Table Properties on the Table menu and setting options on the tabs of the Table Properties dialog box. On the Table tab, you can specify the preferred width of the entire table, as well as the way it interacts with the surrounding text. On the Row tab, you can specify the height of each row, whether a row is allowed to break across pages, and whether a row of column headings should be repeated at the top of each page. On the Column tab, you can set the width of each column, and on the Cell tab, you can set the preferred width of cells and the vertical alignment of text within them.

To adjust table properties:

1   On the **Table** menu, click **Table Properties**.

The Table Properties dialog box appears.

2   Click the tab of the table element whose properties you want to adjust.

3   Make adjustments to the properties as necessary.

4   Click **OK** to close the **Table Properties** dialog box.

Creating Styles for Tables

If none of the table autoformats meets your needs, you can create formatting styles for table text in much the same way you create styles for regular paragraph text.

To create a style for text in a table:

1 On the **Format** menu, click **Styles and Formatting**.

The Styles and Formatting task pane appears.

2 In the **Styles and Formatting** task pane, click **New Style**.

The New Style dialog box appears.

3 Type a name for the new style, click the down arrow to the right of the **Style type** box, and click **Table**.

4 Click the down arrow to the right of the **Apply formatting to** box, and select which text the new style should be applied to.

5 Select the formatting options you want, and click **OK**.

6 Select the text you want to format with the new style, and in the **Pick formatting to apply** list, click the style.

Many of the table formatting tools are available on the Tables and Borders toolbar. You can turn on this toolbar either by clicking Toolbars on the View menu and then clicking Tables and Borders, or by clicking the Tables and Borders button on the Standard toolbar.

In this exercise, you will format the text in a table and add shading to a cell. You'll also apply an autoformat and add a border to a table.

USE the *FormatTable* document in the practice file folder for this topic. This practice file is located in the *My Documents\Microsoft Press\Word 2003 SBS\PresentingInfo\FormattingTable* folder and can also be accessed by clicking *Start/All Programs/Microsoft Press/Word 2003 Step by Step*.
OPEN the *FormatTable* document.

1 In the selection area, point to the first row in the order-form table, and click to select the first row.

2 On the Formatting toolbar, click the down arrow to the right of the **Font** box, and click **Arial**. Then click the down arrow to the right of the **Font Size** box, and click **16**.

B
Bold

3 On the Formatting toolbar, click the **Bold** button.

The bold font style is applied to the text.

Center

4 On the Formatting toolbar, click the **Center** button.

The text appears in the center of the cell.

5 On the **Format** menu, click **Borders and Shading**.

The Borders and Shading dialog box appears.

6 Click the **Shading** tab.

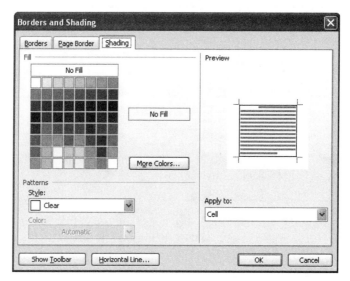

7 In the third column of the seventh row in the color palette, click the **Yellow** box, and then click **OK**.

Word shades the background of the first row in light yellow.

8 Select the second row of the table.

I
Italic

9 On the Formatting toolbar, click the **Bold** button, and then click the **Italic** button.

The headings in the second row are now italic.

Font Color

10 On the Formatting toolbar, click the down arrow to the right of the **Font Color** button, and then in the first column of the third row of the color palette, click the **Red** box.

11 Select the last four rows in the order-form table.

Align Right

12 On the Formatting toolbar, click the **Align Right** button.

Word aligns the text in the last four rows at the right margin.

Tip To change the direction of text in a cell—for example, to rotate column headings so that they read vertically instead of from left to right—select the cell(s), click Text Direction on the Format menu, and then make adjustments in the Text Direction – Table Cell dialog box.

13 Zoom the document to **75%**.

14 Click anywhere in the shipping and handling fees table, and on the **Table** menu, click **Table AutoFormat**.

The Table AutoFormat dialog box appears.

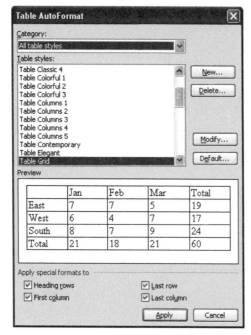

15 Scroll through the **Table styles** list, click **Table List 8**, and then click **Apply**.

Word formats the table in yellow and red.

16 Click anywhere in the special delivery table, and on the **Format** menu, click **Borders and Shading**. Then click the **Borders** tab.

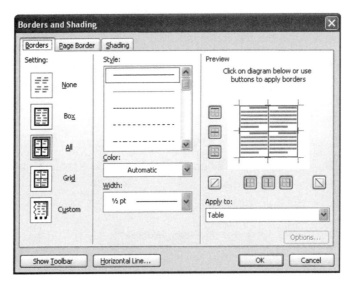

17 In the **Setting** area, make sure the **All** icon is selected.

18 In the **Style** list, click the down scroll arrow (not the scroll bar) twice, and then click the double-line style.

19 Click the down arrow to the right of the **Color** box, and in the first column of the third row of the color palette, click the **Red** box.

20 Click **OK**.

Word adds a red double border to the entire table.

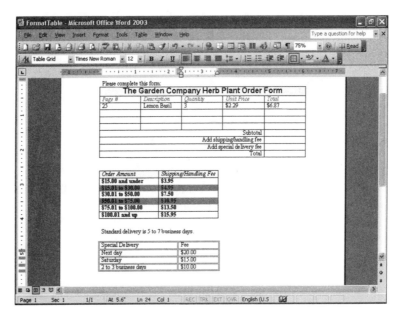

Save

21 On the Standard toolbar, click the **Save** button.

Word saves your changes to the document.

CLOSE the *FormatTable* document.

Working with Table Data

Microsoft Office Specialist

You can perform certain calculations on numbers in a Word table using one of Word's built-in formulas. A *formula* is a mathematical expression that performs calculations, such as adding or averaging values. To construct a formula, you use the Formula dialog box, which you can access by clicking Formula on the Table menu . A formula consists of an equal sign followed by a function name, such as SUM, followed by the location of the cells on which you want to perform the calculation.

This formula totals (sums) the values in the cells above the active cell.

To use a function other than SUM in the Formula dialog box, click the down arrow to the right of the "Paste function" box, and click the function you want in the drop-down list. Word has several built-in functions, including functions to count (COUNT) the number of values in a column or row or to find the maximum (MAX) or minimum (MIN) value in a series of cells.

Although many Word formulas refer to the cells above or to the left of the active cell, you can also use the contents of specified cells or constant values in formulas. To reference a particular cell in a formula, you type the *cell address* in parentheses after the function name. The cell address is a combination of the column letter and the row number, as in *a1* for the cell at the intersection of the first column and the first row. For example, the formula =SUM(b2,b3) totals the values in cells b2 and b3.

When Word's functions don't meet your needs, you can insert a Microsoft Office Excel worksheet in a Word document. Part of The Microsoft Office System, Excel is an electronic spreadsheet program that provides extensive mathematical and accounting capabilities. For example, you can use an Excel worksheet to determine a payment schedule for a loan.

There are three ways to insert Excel worksheet data into a Word document:

- By copying and pasting. You can open the Excel worksheet, copy the data you want to use, and paste it as a table in a Word document.

- By linking. You can use the Object command on the Insert menu to create a link between the source worksheet and the Word document.

- By embedding. You can also use the Object command on the Insert menu to embed a worksheet in a Word document. The worksheet then exists as an Excel object in the document rather than as a separate file, and you can continue to manipulate it using Excel.

Deciding How to Insert an Excel Worksheet

To decide how to insert an Excel worksheet in a Word document, you need to understand how Microsoft Office System programs integrate data from outside sources. This understanding will enable you to decide how to use information created in any other program, not just Excel.

If you need to maintain a connection with the source Excel worksheet or you need to be able to manipulate the data in Excel after it is included in the Word document, you can use Microsoft's *OLE Linking and Embedding* technology. This technology enables you to insert an *object* (a file or part of a file) created in one program into a file created in another program. The object is sometimes called the *source file*, and the file into which you are inserting the information is called the *destination file*. The difference between linking and embedding is the type of connection that is maintained between the source and destination files.

A *linked object* maintains a direct connection (or link) to the source file, and its data is stored there, not in the destination file. The destination file displays only a representation of the linked data. If you want to update the data, you do it in the source file. Then when you open the destination file, the linked object is updated.

An *embedded object* becomes part of the destination file. Its data is stored as well as displayed there and is no longer connected to the source file. If you want to update the data, you do it in the destination file using the source program, but the source file does not change.

Whether an object should be linked or embedded depends on whether the information in the destination file must be synchronized with the information in the source file.

If you do not need to maintain a connection between the source file and the destination file, you can copy and paste information between programs using the Copy and Paste buttons on the Standard toolbar. If you use this method, the source files and the destination files are not connected. The pasted information becomes part of the destination file, and you use the tools in the destination program to edit the pasted information.

Embedding a New Object

You can embed a variety of objects into a Word document including worksheets, charts, graphics, and sound or video clips. You can use existing files, or you can create new ones on the fly while you are working on a Word document.

To embed a new object in a Word document:

1 Click the document where you want to place the object.

2 On the **Insert** menu, click **Object**.

The Object dialog box appears.

3 If necessary, click the **Create New** tab, and in the **Object type** list, click the type of object you want to embed.

4 Select the **Display as icon** check box if you want the embedded object to appear in the document as an icon.

5 Click **OK**.

Word opens the windows and tools you need to create the object. These vary greatly, depending on which object you chose to insert.

6 Create the new object, and then click a blank area of the document to deselect your object.

Tip   After you have copied the worksheet data in Excel, you can use the Paste Special command on Word's Edit menu to link or embed the worksheet data. Paste Special enables you to copy information from one location and paste it in another location using a different format, such as Microsoft Excel Object, Picture, or HTML Format.

To update a linked or embedded worksheet, you double-click it in the Word document. If the worksheet is linked, the source worksheet opens in Excel. When you change the source worksheet, the linked worksheet in the Word document is also updated. If the worksheet is embedded, the Excel row and column headers appear and Excel's menus and toolbars replace Word's so that you can make changes to the worksheet object. The source worksheet remains unchanged.

Tip   If you change a value in a Word table, you must recalculate formulas manually. If you change a value in an Excel worksheet, the formulas are automatically recalculated.

In this exercise, you will calculate data in a table. Then you'll embed an Excel worksheet in a Word document and change the worksheet data.

USE the *DataTable* document and the *InsertTable* workbook in the practice file folder for this topic.
These practice files are located in the *My Documents\Microsoft Press\Word 2003 SBS\PresentingInfo*
\WorkingData folder and can also be accessed by clicking *Start/All Programs/Microsoft Press/Word 2003*
Step by Step.
OPEN the *DataTable* document.

1　Click the lower-right cell of the furniture table (to the right of the cell containing
Total).

2　On the **Table** menu, click **Formula** to open the **Formula** dialog box.

The Formula box shows the formula =*SUM(ABOVE)*, meaning that the formula
will add the numbers in the cells above the current (active) cell.

3　Click the down arrow to the right of the **Number format** box, and click
$#,##0.00;($#,##0.00), which specifies the format for positive and negative
currency values.

4　In the **Number format** box, delete **.00** from both the positive and negative portions
of the format.

5　Click **OK** to display the total cost of the furniture in the cell.

AutoSum

Tip　To quickly total a column or row of numbers, click the last cell in a column or
row of values, and then click the AutoSum button on the Tables and Borders toolbar.

6　Press Ctrl+End to move to the end of the document, and press Enter.

7　On the **Insert** menu, click **Object** to open the **Object** dialog box, and then click
the **Create from File** tab.

8　Click **Browse**, navigate to the *Microsoft Press\Word 2003 SBS\PresentingInfo*
\WorkingData folder, and then double-click the *InsertTable* file.

The InsertTable file appears in the "File name" box.

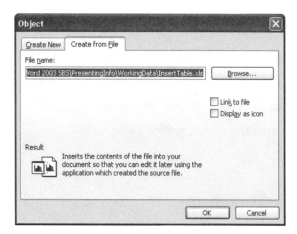

9 Make sure the **Link to file** and **Display as** icon options are not selected, and then click **OK**.

The Excel worksheet appears in the document.

10 Scroll up to see the beginning of the inserted worksheet, and double-click anywhere in the worksheet.

The Excel row and column headers appear above and to the left of the table, and Excel's menus and toolbars replace Word's.

11 Click cell **B4**, type 10000, and then press the Enter key.

New loan amount

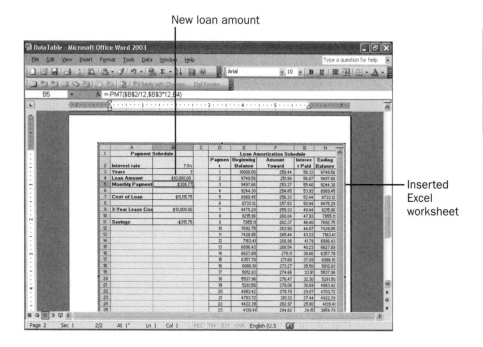

Inserted Excel worksheet

Excel recalculates the data in the table to show the payment schedule for a $10,000 loan.

12 Click anywhere outside the Excel worksheet.

The table is updated with the costs for a loan of $10,000.

Save

13 On the Standard toolbar, click the **Save** button.

Word saves your changes to the document.

CLOSE the *DataTable* document.

Presenting Text in Columns

Microsoft
Office
Specialist

By default, Word displays text in one column, but you can specify that text be displayed in two, three, or more columns to create layouts like those used in newsletters and brochures. In Word, a *column* is a block of text that has its own margins. When you create multiple columns, the text flows, or "snakes", from the bottom of one column to the top of the next. You can insert a column break to force subsequent text to move to the next column.

You can create a multi-column format by using the Columns command on the Format menu or the Columns button on the Standard toolbar. No matter how you set up the columns, you can change their width in the Columns dialog box, and you can format text in columns as you would any other text. For example, you can change the indentation or the alignment of text in a column using the horizontal ruler or buttons on the Formatting toolbar.

In this exercise, you will format text into four columns, reduce the amount of space between the columns, and indent column text. You'll also break the columns at specific locations instead of allowing the text to flow naturally from one column to the next.

USE the *CreateColumn* document in the practice file folder for this topic. This practice file is located in the *My Documents\Microsoft Press\Word 2003 SBS\PresentingInfo\PresentingColumn* folder and can also be accessed by clicking *Start/All Programs/Microsoft Press/Word 2003 Step by Step.*
OPEN the *CreateColumn* document.

1 Press [Enter], and then press [↑] to position the insertion point at the beginning of the document.

2 Type Growing Herbs in Containers, press [Enter], then type If you have no space to plant an herb garden, don't despair. You can plant a variety of herbs in a collection of containers of various shapes and sizes, and then gather them together on a porch, deck, or balcony to create an attractive display., and press [Enter].

3 Change the first paragraph of the document to 26-point, bold text so that this title stands out.

124

4 Click just to the left of the paragraph that begins *Step 1* (do not click in the selection area). Then double-click the letters *EXT* in the status bar to turn on Word's Extend Selection mode, and press Ctrl+End.

Word selects the text from the *Step 1* paragraph through the end of the document.

Tip If you want to format an entire document with the same number of columns, you can simply click anywhere in the document—you don't have to select the text.

5 On the **Format** menu, click **Columns**.

The Columns dialog box appears.

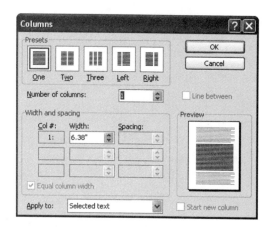

6 Click the up arrow to the right of the **Number of columns** box until the setting is **3**, and click **OK**.

Word inserts a section break above the selection. It then formats the text after the section break in three columns.

7 On the **Edit** menu, click **Select All** to select all the text in the document.

Justify

8 On the Formatting toolbar, click the **Justify** button.

All the paragraphs now align at their left and right margins.

Center

9 Press Ctrl+Home to deselect the text and move to the first paragraph of the document, and then on the Formatting toolbar, click the **Center** button to center the title.

Zoom

10 On the Standard toolbar, click the down arrow to the right of the **Zoom** button, and click **75%**.

More of the document is now displayed in the document window.

11 Click anywhere in the first column.

On the horizontal ruler, Word indicates the margins of the columns.

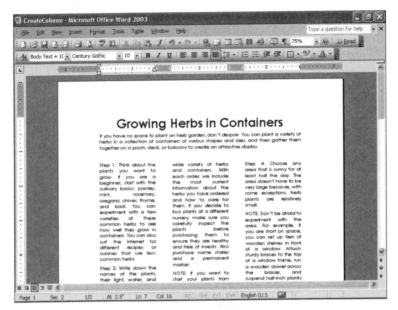

12 On the horizontal ruler, point to the **Right Margin** marker for the second column (the white bar to the right of the 4-inch mark), and when the pointer changes to a double-headed arrow, drag the indicator $^1/_8$ inch (one tick mark) to the right.

Word widens all the columns to reflect the new setting.

Tip Dragging the pointer to the right decreases the spacing between the columns, which decreases the amount of white space on the page. Dragging to the left increases the spacing, which increases the amount of white space.

13 Click anywhere in the *NOTE* paragraph toward the top of the second column.

△
Hanging Indent

14 On the horizontal ruler, drag the **Hanging Indent** marker $^1/_8$ inch (one tick mark) to the right.

All the lines in the *NOTE* paragraph except the first are now indented, offsetting the note from the step.

15 Click anywhere in the *NOTE* paragraph at the top of the third paragraph, and press the ⌜F4⌟ key to apply the same formatting to this paragraph.

16 Scroll to the second page, click just to the left of *Step 8*, click **Break** on the **Insert** menu to open the **Break** dialog box, select the **Column break** option, and then click **OK**.

The text that follows the column break moves to the top of the next column.

17 Click just to the left of *Step 10*, and press ⌜F4⌟.

The columns are now more evenly balanced on the page.

Print Preview

18 On the Standard toolbar, click the **Print Preview** button to view the document formatted in columns.

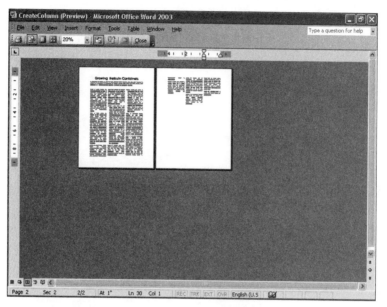

Close

19 On the Print Preview toolbar, click the **Close** button to close the print preview window.

Save

20 On the Standard toolbar, click the **Save** button.

Word saves your changes to the document.

CLOSE the *CreateColumn* document, and if you are not continuing on to the next chapter, quit Word.

Key Points

- You can create a table and format it to make information concise, consistent, and easy to read.

- You can format text in a table using the buttons on the Formatting toolbar, and you can add borders and shading. You can also format a table and its text quickly by applying a table autoformat.

- You can perform calculations on the values in a table using one of Word's built-in formulas. For complex calculations or analyses, you can insert an Excel worksheet in a Word document.

- To vary the layout of a document, you can create two, three, or more columns and format column text as you would any other text.

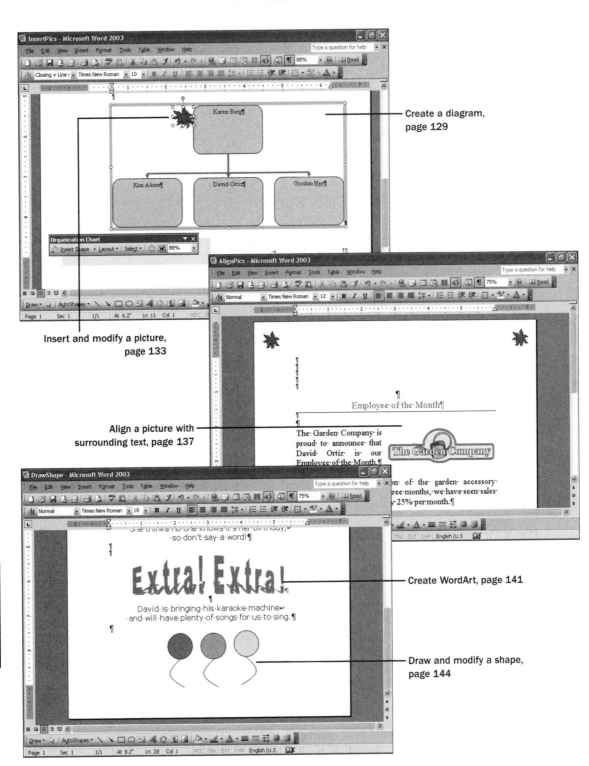

Create a diagram, page 129

Insert and modify a picture, page 133

Align a picture with surrounding text, page 137

Create WordArt, page 141

Draw and modify a shape, page 144

6 Working with Graphics

In this chapter you will learn to:

✔ Create a diagram.

✔ Insert and modify a picture.

✔ Align a picture with the surrounding text.

✔ Create WordArt.

✔ Draw and modify a shape.

You can insert graphics in Microsoft Office Word 2003 to make your documents more visually appealing and to convey information that is difficult to get across in words. A *graphic* is any picture or drawing object. A *picture* is an image created outside of Word—a scanned photograph, clip art, or a file created on a computer with a graphics program. A *drawing object* is an image created within Word—an AutoShape, a diagram, a line, or a WordArt object.

You can use the Drawing toolbar to insert pictures and draw different kinds of objects. After you add a graphic to a document, you can enhance it with colors and special effects. You can also change its position by using layout options and changing how the graphic and other elements on the page relate to each other.

In this chapter, you'll create a diagram, insert pictures, change a picture to appear faintly in the background, change how text and graphics are laid out, insert a WordArt object, and draw and modify shapes.

See Also Do you need only a quick refresher on the topics in this chapter? See the Quick Reference entries on pages xliii–xliv.

 Important Before you can use the practice files in this chapter, you need to install them from the book's companion CD to their default location. See "Using the Book's CD-ROM" on page xiii for more information.

Creating a Diagram

Microsoft Office Specialist

To present hierarchical data or other types of information, you can create and insert diagrams in a document. A *diagram* is a relational representation of information. One common type of diagram is an organization chart. For example, The Garden Company might create an organization chart if it wanted to show the company's personnel structure.

Tip In addition to organization charts, you can create cycle diagrams, radial diagrams, pyramid diagrams, Venn diagrams, and target diagrams.

When you insert an organization chart into a document, the chart has placeholder text that you replace with your own. The boxes and the lines of the organization chart are objects that you can move and change.

In this exercise, you will insert and modify an organization chart.

BE SURE TO start Word before beginning this exercise.
USE the *OrgChart* document in the practice file folder for this topic. This practice file is located in the *My Documents\Microsoft Press\Word 2003 SBS\WorkingGraphic\CreatingDiag* folder and can also be accessed by clicking *Start/All Programs/Microsoft Press/Word 2003 Step by Step.*
OPEN the *OrgChart* document.

1 Press Ctrl+End to move to the end of the document.

2 On the **View** menu, point to **Toolbars**, and then click **Drawing**.

3 On the Drawing toolbar, click the **Insert Diagram or Organization Chart** button.

Insert
Diagram or
Organization
Chart

The Diagram Gallery dialog box appears, with the Organization Chart option selected by default.

4 Click **OK**.

An organization chart is inserted into the document at the insertion point, and the Organization Chart toolbar appears.

Organization Chart toolbar   Placeholder text

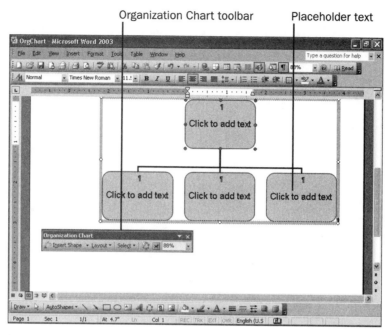

5 In the organization chart, click the top box, and type Karen Berg.

6 Click the first box in the second row, type Kim Akers, click the second box,
type David Ortiz, click the third box, and then type Gordon Hee.

All the boxes now contain names, and the last box is still selected.

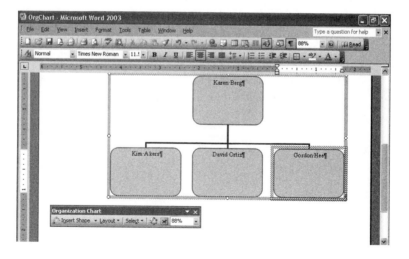

Select

7   On the Organization Chart toolbar, click the down arrow to the right of the **Select** button, and click **All Connecting Lines** in the drop-down list.

All connecting lines in the organization chart are selected.

8   On the **Format** menu, click **AutoShape**.

The Format AutoShape dialog box appears.

9   In the **Line** area, click the down arrow to the right of the **Color** box, and in the first column of the third row of the color palette, click the **Red** box.

10   In the **Arrows** area, click the down arrow to the right of the **Begin style** box, click the second item in the first row, and then click **OK**.

The lines in the organization chart are now red with arrows attached.

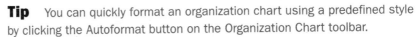

Tip   You can quickly format an organization chart using a predefined style by clicking the Autoformat button on the Organization Chart toolbar.

Autoformat

11   Click the blank area to the right of the organization chart to deselect it.

12   On the Standard toolbar, click the **Save** button to save the document.

Save

CLOSE the *OrgChart* document.

Inserting and Modifying a Picture

Microsoft Office Specialist

You can insert scanned photographs or pictures created in almost any program into a Word document. Pointing to Picture on the Insert menu displays a submenu that you can use to specify the source of the picture, as follows:

- To insert a picture from the clip art collection that comes with Word, you click the Clip Art command on the Picture submenu or click the Insert Clip Art button on the Drawing toolbar, which opens the Clip Art task pane. The Microsoft Office System includes hundreds of professionally designed pieces of clip art that you can use in your documents. For example, you can insert clip art pictures of scenic backgrounds, maps, buildings, or people.

- To insert a picture from a file on your hard disk, removable disk, or network, you use the From File command on the Picture submenu.

- If you have a scanner connected to the computer that you are using, you can scan and insert a picture using the From Scanner command. You can also use this command to insert a picture from a digital camera that's connected to the computer.

After you insert any picture into a document, you can click it to open the Picture toolbar, and then modify the image by using the Picture toolbar buttons.

Button name	Button	Description
Color		Changes the picture to grayscale, black and white, or washed out.
More Contrast		Increases contrast.
Less Contrast		Reduces contrast.
More Brightness		Increases brightness.
Less Brightness		Reduces brightness.
Crop		Crops the picture.
Rotate Left 90°		Rotates the picture to the left.

Button name	Button	Description
Line Style	≡	Changes a line's weight and style.
Compress Pictures		Reduces the file size of pictures.
Text Wrapping		Controls the wrapping of text around a picture.
Format Picture		Opens the Format Picture dialog box, where you can change features such as colors and lines, image size, text wrapping, cropping, color, brightness, and contrast. (This button renames itself depending on what's selected.)
Set Transparent Color		Makes selected colors in the picture see-through. This feature works on bitmap images that don't already have transparent areas. It also works on some clip art.
Reset Picture		Returns the picture to its original state.

The picture toolbar also includes an Insert Picture button that you can use to insert additional images.

In this exercise, you will insert and modify clip art.

USE the *InsertPics* document and *GardenCo* graphic in the practice file folder for this topic. These practice files are located in the *My Documents\Microsoft Press\Word 2003 SBS\WorkingGraphic\InsertingPic* folder and can also be accessed by clicking *Start/All Programs/Microsoft Press/Word 2003 Step by Step*. OPEN the *InsertPics* document.

1 Press the Enter key, and then press the ↑ key to position the insertion point in a blank line at the beginning of the document.

2 On the **Insert** menu, point to **Picture**, and then click **From File**.

The Insert Picture dialog box appears.

Insert Picture

Tip You can also click the Insert Picture button on the Drawing toolbar to open the Insert Picture dialog box.

3 Navigate to the *Microsoft Press\Word 2003 SBS\WorkingGraphic\InsertingPic* folder, and double-click the *Gardenco* file.

The picture is inserted into the document at the insertion point.

4 Click The Garden Company logo to select it, and if the Picture toolbar is not displayed, point to **Toolbars** on the **View** menu, and click **Picture**.

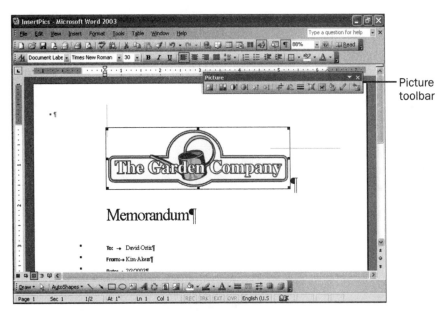

Picture toolbar

5 Point to the handle (the little black square) in the lower-right-corner of the graphic, and when the handle changes to a double arrow, drag up and to the left until the graphic's shadow frame is about at the 4-inch mark on the horizontal ruler and about the $1\frac{1}{4}$-inch mark on the vertical ruler.

Color

6 On the Picture toolbar, click the **Color** button, and then click **Washout**.

The picture's colors decrease in intensity.

Less
Brightness

7 On the Picture toolbar, click the **Less Brightness** button four times to reduce the brightness of the picture.

More Contrast

8 On the Picture toolbar, click the **More Contrast** button two times to give the picture more contrast.

9 Scroll down the document until you see the organization chart, and click the blank area to the left of the top box.

The organization chart is selected, and the Organization Chart toolbar appears.

Insert Clip Art

10 On the Drawing toolbar (not the Organization Chart toolbar), click the **Insert Clip Art** button.

The Clip Art task pane appears.

Troubleshooting If the Picture toolbar obscures the Clip Art task pane, drag the toolbar's title bar to move it out of the way.

11 Click the **Search for** text box of the **Clip Art** task pane, type **plant**, and then click **Go**.

The task pane displays graphics associated with the keyword *plant*.

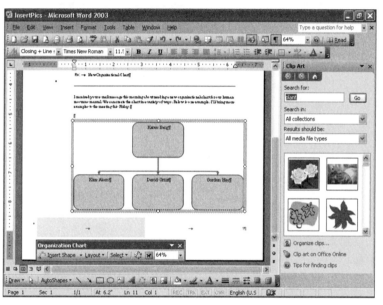

Close

12 In the task pane, click the drawing of the green leaf, and then click the task pane's **Close** button.

The picture is selected in the document, as indicated by the circular handles surrounding its frame.

13 Point to the lower-right handle of the picture, and when the pointer changes to a double arrow, drag up and to the left until the picture is about $\frac{1}{2}$ inch by $\frac{1}{2}$ inch in size.

14 Point to the leaf picture, and when the pointer changes to a four-headed arrow, drag the picture to the left of the Karen Berg box in the organization chart.

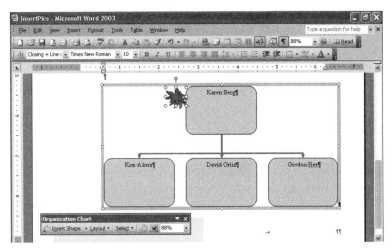

15 Hold down the [Ctrl] key, click the leaf picture, and drag a copy of it to the right of the Karen Berg box.

16 Click the blank area to the right of the organization chart to deselect it.

Save

17 On the Standard toolbar, click the **Save** button to save the document.

CLOSE the *InsertPics* document.

Aligning a Picture with the Surrounding Text

Microsoft Office Specialist

When you insert a picture into a document, it appears as a separate object and pushes any text it's associated with out of the way. You can use the Layout tab of the Format Picture dialog box to help align pictures and wrap text around them. You can choose from seven different text-wrapping styles, and you can wrap text on both sides of a picture, on one side of a picture, or on the largest side of a picture. In addition, you can set the distance between the edge of a picture and the text itself.

You can specify that a picture be positioned as follows:

■ Absolutely. This type of positioning is determined by measurements that you set.

■ Relatively. This type of positioning is determined by the relationship of the picture to another element of the document, such as the margin, the page, a column, or a particular character.

After you have inserted and aligned a picture, you might need to add additional text that could upset the alignment. You can specify whether a picture should remain anchored in its position on the page or should move with its related text. You can also specify whether the picture should be allowed to overlap text.

In this exercise, you will modify the placement and text-wrapping attributes of a picture that has already been inserted into a document.

USE the *AlignPics* document in the practice file folder for this topic. This practice file is located in the *My Documents\Microsoft Press\Word 2003 SBS\WorkingGraphic\AligningPic* folder and can also be accessed by clicking *Start/All Programs/Microsoft Press/Word 2003 Step by Step.*
OPEN the *AlignPics* document.

1 Click the logo for The Garden Company to select it.

Format Picture

2 On the Picture toolbar, click the **Format Picture** button.

Troubleshooting If the Picture toolbar is not displayed, right-click the logo, and click Show Picture Toolbar on the shortcut menu.

The Format Picture dialog box appears.

3 Click the **Layout** tab, and then click **Advanced**.

The Advanced Layout dialog box appears.

4 Click the **Tight** wrapping style, and in the **Wrap text** area, select the **Both sides** option. Then click the **Picture Position** tab.

5 In the **Horizontal** area, select the **Alignment** option, click the down arrow to its right, and then click **Right**. Then click the down arrow to the right of the **relative to** text box, and click **Margin**.

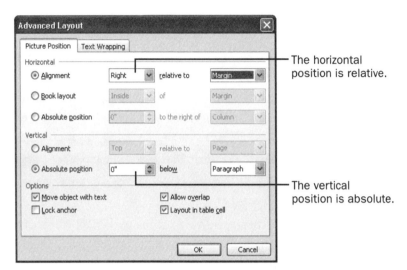

The horizontal position is relative.

The vertical position is absolute.

6 Click **OK** to close the **Advanced Layout** dialog box, and then click **OK** again to close the **Format Picture** dialog box.

The picture is repositioned so that it is aligned with the right margin, with the paragraph text wrapped to its left.

Tip   You might have to move the Picture toolbar out of the way to see the picture.

7 Click to the left of the word *The* at the beginning of the first paragraph, and press ⌨Enter.

The graphic moves with the text.

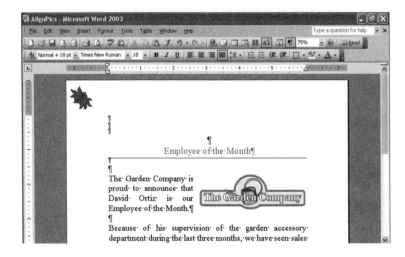

8   In the upper-left corner of the document, click the lower leaf graphic, and then click the **Format Picture** button on the Picture toolbar.

9   Click the **Layout** tab, click the **Advanced** button, and then if necessary, display the **Picture Position** tab.

10   In the **Horizontal** area, select the **Absolute position** option, type 7.75" in the box to the right, and then change the setting in the **to the right of** box to **Page**.

11   In the **Vertical** area, select the **Absolute position** option, type 0.25" in the box to the right, and then change the setting in the **below** box to **Page**.

12   In the **Options** area, select the **Lock anchor** check box, and then click **OK** in each dialog box to close them.

The selected leaf graphic moves to the upper-right corner of the page.

13   Now click the leaf graphic in the upper-left corner, and repeat steps 8 through 12, setting the **Absolute position** relative to the page to 0.25" in both the **Horizontal** and **Vertical** areas.

14   Press Ctrl+Home to move the insertion point to the left of the first blank paragraph mark, and press Enter twice.

The leaf graphics remain anchored in their absolute positions in the corners of the page.

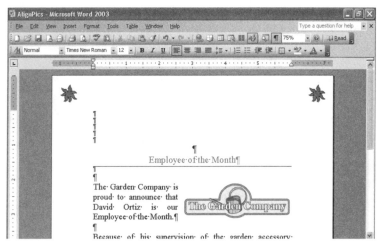

Save

15   On the Standard toolbar, click the **Save** button to save the document.

CLOSE the *AlignPics* document.

Creating WordArt

When you want a fancy text banner that you can't seem to create with font attributes, you can use *WordArt* to create special effects for your text. You can make WordArt text appear curved, outlined, multicolored, shadowed, or three-dimensional.

To create a WordArt object using existing text in your document, you select the text, click the Insert WordArt button on the Drawing toolbar, click a style in the WordArt Gallery dialog box, and then click OK. The Edit WordArt Text dialog box appears with your text selection highlighted so that you can add further formatting to the text. Clicking OK inserts the WordArt object in the document at the insertion point.

Selecting a WordArt object displays the WordArt toolbar, which you can use to edit and format a WordArt object to meet your needs.

Button name	Button	Description
Insert WordArt		Inserts WordArt.
Edit Text	Edit Te_x_t...	Edits the text of existing WordArt.
WordArt Gallery		Opens the WordArt Gallery dialog box, where you can change the style of the WordArt.
Format WordArt		Changes the color, size, and layout options of the WordArt.
WordArt Shape		Changes the shape of the WordArt.
Text Wrapping		Changes the text wrapping around your WordArt.
WordArt Same Letter Heights		Makes the letters in the WordArt the same height.
WordArt Vertical Text		Changes the text from horizontal to vertical.
WordArt Alignment		Changes the alignment of the WordArt.
WordArt Character Spacing		Changes the spacing between characters in the WordArt.

In this exercise, you will insert a new WordArt object. Then you'll turn existing text into a WordArt object and modify the object to look the way you want it.

USE the *WordArt* document in the practice file folder for this topic. This practice file is located in the *My Documents\Microsoft Press\Word 2003 SBS\WorkingGraphic\CreatingArt* folder and can also be accessed by clicking *Start/All Programs/Microsoft Press/Word 2003 Step by Step.*
OPEN the *WordArt* document.

1 Press the ⬇ key twice to move the insertion point to the third paragraph of the document.

Insert WordArt

2 On the Drawing toolbar, click the **Insert WordArt** button.

Drawing

Troubleshooting If the Drawing toolbar is not open on your screen, click the Drawing button on the Standard toolbar.

The WordArt Gallery dialog box appears.

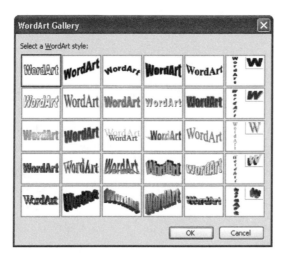

3 Click the style in the fourth column of the third row, and click **OK**.

The Edit WordArt Text dialog box appears, displaying the words *Your Text Here* as a placeholder.

B
Bold

4 Type You're Invited to a Surprise Birthday Party for Karen. Click the down arrow to the right of the **Size** box, click **44**, click the **Bold** button, and then click **OK**.

The text is inserted as an object at the insertion point.

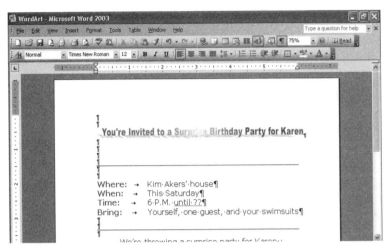

5   Scroll down the document, select the words *Extra! Extra!*, and on the Drawing toolbar, click the **Insert WordArt** button.

6   Click the style in the third column of the fourth row of the **WordArt Gallery** dialog box, and click **OK** twice.

Format WordArt

7   Click the WordArt object you just created, click the **Format WordArt** button on the WordArt toolbar, and then click the **Colors and Lines** tab.

8   Click the down arrow to the right of the **Color** box, and in the first column of the fourth row in the color palette, click the **Pink** box. Then click **OK**.

WordArt
Character
Spacing

9   On the WordArt toolbar, click the **WordArt Character Spacing** button, and then click **Very Loose**.

The spacing between the letters in the WordArt increases.

10   Point to the WordArt object's middle-right handle, and when the pointer changes to a double arrow, drag to the right for an inch or two to stretch the object's frame.

When you release the mouse button, the stretched object snaps to the horizontal center of the page.

WordArt Shape

11   On the WordArt toolbar, click the **WordArt Shape** button, and then in the fifth column of the fourth row of the shape palette, click the **Inflate Top** style.

The WordArt shape changes to an arch.

12   Drag the upper-middle handle upward to exaggerate the curve, and then click a blank area of the document to deselect the WordArt object.

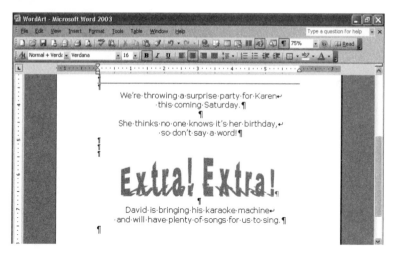

Save

13 On the Standard toolbar, click the **Save** button to save the document.

CLOSE the *WordArt* document.

Drawing and Modifying a Shape

**Microsoft
Office
Specialist**

You can use Word's drawing tools to add shapes (drawing objects) to your documents. Drawing objects can add interest and impact to your message. Popular drawing objects include ovals, rectangles, lines, curves, and AutoShapes—more complex shapes such as stars and banners.

To draw a shape, you click a tool on the Drawing toolbar. Word then displays a drawing canvas. You drag the pointer across the drawing canvas to create a drawing object the size and shape you want. If you add multiple objects to the same drawing canvas, you can size and move the drawing canvas and the objects it contains as one unit.

Tip You don't have to use Word's drawing canvas when creating drawing objects. If you prefer to create them directly in your documents, click Options on the Tools menu, click the General tab, clear the "Automatically create drawing canvas when inserting AutoShapes" check box, and then click OK.

By default, a drawing canvas has no visible attributes of its own, but because it is itself a drawing object, you can apply borders and shading to it just as you can to any other object in Word. You can also manipulate it by using the tools on the Drawing Canvas toolbar. These tools let you fit the drawing canvas to its contents, expand it, scale it, and specify how text should wrap around it.

Often you will draw a shape that isn't quite right. You can select the shape and change it to get the look you want. (When you finish drawing a shape, it is automatically selected. Later you can select the shape by clicking it.) The attributes you can change include the following:

- The fill color inside the object

- The color, thickness, and style of the border around the object

- The shadow effect behind the object

- The three-dimensional aspect, or perspective, from which you are observing the object

- The angle of rotation, or orientation, of the object

- The alignment of the object in relation to the page

- The way text wraps around the object

- The order of the object in a stack of objects

You can also change the size and shape of an object by dragging its handles. You can reposition it by dragging it, or by clicking the Draw button on the Drawing toolbar and pointing to Nudge and then a direction to move the object in small increments.

Tip   If you change the attributes of an object—for example, its fill color and border weight—and you want that object to have those attributes from now on in this document, you can click the object, click the Draw button on the Drawing toolbar and then click Set AutoShape Defaults.

In this exercise, you will insert a few drawing objects into a document and then modify them.

USE the *DrawShape* document in the practice file folder for this topic. This practice file is located in the *My Documents\Microsoft Press\Word 2003 SBS\WorkingGraphic\DrawingShape* folder and can also be accessed by clicking *Start/All Programs/Microsoft Press/Word 2003 Step by Step*.
OPEN the *DrawShape* document.

1   Press [Ctrl]+[End] to position the insertion point at the end of the document.

Oval

2   On the Drawing toolbar, click the **Oval** button.

Troubleshooting   If the Drawing toolbar is not turned on, on the View menu, point to Toolbars, and then click Drawing.

Word adds a page to the document, inserts a drawing canvas, and displays the Drawing Canvas toolbar.

3 Hold down the ⬛shift key, and draw a circle about 1½ inches in diameter in the upper-left corner of the drawing canvas.

Tip To draw objects with equal heights and widths, such as a square or circle, hold down the ⬛shift key while you draw.

When you finish drawing, the circle is selected, as indicated by the handles around it.

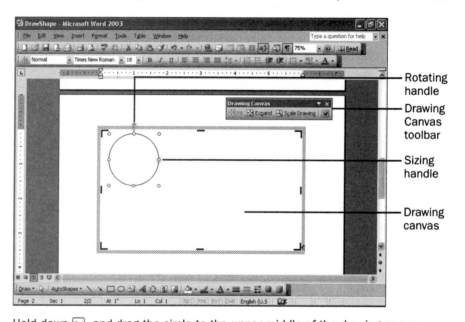

4 Hold down ⬛Ctrl, and drag the circle to the upper middle of the drawing canvas.

Word creates a copy of the circle in the location where you released the mouse button.

5 Hold down ⬛Ctrl, and drag the second circle to create a copy of it in the upper-right corner of the drawing canvas.

Fill Color

6 Click the circle on the left, click the down arrow to the right of the **Fill Color** button on the Drawing toolbar, and in the first column of the fourth row of the color palette, click the **Pink** box.

7 Click the middle circle, and repeat step 6 to fill it with the **Lime** color.

8 Click the right circle, and repeat step 6 to fill it with the **Turquoise** color.

All the circles are now filled with color so that they resemble balloons.

Ϛ
Curve

9 On the Drawing toolbar, click **AutoShapes**, point to **Lines**, and then click the **Curve** button (the first button in the second row).

10 Point to the bottom of the left balloon, click the canvas, drag down and left about an inch, click the canvas, drag down and right about an inch, and then double-click the canvas.

A curved line appears below the left balloon.

11 Hold down ⌃, point to the line, and drag to copy it to the middle balloon. Then drag another line to the right balloon.

All the balloons now have strings, and the line on the right is still selected.

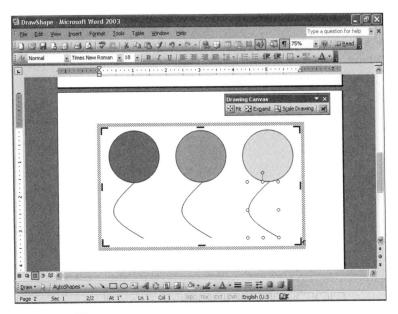

12 Hold down ⌃, and click the turquoise balloon.

Both the balloon and its string are selected.

13 On the Drawing toolbar, click **Draw**, and then click **Group**.

One set of handles appears around the balloon and its string, indicating that the two objects are now grouped as one object.

14 On the Drawing toolbar, click **Draw**, point to **Rotate or Flip**, and then click **Flip Horizontal**.

The balloon and its string are now facing the other way.

15 Press the ↑ key.

The balloon and its string have moved slightly higher in the drawing canvas.

16 Click a blank area of the drawing canvas to deselect the object.

17 On the Drawing Canvas toolbar (not the Drawing toolbar), click the **Scale Drawing** button, point to the lower-right corner of the drawing canvas, and when the pointer changes to a double arrow, drag up and to the left until the drawing canvas is about 3 inches wide.

The balloons shrink in proportion to the canvas. Word moves the drawing canvas to the bottom of the first page of the document, where it now fits.

Text-Wrapping

18 On the Drawing Canvas toolbar, click the **Text Wrapping** button, and click **In Front of Text** on the drop-down menu.

You can now move the drawing canvas independently of the text around it.

19 Drag the drawing canvas to the center of the page, below the document's last paragraph.

The drawing canvas moves with the objects it contains.

20 Click outside of the drawing canvas to deselect it.

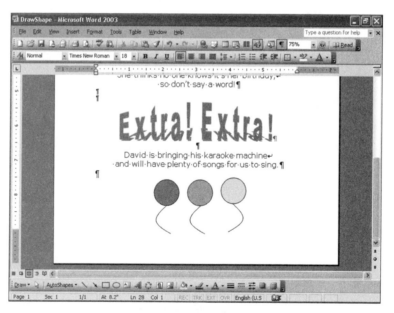

If the Show/Hide ¶ button on the Standard toolbar is turned on, you might want to click it to see the results without the non-printing characters.

Save

21 On the Standard toolbar, click the **Save** button to save the document.

CLOSE the *DrawShape* document, and if you are not continuing on to the next chapter, quit Word.

Key Points

- You can insert and modify diagrams, such as organization charts, to visually convey hierarchical relationships.

- You can insert artwork created with most graphics programs, as well as scanned photographs and images, into a document in Word.

- You can change the position of a graphic in a document in relation to a page element or to the text that surrounds it. You can also specify that your picture move with text, stay locked in position, or overlap the text.

- You can use WordArt to create fancy text banners for your documents.

- You can add drawing objects such as ovals, rectangles, lines, curves, and AutoShapes to your documents. You can also group objects on a drawing canvas to create simple pictures.

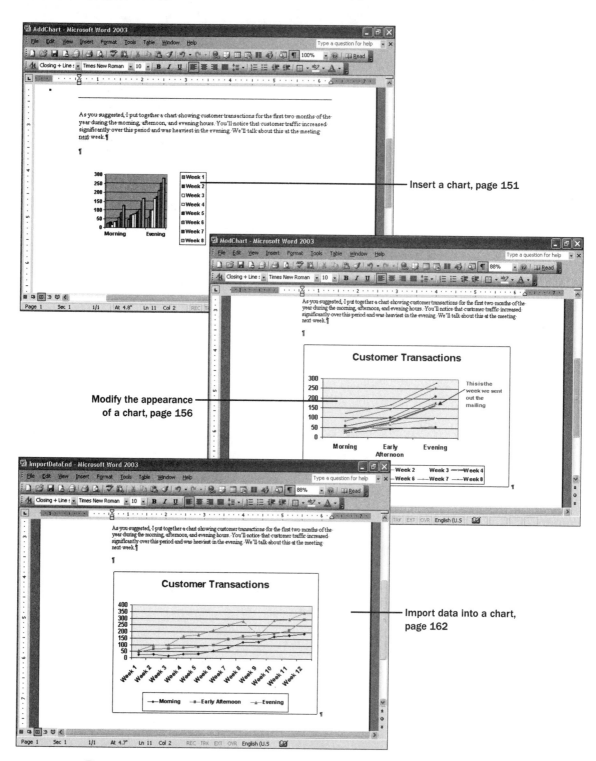

Insert a chart, page 151

Modify the appearance
of a chart, page 156

Import data into a chart,
page 162

Chapter 7 at a Glance

7 Working with Charts

In this chapter you will learn to:

✓ Insert a chart.

✓ Modify the appearance of a chart.

✓ Import data into a chart.

When you want to compare numeric information, you can create a *chart*. Charts are graphics that use lines, bars, columns, "pie" slices, or other markers to represent numbers and other values. Adding a chart to a document creates visual interest and can effectively show trends, illustrate relationships, or demonstrate how information changes over time. For example, The Garden Company might want to use a chart to visually compare quarterly sales by department or the number of people who attended different types of workshops last year.

Microsoft Office Word 2003 and other Microsoft Office System 2003 programs include Microsoft Graph 2003, a program that enables you to insert a chart directly in a document. You plot the numbers, and Graph does the rest. After you have created a chart, you can modify and enhance it to best display your data.

In this chapter, you'll start by creating a chart in a Word document. You'll enter the necessary data and change the look of the chart. You will then import additional data from a Microsoft Office Excel 2003 worksheet into the existing chart.

See Also   Do you need only a quick refresher on the topics in this chapter? See the Quick Reference entries on pages xliv-xlv.

Important   Before you can use the practice files in this chapter, you need to install them from the book's companion CD to their default location. See "Using the Book's CD-ROM" on page xiii for more information.

Inserting a Chart

Microsoft Office Specialist

To create a chart in a Word document, you start by using Microsoft Graph to insert a sample chart and a datasheet into the document. A *datasheet* looks similar to a table and displays data in rows and columns. The chart is linked to the datasheet and plots its data.

After inserting the sample chart and datasheet, you replace the sample data with your own in much the same way you would enter information in a table. Because the datasheet is linked to the chart, when you change the values in the datasheet, the chart changes as well.

Important To make changes to your data, always alter the data in the datasheet, not in the chart. You can change the appearance of the chart, but not the values it plots.

To enter data in an individual *cell*—the intersection of a row and column—you click the cell to select it, and start typing. You can select an entire column by clicking the *column heading*—the gray box at the top of each column, and an entire row by clicking the *row heading*—the gray box to the left of each row. To select the entire datasheet, you can click the Select All button, the gray box in the upper-left corner of the datasheet.

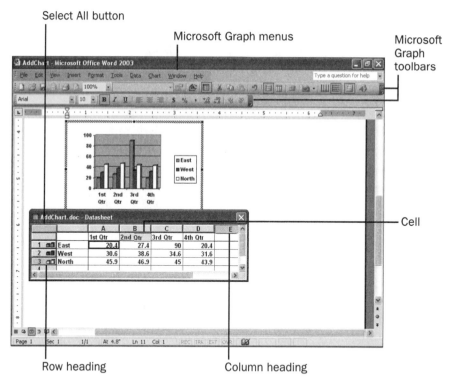

While you are working with a chart in a Word document, the Microsoft Graph commands and buttons replace Word's on the menu bar and toolbars so that you can work with the chart directly in the document.

In this exercise, you will add a chart to a document and then customize the datasheet's sample data.

BE SURE TO start Word before beginning this exercise.

USE the *AddChart* document in the practice file folder for this topic. This practice file is located in the *My Documents\Microsoft Press\Word 2003 SBS\WorkingChart\InsertingChart* folder and can also be accessed by clicking *Start/All Programs/Microsoft Press/Word 2003 Step by Step*.

OPEN the *AddChart* document.

1 Press Ctrl+End.

The insertion point moves to the end of the document.

2 On the **Insert** menu, point to **Picture**, and then click **Chart**.

A sample chart and datasheet appear.

View Datasheet

Troubleshooting If you can see the chart but not the accompanying data-sheet, click the View Datasheet button on Microsoft Graph's Standard toolbar.

3 Drag the title bar of the datasheet window so that the window is positioned below the sample chart.

4 Click the **Select All** button in the upper-left corner of the datasheet, and then press the Del key.

The sample data and sample chart are deleted, leaving a blank datasheet and chart area.

5 Click the first cell in row 1 to the left of column A, type Week 1, and press the Enter key.

Graph enters the heading and moves the insertion point to the next cell in the same column.

6 Pressing Enter to move from cell to cell, type headings for Week 2 through Week 8.

Tip You can use the keyboard to move around the datasheet, as follows: Press Enter to move down in the same column or Shift+Enter to move up, and press Tab to move to the right in the same row or Shift+Tab to move to the left. Or you can press the arrow keys to move up, down, left, or right a cell at a time.

7 Click in the first cell in column A above row 1, type Morning, and press the Tab key.

Graph enters the heading and moves the insertion point to the next cell in the same row.

8 Type Early Afternoon, and press Tab.

9 Type Evening, and press Tab.

10 Point to the border between the column B and column C headings, and when the pointer changes to a double-headed arrow, drag to the right until column B is wide enough to fit its entry.

Tip You can also double-click a border between column headings to size the column to the left to fit its longest entry.

AddChart.doc - Datasheet				
		A	B	C	D
		Morning	Early Afternoon	Evening	
1	Week 1				
2	Week 2				
3	Week 3				
4	Week 4				

Toolbar Options

Troubleshooting Because Graph's toolbars might not be familiar to you, we show them on separate rows. If you want your toolbars to look like ours, click the Toolbar Options button at the right end of one of the toolbars, and then click Show Buttons on Two Rows.

11 Type the following data into the chart's datasheet:

		A	B	C
		Morning	Early Afternoon	Evening
1	Week 1	24	45	58
2	Week 2	29	69	81
3	Week 3	17	74	101
4	Week 4	32	78	167
5	Week 5	35	89	178
6	Week 6	57	102	212
7	Week 7	84	145	254
8	Week 8	123	167	281

As you enter data, the chart changes to reflect what you type.

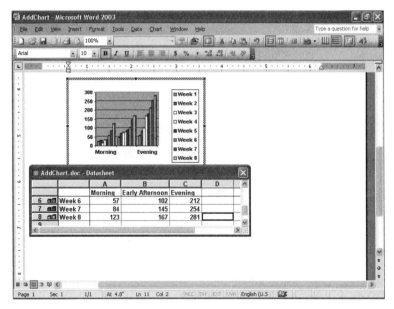

12 Click the cell in column C of row 2 (which contains *81*), type 99 to change the data, and then press Enter.

The column in the chart that represents this value is now slightly taller.

13 Click a blank area of the document to deselect the chart, and scroll up to see the relationship of the chart to the text of the document.

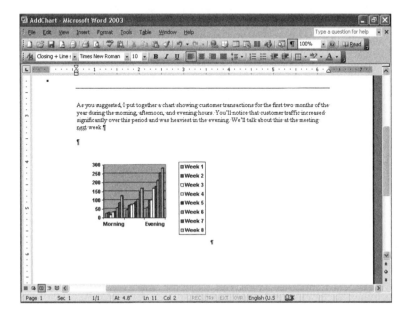

Notice also that Word's own toolbars and menus are once again active.

Save

14 On the Standard toolbar, click the **Save** button to save the document.

CLOSE the *AddChart* document.

Modifying the Appearance of a Chart

If the way a chart plots its underlying data doesn't fit your needs, you can change the chart type. Graph provides 18 different types for presenting your data. Common chart types include the following:

- Column charts, which are good for showing how values change over time.

- Bar charts, which are good for showing the values of several items at a single point in time.

- Line graphs, which are good for showing erratic changes in values change over time.

- Pie charts, which are good for showing how parts relate to the whole.

Each type has both two-dimensional and three-dimensional variations. To change the chart type, you can use the Chart Type button's drop-down list on Graph's Standard toolbar, or the Chart Type dialog box that appears when you click Chart Type on Graph's Chart menu. (You can also create a custom chart type on the Custom Types tab of this dialog box.)

In addition to changing the chart type, you can change the formatting of the chart and its component objects. You start by selecting the chart and then the object you want to modify, either by clicking the object itself or by clicking its name in the Chart Objects box on Graph's Standard toolbar. Common chart objects include the following:

- The chart area, which is the entire area within the frame displayed when you click a chart.

- Axes, which consist of the x-axis (usually horizontal), which plots the categories, and the y-axis (usually vertical), which plots the values. (Three-dimensional charts also have a z-axis.)

- The plot area, which is the rectangular area bordered by the axes.

- Data markers, which are the bars or areas that represent values in the datasheet.

- The data series, which is a group of related data markers.

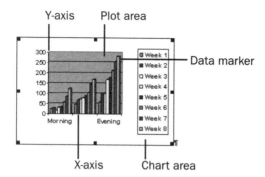

Other chart objects, such as the following, help you identify and interpret the chart data:

- Gridlines, which are lines across the plot area that make it easier to view and evaluate the data.

- A legend, which is a key that identifies the patterns or colors assigned to the data.

- Labels, which are text that identifies what each data series represents.

- A data table, which is a grid attached to a chart that shows the data used to create the chart.

You can turn these optional objects on or off in the Chart Options dialog box.

Having selected an object, you can move, size, or format it. To move a chart or chart object, you drag it to its new location. To size it, you drag a handle. To format it, you use the buttons on Graph's Standard and Formatting toolbars or the dialog box displayed when you click the Selected command on Graph's Format menu.

In this exercise, you will modify the appearance of a chart by changing its chart type, and then you'll size it. Next you will change the color of the plot area and apply a pattern to a data series. You'll hide and show gridlines, move the legend, and add labels to identify the data series. In addition, you will add a formatted data table to show the numeric values used to plot the chart.

USE the *ModChart* document in the practice file folder for this topic. This practice file is located in the *My Documents\Microsoft Press\Word 2003 SBS\WorkingChart\ModifyingChart* folder and can also be accessed by clicking *Start/All Programs/Microsoft Press/Word 2003 Step by Step.*
OPEN the *ModChart* document.

1 Scroll down the document until you can see the chart, and double-click the chart to activate Microsoft Graph.

Troubleshooting Simply clicking the chart selects it for manipulation—such as sizing or moving it—in the Word document. To activate Microsoft Graph, you have to double-click the chart.

The chart and datasheet appear along with Graph's toolbars and menus.

View
Datasheet

2 On Graph's Standard toolbar, click the **View Datasheet** button.

The datasheet is now hidden.

Chart Type

3 On the Standard toolbar, click the down arrow to the right of the **Chart Type** button.

The list of chart types appears.

Line Chart

4 Click the **Line Chart** button (the fourth button in the first column).

The chart type changes to a line chart, which compares data using colored lines instead of columns. The image on the Chart Type button changes to reflect the type of the chart you last selected.

5 Drag the outer right-middle handle to the right until the frame of the chart roughly aligns with the 6-inch mark on the horizontal ruler. Then drag the outer lower-middle handle down to roughly the 7½-inch mark on the vertical ruler.

Troubleshooting You might have to drag the handle part way, stop to scroll further down, and then drag the handle the rest of the way.

Now the labels for all the categories are visible, and the chart is easier to read.

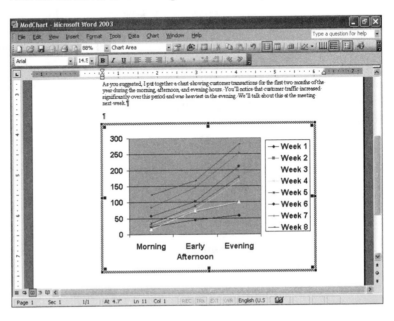

6 Click the plot area—the gray area of the chart—to select it.

The Chart Objects box on Graph's Standard toolbar displays the name of the selected object.

Fill Color

7 On Graph's Standard toolbar, click the down arrow to the right of the **Fill Color** button, and in the fourth column of the fifth row of the color palette, click the **Light Green** box.

Troubleshooting If you don't see the Fill Color button on Graph's Standard toolbar, click the Toolbar Options button at the right end of the toolbar to display hidden buttons.

The background of the chart changes to light green.

Chart Objects

8 On Graph's Standard toolbar, click the down arrow to the right of the **Chart Objects** box, and click **Series "Week 4"** in the drop-down list.

Small black squares appear along the line for the series.

Format Data
Series

9 On the Standard toolbar, click the **Format Data Series** button.

The Format Data Series dialog box appears, showing the Patterns tab.

Tip You can double-click a chart object to display its Format dialog box.

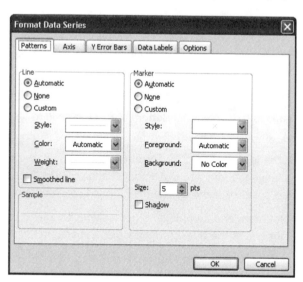

10 In the **Line** area, click the down arrow to the right of the **Color** box, and in the first column of the third row of the color palette, click the **Red** box.

11 Click the down arrow to the right of the **Weight** box, and in the drop-down list, click the heaviest weight. Then click **OK**.

The Week 4 data series is now represented by a heavy red line.

Value Axis
Gridlines

12 On Graph's Standard toolbar, click the **Value Axis Gridlines** button to remove the horizontal gridlines from the chart.

13 On the **Chart** menu, click **Chart Options**.

The Chart Options dialog box appears, showing the Gridlines tab.

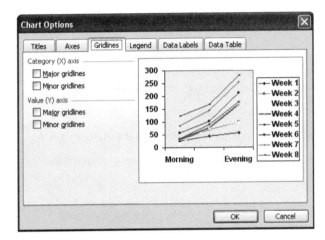

14 In the **Value (Y) axis** area, select the **Major gridlines** check box to turn the gridlines back on.

15 Click the **Titles** tab, and in the **Chart title** text box, type Customer Transactions.

16 Click the **Legend** tab, select the **Bottom** option (which is at the top of the list of options), and then click **OK**.

17 Right-click the legend, and click **Format Legend** on the shortcut menu, click the **Font** tab, change the font size to **10** points, and click **OK**. If necessary, adjust the size and position of the legend until it has two even, centered lines.

18 Click the plot area, and then drag its right-middle handle to the left until it aligns with the right end of the title, creating a blank space on the right.

19 On the Drawing toolbar, click the **Text Box** button, and move the pointer over the chart.

Text Box

Troubleshooting   If you don't see the Drawing toolbar, right-click one of the visible toolbars, and click Drawing in the drop-down list.

20   Point to a spot about $\frac{1}{8}$ inch to the right of the upper-right corner of the plot area, and drag diagonally down and to the right until the text box is the height of the plot area and the width of the available space on the right.

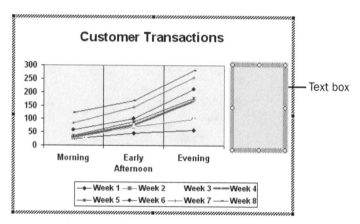

21   Type This is the week we sent out the mailing, select the text, and change its size to **10** points (Formatting toolbar) and its color to **Red** (Drawing toolbar).

Arrow

22   On the Drawing toolbar, click the **Arrow** button (not the Select Objects button, and not the Arrow Style button), and drag a line from the text you just entered to the Week 4 data series (the heavy red line).

The text draws attention to the jump in the number of evening customers and the overall increase from this week on.

23   Right-click a blank space in the chart area, and click **Format Chart Area** on the shortcut menu. In the **Border** area of the **Patterns** tab of the Format Chart Area dialog box, click **Automatic**, and then click **OK**.

Graph puts a border around the entire chart.

24   Make any other formatting adjustments you feel are necessary, and then click outside the chart to deselect it.

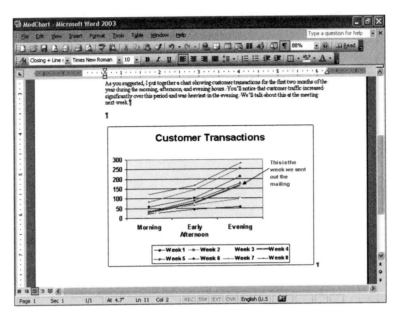

25 On the Standard toolbar, click the **Save** button to save the document.

Save

CLOSE the *ModChart* document.

Importing Data into a Chart

Microsoft
Office
Specialist

Instead of typing data in a datasheet to create a chart, you can enter data by importing it from another source, such as a Word table, a Microsoft Excel workbook, or a Microsoft Access database. For example, if the owner of The Garden Company tracks quarterly sales by department in an Excel worksheet, she can import that information into a chart in a report created in Word.

To import data, you select the cells in the datasheet where you want the data to be placed, click the Import File button on Graph's Standard toolbar, and then select a data file. The Import Data Options dialog box appears and asks you to select the data you want to import. If you do not want incoming data to overwrite existing data, clear the "Overwrite existing cells" check box before clicking OK.

Instead of importing data for a chart from a Word table, you might find that copying and pasting the information into the chart's datasheet is easier. To do so, select the data in the table, right-click the selection, and then click Copy on the shortcut menu. In your chart's datasheet, you then click the cell in which you want the copied data to begin and click the Paste button on the Standard toolbar. Copying and pasting to a chart's datasheet from an Excel worksheet or an Access database is equally easy.

In this exercise, you will import data stored in a range of cells in an Excel worksheet into a chart in a Word document.

USE the *ImportData* document and the *FileImport* workbook in the practice file folder for this topic. These practice files are located in the *My Documents\Microsoft Press\Word 2003 SBS\WorkingChart \ImportingData* folder and can also be accessed by clicking *Start/All Programs/Microsoft Press/Word 2003 Step by Step*.
OPEN the *ImportData* document.

1 Press [Ctrl]+[End] to move to the end of the document, and then double-click the chart to activate it in Microsoft Graph.

The datasheet appears along with Graph's toolbars and menus.

View
Datasheet

Troubleshooting If the datasheet doesn't appear when you activate the chart, click the View Datasheet button on Graph's Standard toolbar.

2 Move the datasheet up by dragging its title bar. Then adjust its size by dragging its lower-right corner down until you can see about 18 rows.

Import File

3 Click the first cell in row 9, and on Graph's Standard toolbar, click the **Import File** button.

The Import File dialog box appears.

4 Navigate to the *My Documents\Microsoft Press\Word 2003 SBS\WorkingChart \ImportingData* folder, and double-click the *FileImport* workbook.

The Import Data Options dialog box appears, listing the four worksheets in this workbook.

5 In the **Select sheet from workbook** box, click (don't double-click) **weeks 9-12**.

The data you want to import from this worksheet is stored in the block (or range) of cells located in cells A2 through D5 of this worksheet.

Tip   Each worksheet cell is identified by an address consisting of its column letter and row number. A range of cells is identified by the address of the cell in the upper-left corner and the address of the cell in the lower-right corner, separated by a colon—for example, A2:D5.

6   Select the **Range** option, and type **A2:D5** in the adjacent box.

7   Clear the **Overwrite existing cells** check box to add the incoming data to the existing chart data, and click **OK**.

The data from the Excel worksheet appears in the datasheet.

8   On Graph's Standard toolbar, click the **View Datasheet** button to hide the datasheet.

With the addition of the imported data, the chart has become very crowded.

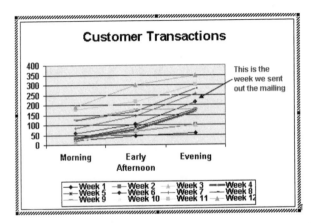

9   Click the text that starts *This is the week*, click the border that appears around this text box, and press ⌫. Then select and delete the arrow.

10   Click the plot area (be careful not to click a gridline), and drag the right-middle handle to the right to take up the space vacated by the text box.

11   On Graph's Standard toolbar, click the **By Column** button.

By Column

Graph changes the plot orientation of the data, making the data easier to read.

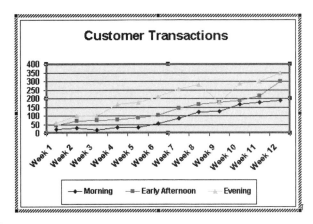

Save

12   On the Standard toolbar, click the **Save** button to save the document.

CLOSE the *ImportData* document, and if you are not continuing on to the next chapter, quit Word.

Key Points

- A chart is often the most efficient and visually appealing way to present certain types of information. You can create, modify, and format various types of charts.

- When you change the values in the datasheet, the chart changes as well.

- You can change the chart's type, and you can change the appearance of the chart and its component objects, such as the title, gridlines, and legend.

- You can import data for a chart from another source, such as a Word table, Excel workbook, or Access database.

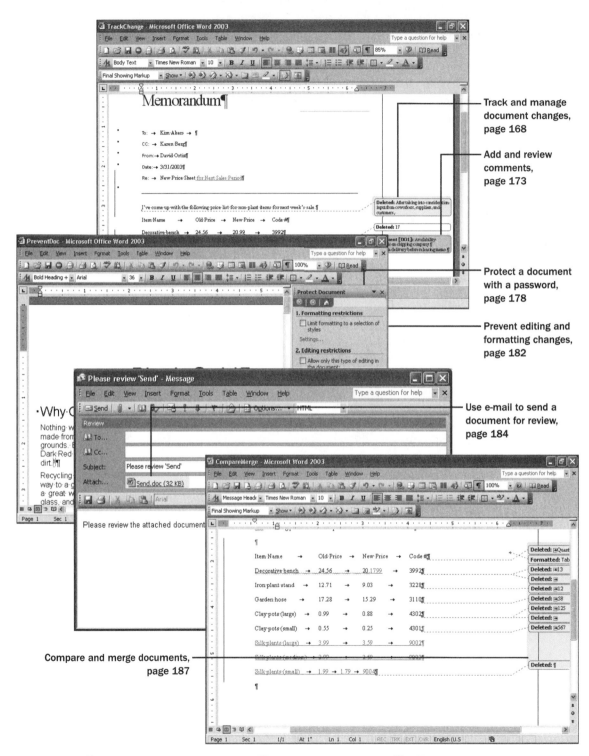

Track and manage
document changes,
page 168

Add and review
comments,
page 173

Protect a document
with a password,
page 178

Prevent editing and
formatting changes,
page 182

Use e-mail to send a
document for review,
page 184

Compare and merge documents,
page 187

Chapter 8 at a Glance

8 Collaborating with Others

In this chapter you will learn to:

✔ Track and manage document changes.

✔ Add and review comments.

✔ Protect a document with a password.

✔ Prevent editing and formatting changes.

✔ Use e-mail to send a document for review.

✔ Compare and merge documents.

After you create a draft of a document, you might distribute it to your coworkers and ask for their comments and revisions. Collaborating with others in this way helps you produce accurate and thorough documents.

With Microsoft Office Word 2003, you can easily distribute a document to reviewers electronically so that they can read, revise, and comment on the document without printing it. For example, an assistant at The Garden Company might collaborate with the head buyer to revise a memo to the owner of the company. Reviewers edit the document using the Track Changes feature so that you can see what they've changed. Reviewers can also insert notes. You can review, accept, and reject changes and comments by using buttons on the Reviewing toolbar. If different reviewers have inserted changes and comments in different versions of the document, you can merge all the versions and then review them in a single document.

If you don't want reviewers to edit your work, you can protect a document so that others can read but not change it. For greater protection, you can assign a password so that only people who know the password can open the document.

In this chapter, you will revise a memo and related documents. You will track changes, review comments, and accept and reject revisions. You will also protect a document with a password and set editing and formatting permissions for another document so that only authorized people can make changes to it. After sending the documents for review via e-mail, you will merge edited versions so that you can see all the changes and comments in one document.

> **See Also** Do you need only a quick refresher on the topics in this chapter? See the Quick Reference entries on pages xlv-xlviii.

> **Important** Before you can use the practice files in this chapter, you need to install them from the book's companion CD to their default location. See "Using the Book's CD-ROM" on page xiii for more information.

Tracking and Managing Document Changes

Microsoft Office Specialist

New in Office 2003

Reading Mode
Markup toolbar
Setting insertions and deletions to different colors

When two or more people collaborate on a document, one person usually creates and "owns" the document and the others review it, suggesting changes to make it more accurate, logical, or readable. Reviewers can turn on the Track Changes feature so that the revisions they make to the document are recorded without the original text being lost.

To turn on change tracking, you click Track Changes on the Tools menu. You then edit the text as usual. Word shows changed text in a different color from the original text and uses *revision marks*, such as underlines, to distinguish the revised text from the original text. In Print Layout view, Word identifies the change and its type, such as a deletion, in a *comment balloon*—a text box that appears in the margin of the document—and displays a vertical line in the margin to the left of any changed text to help you locate changes in the document.

Inserted text   Deleted text

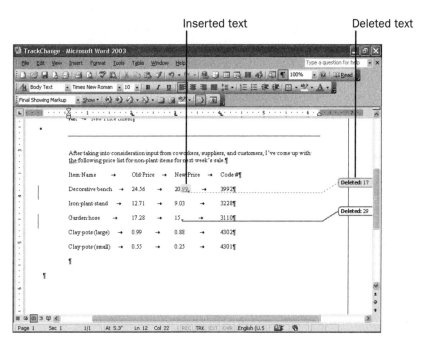

To help you manage changes, you can turn on the Reviewing toolbar by right-clicking any visible toolbar and clicking Reviewing on the shortcut menu. You can then use the buttons on this toolbar to work with tracked changes in the following ways:

■ If revision marks are distracting, you can track changes without showing them on the screen. Word then shows the text as it would be if you were making changes without tracking them. To hide revision marks, click the down arrow to the right of the Display for Review box, and then click Final. To display the changes again, click the down arrow again, and click Final Showing Markup.

■ When revisions are visible in the document, you can click the down arrow to the right of the Show button to specify that only certain types of revisions be displayed.

■ You can move among the changes by using the Next and Previous buttons.

■ You can use the Accept Change or Reject Change/Delete Comment button to incorporate a change into the document or delete it and restore the original text. To accept all the changes at once, click the right arrow to the right of the Accept Change button, and then click Accept All Changes in Document. To reject all the changes at once, click the down arrow to the right of the Reject Change button, and then click Reject All Changes in Document.

If you want a record of changes made to a document, you can save different *versions* of it. Saving versions saves disk space because Word saves only the differences between versions, not an entire copy of each document. After you've saved several versions of the document, you can review, open, print, and delete earlier versions. You can also have Word save a version of your document each time the document is closed, which is useful when you need a record of who made changes and when, as in the case of a legal document. To save a version every time you close a document, you use the Versions command on the File menu.

In this exercise, you will open a document, turn on change tracking, make changes to the document, accept and reject changes, and create a second version of the document.

BE SURE TO start Word before beginning this exercise.
USE the *TrackChange* document in the practice file folder for this topic. This practice file is located in the *My Documents\Microsoft Press\Word 2003 SBS\CollaboratingOther\TrackingChange* folder and can also be accessed by clicking *Start/All Programs/Microsoft Press/Word 2003 Step by Step*.
OPEN the *TrackChange* document.

1 On the **View** menu, point to **Toolbars**, and then click **Reviewing**.

The Reviewing toolbar appears.

Track Changes

2 On the Reviewing toolbar, click the **Track Changes** button.

Any changes that you make will now be tracked.

Important When the Track Changes feature is turned on, the Track Changes button is orange and has a border, and the letters *TRK* on the status bar are black instead of gray. When change tracking is turned off, the Track Changes button has no border, and *TRK* is gray on the status bar.

3 Scroll the document to see the product information, click to the right of *20.17*, the new price for the decorative bench, and press the ⌴Backspace⌴ key twice.

Word displays a balloon with the text *Deleted: 17* to describe the type and content of your change.

4 Type 99.

The price changes from $20.17 to $20.99, with 99 in a different color.

5 Click to the right of *$15.29*, the new price for the garden hose.

6 Press ⌴Backspace⌴ twice to delete *29*.

The document now shows two balloons, each identifying text that has been deleted.

Inserted text   Balloon

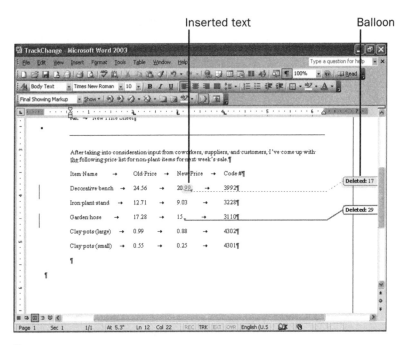

7 Type 99.

8 Point to *99* in the price for the decorative bench.

A ScreenTip tells you who made the change, when the change was made, and the type of change.

Tip   When you point to a change on the screen, the ScreenTip displays the name that was entered when the operating system was installed. If no name was entered, the ScreenTip shows *User* as the name. You can change the name by clicking Options on the Tools menu, clicking the User Information tab, typing a name in the Name box, and then clicking OK.

9   Press ⌷Ctrl⌷+⌷Home⌷ to move to the beginning of the document.

Next

10   On the Reviewing toolbar, click the **Next** button.

Word selects the first change in the document—the number 99 in the decorative bench price.

Accept Change

11   On the Reviewing toolbar, click the **Accept Change** button, and then click the price to deselect it.

Word accepts the change, and the price of the decorative bench now appears as *$20.99* without revision marks. A balloon still shows that you deleted *17* from this text.

Tip   To accept a change, you can also right-click the change and then click Accept Insertion or Accept Deletion on the shortcut menu.

12   Click *99* in the new garden hose price.

Reject
Change/Delete
Comment

13   On the Reviewing toolbar, click the **Reject Change/Delete Comment** button, and then click the same button again.

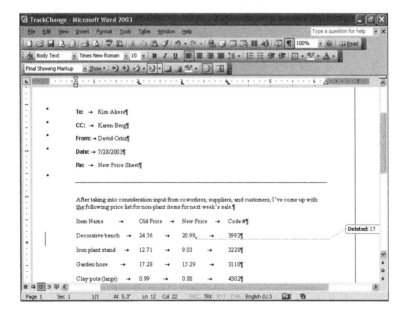

The first click rejects the new price that you entered, and the second rejects the deletion of *29*.

14 On the **File** menu, click **Versions**.

The "Versions in TrackChange" dialog box appears, showing who saved the original version of the document (in this case, the author is unknown).

15 Click **Save Now** to open the **Save Version** dialog box, type New price for decorative bench in the **Comments on version** box, and click **OK**.

Word closes the Versions in TrackChange dialog box and saves the current version of the document.

16 On the **File** menu, click **Versions** to open the **Versions in TrackChange** dialog box again.

Tip   You can also double-click the Versions icon on the status bar to open the Versions in TrackChange dialog box.

The new version appears in the "Existing versions" area.

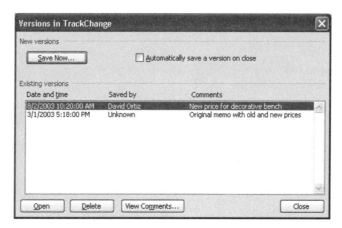

17 Click the **Close** button to close the **Versions in TrackChange** dialog box.

18 On the Standard toolbar, click the **Save** button to save the document.

Save

CLOSE the *TrackChanges* document.

Entering Handwritten Changes

Microsoft Word 2002 introduced handwriting recognition—the ability to enter text in a document using the mouse or a device such as a Tablet PC. You could leave this text in handwritten form or convert it to text using Word's optical character recognition (OCR) function.

The ink features in Word 2003 significantly expand these capabilities. Now you can use a Tablet PC to mark up a Word document in your own handwriting, just as though you were marking up the document on paper. You can circle words or paragraphs, cross things out, draw arrows, and sketch diagrams to make your point.

To use these ink features, you must be running Word on a Tablet PC. To add ink annotations in Print Layout view, tap Ink Annotations on the Insert menu. To add ink annotations in Reading Layout view:

1   On the Reading Layout toolbar, tap the **Actual Page** button.

2   On the Reviewing toolbar, tap the **Insert Ink Annotations** button.

The Ink Annotations toolbar appears.

3   Add your annotations to the document.

4   When you are finished, tap the **Stop Inking** button on the Ink Annotations toolbar.

In addition to entering annotations directly in the document with Word's Ink Annotations feature, you can use the Ink Comment command to insert handwritten text in comment balloons.

Other people don't need a Tablet PC to see your handwritten notes. Your annotations appear as objects in the Word document, where they can be moved and sized, or deleted when they are no longer necessary.

Adding and Reviewing Comments

In addition to making changes to a document in revision marks, you can insert notes, or *comments*, to ask questions or explain suggested edits. To insert a comment, you select the text to which the comment refers, click the Insert Comment button on the Reviewing toolbar, and type what you want to say in the comment balloon that appears. In the document Word inserts colored brackets around commented text and displays the comment in the balloon in the margin of the document.

To review comments, you click the Next and Previous buttons to move from one comment to another, reading the comments in their balloons. You can point to commented text to see a ScreenTip showing the name of the person who made the comment and the date and time of the comment. To edit or delete a comment, you right-click the commented text and click Edit Comment or Delete Comment on the shortcut menu. To respond to a comment, you can either add text to an existing comment balloon or you can click the text of the comment and then click the Insert Comment button to add a new comment balloon.

Tip   If the complete text of a comment isn't visible in its balloon, you can click the Reviewing Pane button on the Reviewing toolbar to open the Reviewing pane, where you can see the entire comment. In addition to displaying the text of comments in the main part of the document, the Reviewing pane also tracks changes to headers and footers, and to footnotes and endnotes. Click the Reviewing Pane button again to hide the pane.

If you find comment balloons distracting, you can turn them off. To show or hide balloons, click Options on the Tools menu to open the Options dialog box, click the Track Changes tab, and in the Balloons area, click the down arrow to the right of the Use Balloons (Print and Web Layout) box. Then click the option you want. When balloons are turned off, you can still review comments in the Reviewing pane.

In this exercise, you will show and review comments in a document, add a comment, delete one that is no longer needed, and then hide the remaining comments.

USE the *RevComment* document in the practice file folder for this topic. This practice file is located in the *My Documents\Microsoft Press\Word 2003 SBS\CollaboratingOther\AddingComment* folder and can also be accessed by clicking *Start/All Programs/Microsoft Press/Word 2003 Step by Step*.
OPEN the *RevComment* document.

1   If Markup is not active on the **View** menu, click **Markup**, and if the Reviewing toolbar is not displayed, right-click a visible toolbar, and click **Reviewing**.

Troubleshooting   If Markup is active, the icon to its left is orange. Don't click Markup on the menu if it is already active, or you will turn it off.

Next

2   On the Reviewing toolbar, click the **Next** button to display the first comment in the document, and then scroll vertically and horizontally to display the entire comment balloon.

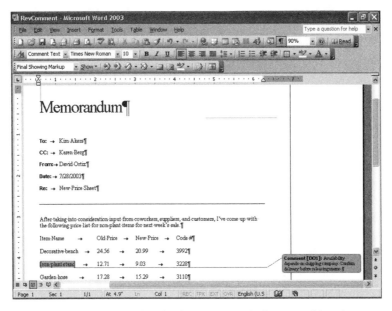

The insertion point appears in the comment balloon, and brackets surround the commented text, *Iron plant stand*.

3 On the Reviewing toolbar, click the **Next** button.

The insertion point appears in the next comment balloon, and brackets surround *Clay pots (small)*.

4 Point to *Iron plant stand*, and read the ScreenTip that appears.

The ScreenTip displays information about who inserted the comment.

5 Select the words *Garden hose* in the document.

6 On the Reviewing toolbar, click the **Insert Comment** button.

Insert Comment

Word surrounds *Garden hose* with brackets and displays a new comment balloon in the right margin.

7 In the comment balloon, type Preferred customers receive an extra 10% discount on hoses.

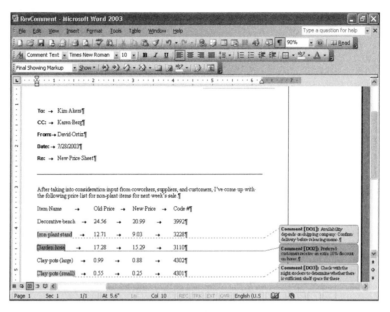

8 Click a blank area of the document to deselect the comment balloon.

9 Right-click anywhere in the words *Iron plant stand*, and click **Delete Comment**.

Word deletes the comment and its balloon.

Reviewing Pane

10 On the Reviewing toolbar, click the **Reviewing Pane** button.

The Reviewing pane opens at the bottom of the Word window, showing the remaining comments about the garden hoses and clay pots.

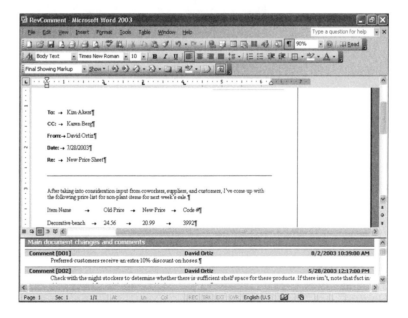

Tip To change the size of the Reviewing pane, point to the top border of the Reviewing pane, and when the pointer changes to a double-headed arrow, drag the border up or down.

11 Scroll the **Reviewing** pane, click to the right of *intact* (the last word in the second comment), press [Space], type your initials, type a colon (:), press [Space], and then type I'm not sure
if there is enough shelf space.

The text appears in the selected comment in the Reviewing pane.

12 On the Reviewing toolbar, click the **Reviewing Pane** button to close the pane.

13 Right-click *Clay pots (small)*, and click **Edit Comment** on the shortcut menu.

The insertion point appears at the end of the comment attached to *Clay pots (small)*.

14 On the Reviewing toolbar, click the **Insert Comment** button to create a new comment balloon in response to the selected comment.

15 Type I checked with the shipping company. They are ready to go.

The text appears in the new comment balloon.

16 Double-click *3992* in the decorative bench code to select the number.

17 On the Reviewing toolbar, click the **Insert Comment** button, and type Kim, is this product code correct?

The text appears in a new comment balloon.

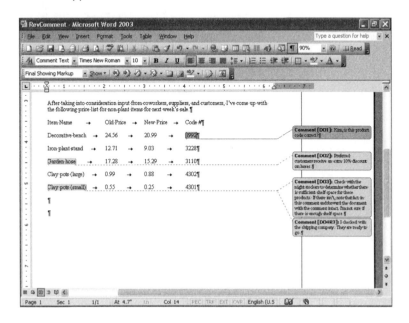

18 On the Reviewing toolbar, click the down arrow to the right of the **Show** button, and then click **Comments** to hide them.

Save

19 On the Standard toolbar, click the **Save** button to save the document.

CLOSE the *RevComment* document, and turn off the Reviewing toolbar.

Protecting a Document with a Password

Microsoft Office Specialist

Sometimes, you will want only certain people to be able to open a document. To protect a document, you can click Options on the Tools menu and display the Security tab of the Options dialog box. To set a password, enter it in the "Password to open" box and click OK.

To open a protected document, you need to enter the password exactly as it was set, including spaces, symbols, and uppercase and lowercase characters. When you set a password, take a moment to write it down in a safe place. Word doesn't keep a list of passwords. If you lose or forget the password for a protected document, you will not be able to open it.

If you want other people to be able to read or copy the document but not change it, you can select the "Read-only recommended" check box on the Security tab of the Options dialog box. Then when someone opens the document, Word displays a message suggesting that a *read-only* version of the document be opened. For even more control, Word also gives you the option to require a password to modify a document. That way, anyone who doesn't know the password has no choice but to open a read-only version. Setting a document as read-only is useful when you want a document, such as a company-wide bulletin, to be distributed and read but not changed. It does not prevent people from opening the file or from saving a copy with a different name so that they can edit the copy.

In this exercise, you will set a password for a document. You'll save and close the document, and then you'll test the document's security by entering an incorrect password. You will open a read-only version of the document and then reopen it with the correct password. Finally, you'll remove the protection from the document.

USE the *ProtectDoc* document in the practice file folder for this topic. This practice file is located in the *My Documents\Microsoft Press\Word 2003 SBS\CollaboratingOther\ProtectingDoc* folder and can also be accessed by clicking *Start/All Programs/Microsoft Press/Word 2003 Step by Step*.
OPEN the *ProtectDoc* document.

1 On the **Tools** menu, click **Options**.

The Options dialog box appears.

2 Click the **Security** tab to display security options.

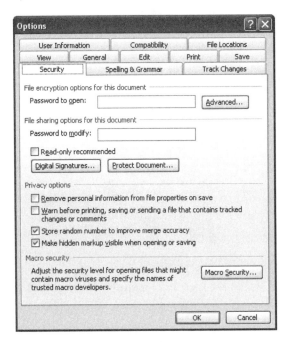

3 In the **Password to modify** box, type tgc3.

As you type the password, dots appear instead of the characters to keep the password confidential.

Tip Don't use common words or phrases as passwords, and don't use the same password for multiple documents.

4 Click **OK** to close the **Options** dialog box.

The Confirm Password dialog box appears.

5 In the **Reenter password to modify** box, type tgc3.

6 Click **OK** to set the password.

Save

7 On the Standard toolbar, click the **Save** button

The document is saved.

Close Window

8 Click the **Close Window** button at the right end of the menu bar.

The ProtectDoc document closes.

9 On the Standard toolbar, click the **Open** button.

10 In the **Open** dialog box, navigate to the *My Documents\Microsoft Press \Word 2003 SBS\CollaboratingOther\ProtectDoc* folder, and then double-click the *ProtectDoc* file.

Because this document is protected by the password you just set, the Password dialog box appears.

11 In the **Password** box, type tgc1, and click **OK**.

A message tells you that you typed an incorrect password.

12 In the message box, click **OK**.

13 In the **Password** dialog box, click **Read Only**.

The ProtectDoc document opens as a read-only document, as indicated by *(Read-Only)* in the title bar.

14 Click the **Close Window** button at the right end of the menu bar.

15 On the Standard toolbar, click the **Open** button, navigate to the *My Documents \Microsoft Press\Word 2003 SBS\CollaboratingOther\ProtectDoc* folder, and double-click the *ProtectDoc* file.

16 In the **Password** dialog box, type tgc3, and click **OK**.

This time you typed the correct password, so the document opens.

17 On the **Tools** menu, click **Options**.

18 On the **Security** tab of the **Options** dialog box, select the contents of the **Password to modify** box, press [Del], and then click **OK**.

The document's password protection is removed.

19 On the Standard toolbar, click the **Save** button to save the document.

CLOSE the *ProtectDoc* document.

Information Rights Management

If you work for a company that frequently handles sensitive or proprietary information, the ability to protect that information from unauthorized access—whether from nosy employees or from computer criminals—can be critical. The Information Rights Management feature available with Microsoft Office 2003 provides the basis for a secure information system.

If your company or organization has implemented the Information Rights Management feature, you can restrict who can change, print, or copy a document, and you can limit these permissions for a specific period of time. If Microsoft Windows Rights Management Services is running on your company's Microsoft Windows Server 2003 system, your system administrator can establish policies that further restrict how documents can be manipulated and circulated and can create templates for use with confidential or otherwise sensitive documents.

To set the permissions for the open document:

1   Click the **Permission** button on the Standard toolbar.

The Permission dialog box opens.

2   Select the **Restrict permission to this document** check box to activate the other features in the dialog box.

3   To grant users permission to only read the document, enter their e-mail addresses in the **Read** box. To grant users permission to read, edit, and save changes to the document (but not print it), enter their e-mail addresses in the **Change** box. You can also click the **Read** or **Change** buttons to select names from your **Outlook Address Book**.

4   If you want to grant additional permissions, such as permission to print or copy document contents, or if you want to set an expiration date for permissions, click the **More Options** button, set the permissions, and then click **OK**.

If you send a document with restricted permissions to someone who uses a version of Microsoft Office that's older than Microsoft Office 2003, that person can still use the document by opening it in a version of Microsoft Internet Explorer that has been updated with rights management software.

Preventing Editing or Formatting Changes

Sometimes you will want people to be able to open and view a document but not make changes to it. Sometimes you will want to allow changes, but only if you know about them. You can specify that only comments can be inserted in the document, or you can require that changes must be made using change tracking. To prevent anyone from introducing inconsistent formatting into a document, you can specify a selection of styles that must be used.

To protect a document from unauthorized changes, you click Protect Document on the Tools menu to display the Protect Document task pane. You can then use the task pane's options to specify the types of changes that are allowed.

In this exercise, you'll set editing and formatting restrictions for groups and individuals to selectively allow modifications to a protected document.

USE the *PreventDoc* document in the practice file folder for this topic. This practice file is located in the *My Documents\Microsoft Press\Word 2003 SBS\CollaboratingOther\PreventingEdit* folder and can also be accessed by clicking *Start/All Programs/Microsoft Press/Word 2003 Step by Step*.
OPEN the *PreventDoc* document.

1 On the **Tools** menu, click **Protect Document**.

The Protect Document task pane appears.

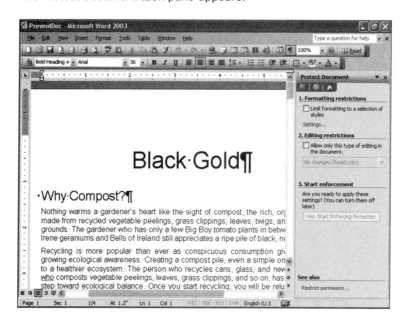

2   In the **Formatting restrictions** area of the task pane, select the **Limit formatting to a selection of styles** check box, and then click **Settings**.

The Formatting Restrictions dialog box appears.

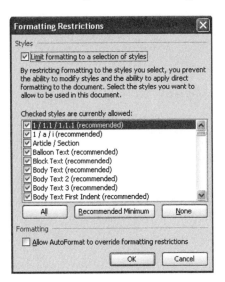

3   Scroll through the list of styles in the **Checked styles are currently allowed** box, click **Recommended Minimum**, and scroll through the list again.

The styles reflect those in the template attached to the open document. The recommended minimum styles are those needed by Word for features such as tables of contents.

4   Click **OK** to implement the restricted set of styles.

Word displays a message stating that the document might contain formatting that has been applied directly rather than through styles and restricted styles, and asking if you want it removed.

5   Click **Yes**, and then scroll through the document, noticing the changes.

Troubleshooting   If you see a message about collecting information, click Don't Send so that you can continue with the exercise.

6   In the **Editing restrictions** area of the task pane, select the **Allow only this type of editing in the document** check box.

7   Click the down arrow to the right of the box below, and click **Tracked changes** in the drop-down list.

8   Click the **Yes, Start Enforcing Protection** button.

Word displays the Start Enforcing Protection dialog box.

You enter a password if you want only those people who know the password to be able to turn off document protection.

9 Without entering a password, click **OK**.

With the exception of the Style box, the buttons on the Formatting toolbar are now dimmed, indicating that they are unavailable. The Protect Document task pane tells you that you can make only tracked changes and can format only with certain styles.

10 Select the *Black Gold* heading, and click **Format** on the menu bar.

Most of the formatting commands are not available to you, indicating that the formatting restrictions are in effect.

CLOSE: the *PreventDoc* document without saving your changes, and then close the Protect Document task pane.

Using E-Mail to Send a Document for Review

Microsoft Office Specialist

After you create a document, you can quickly send it via e-mail to another person for review from within Word. You do not have to start your e-mail program. To share your documents with others, point to Send To on the File menu. The Send To submenu includes the Mail Recipient (for Review) and Mail Recipient (as Attachment) commands. Click one of these commands to open a message window with the current document as an attachment. If you click Mail Recipient (for Review), the message *Please review the attached document* accompanies the attachment.

Before sending the message, all you have to do is enter the e-mail addresses of anyone you want to receive the message and its attachment. The subject line already contains the name of the document you are sending.

New in Office 2003
Shared Workspaces

Tip   If your team is running Microsoft Windows SharePoint Services, sending an e-mail attachment is one way to create a Document Workspace, which is a team Web site where your group can collaborate on files and discuss a project. Before you send your message, click Attachment Options in the message header. This opens the Attachment Options task pane, where you can click the "Shared attachments" option and specify the URL for the Document Workspace server (you must have permission to access this server). You can also establish a Document Workspace for any document by opening the Shared Workspace task pane and clicking Create. After you've created the Document Workspace, you can use the Shared Workspace task pane to add new members to the Document Workspace, give them assignments, and monitor progress. You can also use a Web browser to view this team Web site.

Attaching a Digital Signature

Microsoft Office Specialist

When you create a document that will be circulated to other people via e-mail or the Web, you might want to consider attaching a *digital signature*, which is an electronic stamp of authentication. Certified digital signatures can be obtained from companies such as VeriSign. The digital signature confirms the origin of the document and that no one has tampered with it since it was signed.

To add a digital signature to a Word document:

1   With the document open, click **Options** on the **Tools** menu, and click the **Security** tab.

2   Click **Digital Signatures**, and in the **Digital Signature** dialog box, click **Add**.

3   In the **Select Certificate** dialog box, click a certificate in the list, and click **OK**.

4   Click **OK** twice to close the **Digital Signature** and **Options** dialog boxes.

5   On the Standard toolbar, click the **Save** button to save the document.

To view the digital signatures attached to a signed document:

1   Click **Options** on the **Tools** menu, and click the **Security** tab.

2   Click **Digital Signatures** to open the **Digital Signature** dialog box, where you can view a list of signers and see who issued their digital IDs.

3   Click **OK** twice to close the **Digital Signature** and **Options** dialog boxes.

In this exercise, you will attach three documents to an e-mail message so that you can send them for review.

BE SURE TO have an e-mail program installed on your computer and an e-mail account set up before beginning this exercise. Microsoft Office Outlook 2003 is recommended. You can use another e-mail program, but the steps for attaching and sending a message might vary from those given in this exercise. USE the *Send*, *Attach1*, and *Attach2* documents in the practice file folder for this topic. These practice files are located in the *My Documents\Microsoft Press\Word 2003 SBS\CollaboratingOther\SendingDoc* folder and can also be accessed by clicking *Start/All Programs/Microsoft Press/Word 2003 Step by Step*. OPEN the *Send* document.

1 On the **File** menu, point to **Send To,** and then click **Mail Recipient (for Review).**

Tip To send a copy of the current document as the body of an e-mail message rather than as an attachment to the message, click the E-Mail button on the Standard toolbar.

2 If the **Choose Profile** dialog box appears with information about your Internet or network profile, click **OK.**

The message window opens with the name of the document in the Subject line and the default message in the message pane.

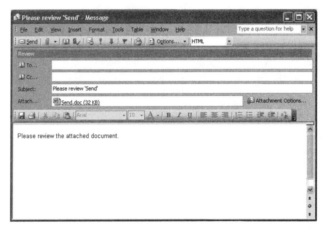

3 In the **To** box, type your own e-mail address.

Insert File

4 Click the **Insert File** button, and if the *SendingDoc* folder does not appear in the **Insert File** dialog box, navigate to the *My Documents\Microsoft Press\Word 2003 SBS \CollaboratingOther\SendingDoc* folder.

5 Click *Attach1*, hold down ⌃, click *Attach2*, and then click **Insert**.

In the message window, the Attach box shows that three files are attached to the message.

Importance: High

6 On the message window's toolbar, click the **Importance: High** button.

The message will be delivered with a red exclamation mark indicating that it is important.

7 Click anywhere in the message pane, and select the message text.

8 On the message window's Formatting toolbar, click the **Bold** button.

Bold

Font Color

9 Check the down arrow to the right of the **Font Color** button, click **Blue** in the color palette, and then press the ⟨End⟩ key.

The text is bold and blue, making it stand out.

10 On the message window's toolbar, click the **Send** button.

The e-mail message with the attached documents is sent out for review. In this case, the e-mail message should be received into your own Inbox the next time you log on to your e-mail program.

Save

11 On the Standard toolbar, click the **Save** button to save the document.

CLOSE the *Send* document.

Comparing and Merging Documents

Microsoft Office Specialist

Sometimes you might want to compare several versions of the same document. For example, if you have sent a document out for review by colleagues, you might want to compare their edited versions with the original document. Or you might want to compare an earlier version of a document with the current version. Instead of comparing multiple open documents, you can make this process much easier by using Word to compare the documents and merge the changes into one document.

When you compare and merge documents, Word shows the differences as tracked changes. If several reviewers return their changes and comments in separate documents, you can merge all their changes into a single document so that you can review them in one document. From within that one document, you can view all the changes from all the reviewers or view only those from a specific reviewer.

In this exercise, you merge a document with two other versions of it.

USE the *CompareMerge, Merge1,* and *Merge2* documents in the practice file folder for this topic. These practice files are located in the *My Documents\Microsoft Press\Word 2003 SBS\CollaboratingOther \ComparingDoc* folder and can also be accessed by clicking *Start/All Programs/Microsoft Press/Word 2003 Step by Step.*
OPEN the *CompareMerge* document.

1 On the **Tools** menu, click **Compare and Merge Documents**.

The Compare and Merge Documents dialog box appears.

2 Navigate to the *My Documents\Microsoft Press\Word 2003 SBS\CollaboratingOther \ComparingDoc* folder.

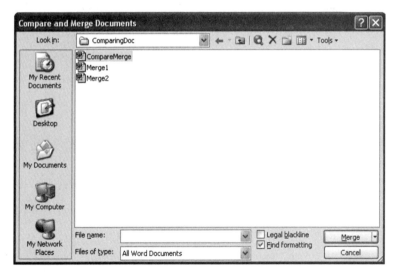

3 Click (don't double-click) **Merge1**, click the down arrow to the right of the **Merge** button, and then click **Merge into current document**.

The changes from the Merge1 document are transferred to the current document. Each reviewer's changes are identified by a different color.

Tip When you compare versions of a document, you see the reviewers' changes in revision marks even if the reviewers did not track their changes as they edited.

4 On the **Tools** menu, click **Compare and Merge Documents**, navigate to the *My Documents\Microsoft Press\Word 2003 SBS\CollaboratingOther\ComparingDoc* folder, click (don't double-click) **Merge2**, click the down arrow to the right of the **Merge** button, and then click **Merge into current document**.

The changes from this version of the document are added to those of the other two versions.

5 Scroll down the document to see the product information.

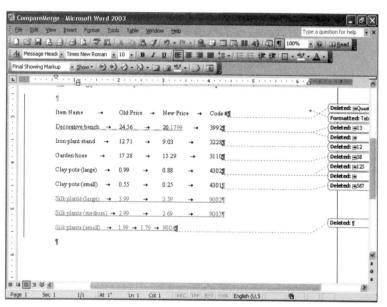

6 On the Reviewing toolbar, click the down arrow to the right of the **Show** button, point to **Reviewers**, and then click **David Ortiz**.

The revisions made by David Ortiz are hidden.

7 On the Reviewing toolbar, click the down arrow to the right of the **Show** button, point to **Reviewers**, and then click **All Reviewers**.

The revisions made by all reviewers appear.

8 On the Reviewing toolbar, click the down arrow to the right of the **Show** button, and click **Formatting**.

Only insertions and deletions, not formatting changes, appear in the document.

9 Press Ctrl+Home to move to the top of the document.

The title of the document has been changed by one of the reviewers.

Next

10 On the **Reviewing** toolbar, click the **Next** button.

The suggested title is highlighted.

Accept Change

11 On the **Reviewing** toolbar, click the **Accept Change** button.

12 On the Reviewing toolbar, click the **Next** button.

Reject
Change/Delete
Comment

13 On the Reviewing toolbar, click the **Reject Change/Delete Comment** button to reject the former title, and then click the **Next** button to find the next revision.

14 On the Reviewing toolbar, click the **Reject Change/Delete Comment** button to reject the change.

The added text is removed.

15 On the Reviewing toolbar, click the down arrow to the right of the **Display for Review** box, click **Final**, and then scroll through the document.

The revision marks are hidden so that the document looks the way it would if all the changes were accepted.

16 On the Reviewing toolbar, click the down arrow to the right of the **Display for Review** box, and click **Final Showing Markup**.

The revision marks reappear.

17 On the Reviewing toolbar, click the down arrow to the right of the **Accept Change** button, and click **Accept All Changes in Document**.

All the changes are accepted.

Save

18 On the Standard toolbar, click the **Save** button to save the document.

CLOSE the *CompareMerge* document, and if you are not continuing on to the next chapter, quit Word.

Key Points

■ When you collaborate on a document, you can turn on the Track Changes feature so that the revisions you make to the document are recorded without the original text being lost.

■ You can insert comments in a document to ask questions or explain suggested edits. In the document, Word inserts colored brackets around commented text and displays the comment in a balloon in the margin of the document.

■ You can protect a document with a password so that only certain people can open it.

■ You can restrict who can make editing and formatting changes to a document. You can also specify that only comments can be inserted in the document, or you can require that changes be made using change tracking.

■ You can send a document for review via e-mail, and then when you receive the reviewed versions, you can merge them so that all the changes are recorded in one document.

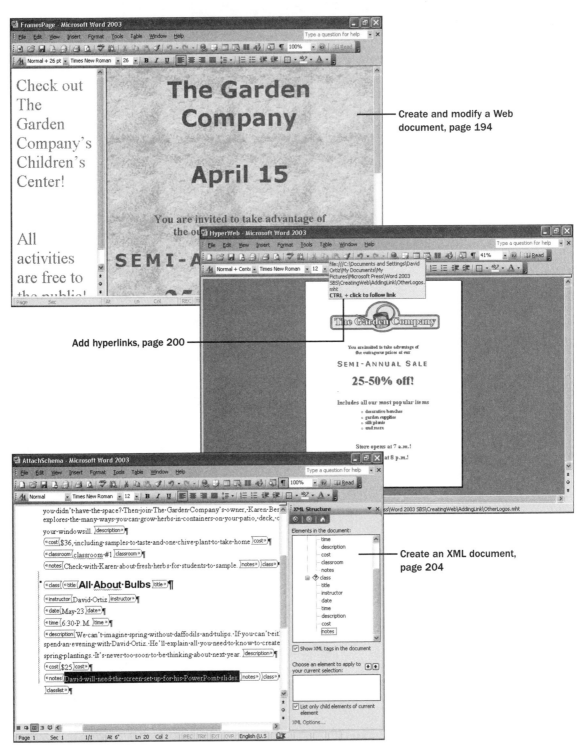

Create and modify a Web document, page 194

Add hyperlinks, page 200

Create an XML document, page 204

9 Creating Documents for the Web

In this chapter you will learn to:

✔ Create and modify a Web document.

✔ Add hyperlinks.

✔ Create an XML document.

If you have ever explored the Web to check the news, find sports scores, or research a topic, you know that the Web is appealing, informative, and immediate. It's also a great business or publishing tool if you are trying to reach a broad audience. It's not difficult to transform your documents into *Web pages* so that people can read them on the Web. For example, The Garden Company might want to publish a Web newsletter to provide information about gardening while advertising its merchandise and services. Customers and gardening enthusiasts can then read the newsletter in a *Web browser*.

Professional Web designers use special programs, such as Microsoft FrontPage, to design sophisticated *Web sites* (collections of related Web pages). However, you can use Microsoft Office Word 2003 to create simple Web pages or to convert existing documents to Web pages. With Word, you can save a document as a Web page, preview it in your Web browser, and then modify the page as necessary. You can also add *hyperlinks* (also called *links*) to the document to provide a quick way of jumping to other documents, Web pages, or e-mail addresses.

When you convert a document to a Web page, Word translates the styles and formatting in the document to *Hypertext Markup Language (HTML)* codes, called *tags*, that tell your Web browser how to display the document. You can also convert a document using *Extensible Markup Language (XML)*. XML is a system for defining, validating, and sharing documents that uses tags to distinguish document structures, attributes to define extra document information, and transforms to extract different items of tagged information for different purposes.

In this chapter, you will create a Web document from a Word document, create and modify a page in which information is displayed in frames, and then add links. You'll also convert a Word document into an XML document.

See Also   Do you need only a quick refresher on the topics in this chapter? See the Quick Reference entries on pages xlviii–xlix.

Important   Before you can use the practice files in this chapter, you need to install them from the book's companion CD to their default location. See "Using the Book's CD-ROM" on page xiii for more information.

Creating and Modifying a Web Document

Microsoft Office Specialist

You can save any Word document as a Web page—a special document designed to be viewed in a Web browser such as Microsoft Internet Explorer. When you convert a document, most of the formatting is preserved, though some formatting, such as text wrapping around pictures and objects, is not converted and some features, such as table formatting, character formatting, page layout features, and security and document protection, are not supported by all Web browsers.

Tip   If you know which Web browser people will use to view your Web page, it's a good idea to specify that browser and have Word disable any features that won't work.

To see how a document will be displayed in a Web browser, you can preview it as a Web page, or you can click the Web Layout View button to see how it will look. You can then edit the page as necessary to achieve the effect you want. When you're satisfied with the results, you save the document as a Web page.

You can convert existing Word documents to Web pages using the Save as Web Page command on the File menu. You can also create new Web pages from within Word, by using a Web page template. You can access a template in the following ways:

- Click New on the File menu, click "On my computer" in the Templates area of the New Document task pane, and click the Web Pages icon on the General tab of the Templates dialog box.

- Click New on the File menu, click "Templates on Office Online" in the Templates area of the New Document task pane, and make a selection on the Templates page of the Microsoft Office Online Web site.

After you save a Word document as a Web page, you can open it in Word and modify it, just as you would a normal Word document. You can also use Word to open Web pages created in other programs and saved with a *.htm* or *.html* file name extension. Making changes can be as basic as replacing text and adjusting alignment or as advanced as moving and inserting graphics. You can also display a Web document in an area called a *frame* on a special type of page called a *frames page*, and then include other items of interest in the other frames so that they can be viewed at the same time as the document.

When you finish modifying the document, you can save it as a Web page or a regular Word document.

In this exercise, you will set options for displaying a document in Microsoft Internet Explorer 5.0 or later. You will then preview and save the document as a Web page. You will create a frames page, modify the page, and then save your changes.

BE SURE TO start Word before beginning this exercise. Also be sure you have a Web browser installed on your computer. (Internet Explorer 5.0 or later is recommended; the functionality and settings might be different for other browsers.)

USE the *CreateWeb* document in the practice file folder for this topic. This practice file is located in the *My Documents\Microsoft Press\Word 2003 SBS\CreatingWeb\CreatingWebDoc* folder and can also be accessed by clicking *Start/All Programs/Microsoft Press/Word 2003 Step by Step*.

OPEN the *CreateWeb* document.

1 On the **Tools** menu, click **Options**.

The Options dialog box appears.

2 If necessary, click the **General** tab, and then click **Web Options**.

The Web Options dialog box appears.

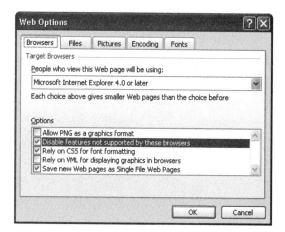

3 On the **Browsers** tab, click the down arrow to the right of the **People who view this Web page will be using** box, and then click **Microsoft Internet Explorer 5.0 or later**.

4 In the **Options** list, verify that the **Disable features not supported by these browsers** check box is selected, and click **OK**.

5 Click **OK** to close the **Options** dialog box.

Maximize

6 On the **File** menu, click **Web Page Preview** to open the page in your Web browser, and then at the right end of your Web browser's title bar, click the **Maximize** button.

The CreateWeb document is displayed in your Web browser as a Web page.

7 Close the Web browser window.

8 On the **File** menu, click **Save as Web Page**.

The Save As dialog box appears.

9 Navigate to the *Microsoft Press\Word 2003 SBS\CreatingWeb\CreatingWebDoc* folder, and in the **File name** box, type WebDoc.

Tip When you save a document as a Web page, you can specify a page title for the document. This title appears in the title bar of the Web browser, and it can be different from the file name. To specify a Web page title, click Change Title in the Save As dialog box, type the title in the "Page title" box, and click OK.

10 Click the down arrow to the right of the **Save as type** box, click **Web Page** in the drop-down list, and click **Save**.

A message tells you that some features in this document are not supported by Internet Explorer 5.0.

11 Click **Continue**.

Because the document is now a Web document, it appears in Word in Web Layout view.

Tip We've closed the Drawing toolbar and toggled off the Show/Hide ¶ button and the ruler to reduce visual clutter.

12 On the **Format** menu, point to **Frames**, and then click **New Frames Page**.

As indicated in the title bar, Word displays a new document. This document consists of one area, or frame, with WebDoc displayed in it. Word also displays the Frames toolbar.

13 On the Frames toolbar, click **New Frame Left**, and then close the Frames toolbar.

A frame roughly half the width of the screen appears to the left of the frame that displays the WebDoc document.

14 Point to the border between the two frames, and when the pointer changes to a double-headed arrow, drag the border until the frame on the left is half its original width.

15 In the left frame, type Check out The Garden Company's Children's Center!, and press [Enter] three times.

16 Type All activities are free to the public!, and press [Enter].

Font Color

17 Select all the text in the left frame, click the down arrow to the right of the **Font Size** box, and click **26**. Then click the down arrow to the right of the **Font Color** button, and in the second column of the second row of the color palette, click the **Orange** box, and press [End].

18 Scroll the frame that displays the *WebDoc* document.

The document scrolls, but the message in the adjacent frame doesn't.

19 On the **File** menu, click **Save**, type **FramesPage** as the name of the file, verify that the file will be saved in the *Microsoft Press\Word 2003 SBS\CreatingWeb \CreatingWebDoc* folder, and click **Save**.

Word saves the frames document, which contains text in the left frame and an instruction to display the WebDoc document in the right frame.

20 Close the *FramesPage* document.

21 On the Standard toolbar, click the **Open** button.

Open

The Open dialog box appears.

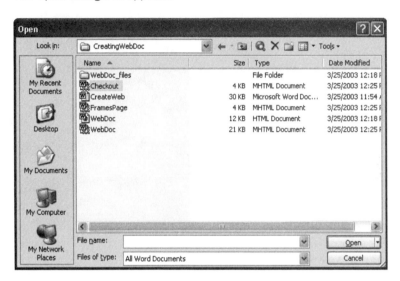

Troubleshooting If your Open dialog box view is different, click the Views button on the toolbar until the Details view is displayed.

The CreatingWebDoc folder now contains CreateWeb (the original Word document); WebDoc (the Web document you saved in HTML); and three MHTML files that contain the information for the frames page, the text in the left frame, and the text in the right frame.

22 Double-click the *WebDoc* MHTML document (not the *WebDoc* HTML document).

23 With the insertion point to the left of *The Garden Company*, press `End`, and then press `Enter` twice.

24 Type April 15.

25 On the Standard toolbar, click the **Save** button to save the Web document, and then close it.

Save

26 On the Standard toolbar, click the **Open** button, and then double-click the *FramesPage* MHTML document.

The edited document appears in the right frame of the frames page.

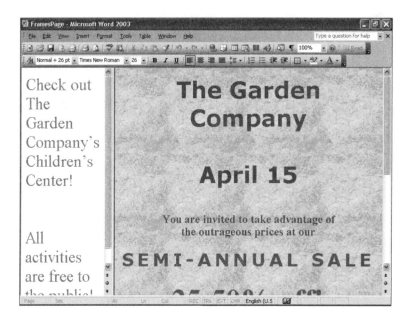

CLOSE the *FramesPage* document.

Adding Hyperlinks

Microsoft Office Specialist

Web pages use hyperlinks (links) as a quick way to perform tasks such as opening another Web page, downloading a file, or sending an e-mail message. You can insert hyperlinks into a Web document or a regular Word document by clicking the Insert Hyperlink button on the Standard toolbar to display the Insert Hyperlink dialog box. Then use the buttons on the "Link to" bar to set up a link to another file or Web page, to another place in the same document (such as a heading or *bookmark*), to a new document, or to an e-mail address.

Tip To link to another Web page, you specify a *Uniform Resource Locator (URL),* which is a unique address for the Web page, such as *www.microsoft.com.* When you type a URL, you do not have to type *http://* in front of it—your Web browser will add *http://* for you.

When you insert a hyperlink into a document, you can click Target Frame in the Insert Hyperlink dialog box and use the Set Target Frame dialog box to control how the linked page is displayed in the document. You can display the linked page in the same window as the original page, in a new window, or in a frame.

Text hyperlinks appear in Word documents as blue underlined text, which is similar to the way that they appear in most browsers. You can jump to the target of a hyperlink in a Word document by holding down the [Ctrl] key and clicking the link. When you view the Web document in your browser, you can simply click the link to follow it.

To edit a hyperlink, you right-click it and then click one of the commands on the shortcut menu, which allow you to change the destination of the hyperlink, change the display text, or convert the hyperlink to regular text.

In this exercise, you will insert, test, and modify a hyperlink.

USE the *HyperWeb* and *OtherLogos* documents in the practice file folder for this topic. These practice files are located in the *My Documents\Microsoft Press\Word 2003 SBS\CreatingWeb\AddingLink* folder and can also be accessed by clicking *Start/All Programs/Microsoft Press/Word 2003 Step by Step*.
OPEN the *HyperWeb* document.

1 Right-click The Garden Company logo, and click **Hyperlink** on the shortcut menu.

The Insert Hyperlink dialog box appears, displaying the contents of the AddingLink folder.

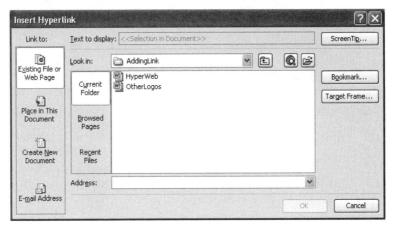

2 In the list of folders and file names, click (don't double-click) the *OtherLogos* file, and then click **Target Frame**.

The Set Target Frame dialog box appears with Page Default (none) as the current frame setting.

3 Click **OK** to accept the default selection, and click **OK** to close the **Insert Hyperlink** dialog box.

4 Point to the logo again.

Word displays a ScreenTip that shows the path of this hyperlink to the OtherLogos file and information about how to follow the link in Word.

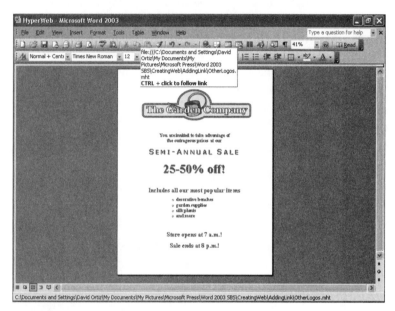

5 Hold down ⟦Ctrl⟧, and then click the logo.

The OtherLogos file is displayed in your Web browser window.

6 Close the browser window.

Center

7 Back in Word, zoom to **75%**, press ⟦Ctrl⟧+⟦End⟧, press ⟦Enter⟧, and click the **Center** button on the Formatting toolbar.

Insert
Hyperlink

8 Type Contact us for more information, select the text, click the **Insert Hyperlink** button on the Standard toolbar, and on the **Link to** bar of the **Insert Hyperlink** dialog box, click **E-mail Address**.

The dialog box changes so that you can enter the information appropriate for an e-mail hyperlink.

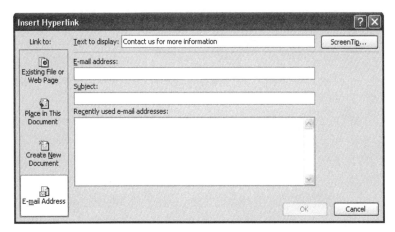

9 In the **E-mail address** box, type David@gardenco.msn.com, and click **OK**.

The hyperlinked text is displayed in blue with an underline. Pointing to it displays a ScreenTip with the hyperlink's destination.

10 On the **File** menu, click **Save As**. Change the **Save as type** setting to **Web Page**, type **HyperWebPage** in the **File name** box, and click **Save**. Then click **Continue**.

The Web document is displayed in Web Layout view.

11 Open your Web browser, and on the **File** menu, click **Open**. In the **Open** dialog box, click **Browse**, navigate to the *My Documents\Microsoft Press\Word 2003 SBS \CreatingWeb\AddingLink* folder, double-click *HyperWebPage*, and click **OK**.

12 Click the company logo.

The OtherLogos document opens in the same browser window.

13 Close the browser window.

14 Back in Word, right-click the text hyperlink at the bottom of the page, and click **Edit Hyperlink**.

The Edit Hyperlink dialog box appears with the current destination for this link in the E-mail address box.

15 In the **E-mail address** box, replace *David* with Kim, and click **OK**.

16 Hold down [Ctrl], and click the hyperlink.

Your e-mail program opens, with the specified e-mail address in the To line.

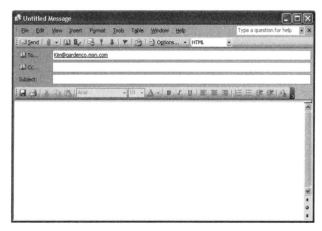

17 Close the message window, clicking **No** to discard the message.

18 On the Standard toolbar, click the **Save** button to save the document.

Save

CLOSE the *HyperWebPage* document.

Creating an XML Document

Microsoft Office Specialist

New in Office 2003

XML capabilities

Web documents are coded with Hypertext Markup Language (HTML) so that they can be displayed in a Web browser, no matter what that browser might be. HTML is a small, fixed subset of the *Standard Generalized Markup Language (SGML)*, a comprehensive system for coding the structure of text documents and other forms of data so that they can be used in a variety of environments. The Extensible Markup Language (XML) is another subset of SGML. However, instead of being fixed like HTML, XML can be customized (extended) to store data so that it can be used in many ways or in many environments—for example, as text, in a database or spreadsheet, or as a Web page.

To save a Word document in XML format, you need to attach an *XML schema* to it. This schema describes the structure allowed in the document, including the names of structural elements and what elements can contain what other elements. For example, a numbered list might be defined as an element that can contain only numbered items—no regular paragraphs, graphics, or sidebars. Generally, companies employ a specialist with in-depth knowledge of XML to create custom schemas, but after a schema is created, anyone can attach it to a Word document and convert the format to an XML document.

Tip If you don't have a custom schema, you can still save a Word document as an XML document by using Word's built-in XML schema, which is called WordML. To use WordML, create a Word document and then save it as an XML document. Word will apply XML tags that define the document's structure and store formatting information.

In this exercise, we can't teach you all the details of XML programming, but you will learn how to attach a schema to a Word document and tag elements to create valid structure. Then you'll save the file as an XML document.

USE the *AttachSchema* document in the practice file folder for this topic. This practice file is located in the *My Documents\Microsoft Press\Word 2003 SBS\CreatingWeb\CreatingXML* folder and can also be accessed by clicking *Start/All Programs/Microsoft Press/Word 2003 Step by Step*.
OPEN the *AttachSchema* document.

1   On the **Tools** menu, click **Templates and Add-Ins**.

2   In the **Templates and Add-ins** dialog box, click the **XML Schema** tab, and then click Schema Library.

3   In the **Schema Library** dialog box, click **Add Schema**.

    The Add Schema dialog box appears.

4   If the contents of the My Documents folder are not displayed, click the **My Documents** icon on the Places bar. Then navigate to the *Microsoft Press\Word 2003 SBS \CreatingWeb\CreatingXML* folder, and double-click *GardenClassSchema*.

    The Schema Settings dialog box appears.

5   In the **Alias** box, type May Class Schema, and click **OK**.

    Word adds the schema to the Schema Library.

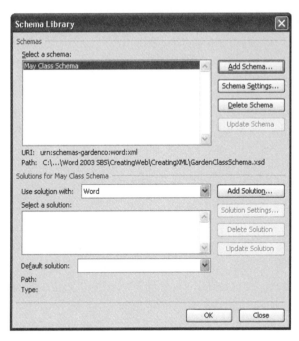

6 Click **OK** to close the **Schema Library** dialog box.

7 On the **XML Schema** tab of the **Templates and Add-ins** dialog box, select the **May Class Schema** check box in the **Checked schemas are currently attached** box.

8 In the **Schema validation options** area, make sure the **Validate document against attached schemas** check box is selected.

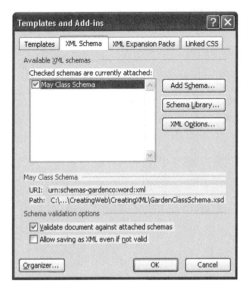

9 Click **XML Options** to display the **XML Options** dialog box.

10 In the **Schema validation options** area, make sure the **Hide schema violations in this document** check box is cleared. Then in the **XML view options** area, make sure the **Hide namespace alias in XML Structure task pane** check box is cleared, and then select the **Show advanced XML error messages** check box.

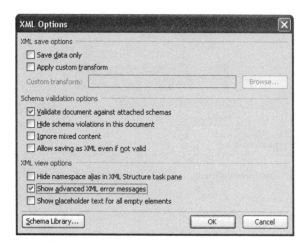

11 Click **OK** to close the **XML Options** dialog box, and then click **OK** again to close the **Templates and Add-ins** dialog box.

The XML Structure task pane opens.

12 In the **XML Structure** task pane, make sure the **Show XML tags in the document** check box is selected.

Tip When you don't need to see XML tags in a document, you can toggle them off by clearing the "Show XML tags in the document" check box.

13 Click anywhere in the document window. Then in the **Choose an element to apply to your current selection** box at the bottom of the **XML Structure** task pane, click **classlist {May Class Schema}**.

Word asks whether you want to apply this element to the entire document.

14 Click **Apply to Entire Document**.

Word selects all the text in the document, adds an opening XML tag and a closing XML tag at either end of the document to indicate that the entire document is now a classlist element, and lists the element in the "Elements in the document" box in the XML Structure task pane.

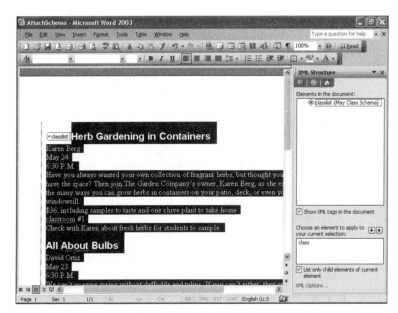

15 Select all the text from *Herb Gardening in Containers* down to *Check with Karen about fresh herbs for students to sample.* In the **Choose an element to apply to your current selection** box, click **class**.

Word tags the selection as a class element.

Tip By default, the "List only child elements of current element" check box is selected. This simplifies the list of elements by showing only the ones that are valid in the current location. If you want to see a complete list of elements allowed in this schema, clear this check box. Invalid elements are then flagged with a slash inside a circle (the "not allowed" symbol).

16 Select the *Herb Gardening in Containers* heading, and tag it as **title**.

Show/Hide ¶

17 On the Standard toolbar, click the **Show/Hide** ¶ button, and then select each of the next six paragraphs one at a time, and tag them in turn as **instructor**, **date**, **time**, **description**, **cost**, and **classroom**.

As you tag each new element, Word adds that element to the growing structure in the "Elements in the document" box. An X next to the class element tells you that the structure is not valid according to the schemas rules, and three dots under the classroom element tell you that the schema calls for an element that is missing.

18 Point to the X beside **class**.

A ScreenTip tells you that "Text is not allowed in the context of element 'class' according to DTD/Schema." In other words, untagged text is not valid; all text must be enclosed in valid start and end element tags.

19 Select *Check with Karen about fresh herbs for students to sample.*—the only remaining untagged text in the class element (don't include the closing class tag).

20 Scroll the **Choose an element to apply to your current selection** list, and click **notes**.

Word tags the element, and the X next to class disappears.

21 Select all the text from *All About Bulbs* down to *David will need the screen set up for his PowerPoint slides.* In the **Choose an element to apply to your current selection** box, click **class**.

22 Select each of the paragraphs in this class in turn, and tag them as **title**, **instructor**, **date**, **time**, **description**, **cost**, and **notes**.

Important When you select the first and last paragraphs, be sure not to include the tags for the class element.

In the "Elements in the document" area of the XML Structure task pane, a question mark appears next to the second class element, and a wavy purple line appears in the left margin to show you the section with invalid structure.

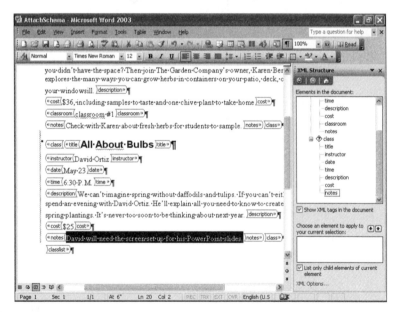

23 Point to the question mark.

Word tells you that the "Content for element 'class' is incomplete according to DTD/Schema."

24 In the *All About Bulbs* class in the document window (not the XML Structure task pane), click to the right of the **cost** end tag, and press [Enter].

25 Type classroom #2. Then select that text, and tag it as **classroom**.

The "Elements in the document" box of the XML Structure task pane shows that the document's structure is now fully valid, and you are now ready to save it.

Troubleshooting If the "Allow saving as XML even if not valid" check box is cleared in the XML Options dialog box, Word will not allow you to save a document as XML unless the structure is valid. If Word tells you that it cannot save your document as XML because its structure violates the rules set by the schema, you have three choices: save the file as a Word document; click Cancel and change the option in the XML Options dialog box; or click Cancel and go back to the "Elements in the document" box of the XML Structure task pane to correct the structure of marked elements.

26 On the **File** menu, click **Save As**.

27 In the **Save As** dialog box, click the down arrow to the right of the **Save as type** box, and click **XML Document** in the drop-down list.

28 Click **Save** to save the AttachSchema XML document.

CLOSE the *AttachSchema* XML document, and if you are not continuing on to the next chapter, quit Word.

Using Attributes and Transforms

If the schema that you are using has defined attributes for any of its elements, you can assign the attributes from the XML Structure task pane.

To assign an attribute to an element:

1 Right-click the element in the **XML Structure** task pane, and then click **Attributes**.

The Attributes dialog box appears.

2 Select an attribute from the **Available attributes** box, and click **Add**.

3 Click **OK**.

The power of XML is its adaptability. By applying different transforms to an XML document, you can pull only the data you need, put it in the necessary format, and send it in different directions. For example, if The Garden Company has an XML document that is a list of gardening classes, they can apply a transform that extracts the title, description, instructor, cost, date, and time of the class and then formats that information as a Web page for customers. They can also apply a different transform that extracts the date, classroom, and notes and then formats that information as a memo for setup staff.

To apply a transform to an XML document:

1   On the **File** menu, click **Save As**.

    The Save As dialog box appears.

2   In the **File name** box, type a name for the file.

3   Click the down arrow to the right of the **Save as type** box, and click **XML Document** in the drop-down list.

    The "Apply transform" check box appears to the right of the "File name" box.

4   Select the **Apply transform** check box, and then click **Transform**.

5   In the **Choose an XSL Transformation** dialog box, navigate to the folder where the transform you want to apply is stored, and double-click the transform.

6   Click **Save**.

    Word warns you that saving a file through a transform without WordML could remove features such as formatting and pictures.

7   To save the file without WordML, click **Continue**. To save the file with WordML, click **Keep WordML**.

Key Points

- You can save any Word document as a Web page, and you can preview the page and edit it as necessary.

- You can insert hyperlinks into a Web document or any other type of Word document to link to another Web page, file, e-mail address, or bookmark.

- You can convert a Word document into an XML document that can be used by other programs in other environments.

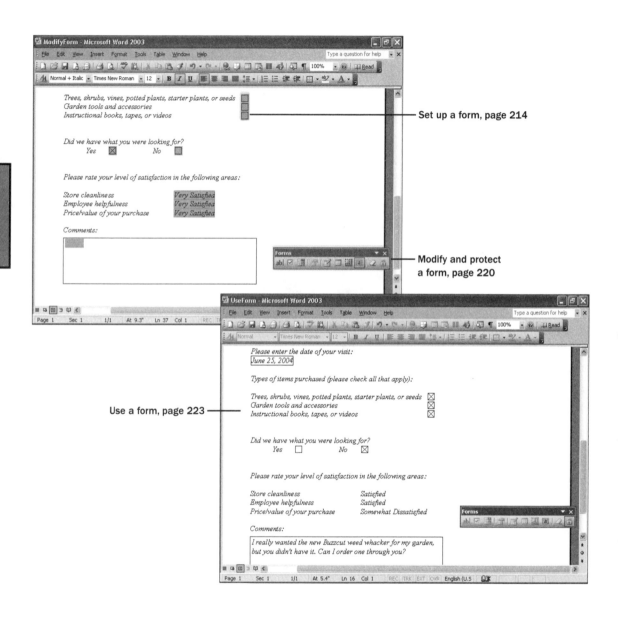

Set up a form, page 214

Modify and protect a form, page 220

Use a form, page 223

Chapter 10 at a Glance

10 Creating Forms

In this chapter you will learn to:

✔ Set up a form.

✔ Modify and protect a form.

✔ Use a form.

Using a Microsoft Office Word 2003 form is a convenient way to collect information consistently. A *form* is a document containing text instructions and questions, together with blank areas where users can enter their responses. With a form, you can ask specific questions and get the responses in the format that you want. For example, The Garden Company might use forms to register customers for a training class and to collect feedback at the end of the class.

To set up a Word form, you associate each blank area where users enter information with a *form field*. Word includes many different types of form fields, such as text boxes for name entries, date and time fields for dates and times, fields that perform calculations, and fields that enable users to select from predefined options.

After you have created a form, you can print it so that users can respond on paper, or you can distribute the form electronically. In the latter case, you can protect the form document so that users can enter information in the fields but cannot otherwise change the form's contents or layout.

In this chapter, you'll create a form for a customer satisfaction survey. You will insert various form fields and then modify them. When you are satisfied with the form, you will protect it so that users cannot do anything but fill in the form fields. Finally, you'll test the form by filling it in.

See Also Do you need only a quick refresher on the topics in this chapter? See the Quick Reference entries on pages I–li.

Important Before you can use the practice files in this chapter, you need to install them from the book's companion CD to their default location. See "Using the Book's CD-ROM" on page xiii for more information.

Setting Up a Form

Microsoft
Office
Specialist

To create a form, you type all the information that does not change from one form to the next, and you insert form fields for all the information supplied by users. In Word, you can insert several types of form fields, as follows:

- *Text form fields* include six types:

  - Regular text fields can accept any combination of keyboard characters, including letters, numbers, or symbols. This text field is useful for comments and short text answers.

  - Number fields accept only numeric values, making them appropriate for a quantity or price field on an order form.

  - Date fields enable users to type a date in a specified format, such as *12/21/2004*.

  - Current date fields instruct Word to enter the current date maintained by your computer.

  - Current time fields instruct Word to enter the current system time.

  - Calculation fields perform a calculation based on the formula and values you supply, such as totaling the values in specified number fields.

- *Check-box form fields* enable you to provide options that users can select. Users can select all, some, or none of the options. Check boxes are also good for true/false and yes/no responses.

- *Drop-down form fields* enable you to limit users' responses to one of several predefined options. You specify all the possible options, and users choose one, ensuring that they enter consistent and accurate information.

For example, suppose the marketing manager of The Garden Company wants to conduct a survey to find out how people discovered the store and to measure their level of satisfaction. The survey will be e-mailed to all customers on the customer list, with a discount offer for those who fill in and return the survey. When users enter responses in text form fields, responses must be interpreted and tallied by hand. To make tallying easier, the survey can instead include a drop-down form field with a list of all the possible information avenues—advertisement, mailing, word of mouth, and so on—and it can include check-box form fields to gather *excellent, very good, good, fair,* and *poor* responses to questions such as "How would you rate our service?"

After you insert a form field into a document, you can click the Form Field Options button on the Forms toolbar to set *form field properties*, such as the type of a text field, the maximum length of entries, and the options in a drop-down form field. The properties you can set vary depending on the form field type.

In this exercise, you will insert text form fields, check-box form fields, and drop-down form fields to create a form.

BE SURE TO start Word before beginning this exercise.
USE the *CreateForm* document in the practice file folder for this topic. This practice file is located in the *My Documents\Microsoft Press\Word 2003 SBS\CreatingForm\SettingUp* folder and can also be accessed by clicking *Start/All Programs/Microsoft Press/Word 2003 Step by Step*.
OPEN the *CreateForm* document.

1 On the **View** menu, point to **Toolbars**, and then click **Forms**.

The Forms toolbar appears.

2 Scroll down the document, and click the blank line below *Please enter the date of your visit*.

Text Form Field

3 On the Forms toolbar, click the **Text Form Field** button.

Word inserts a text form field with the default text format.

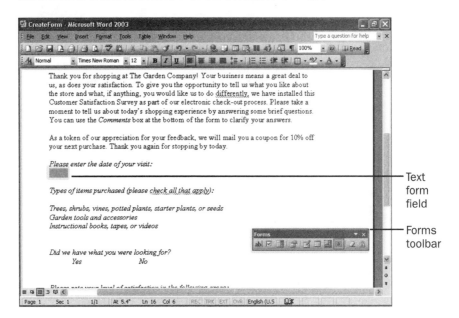

Form Field
Options

4   On the Forms toolbar, click the **Form Field Options** button.

The Text Form Field Options dialog box appears.

5   In the **Text Form Field Options** dialog box, click the down arrow to the right of the **Type** box, and then click **Date**.

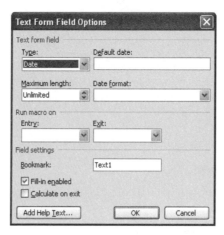

6   Click the down arrow to the right of the **Date format** box, click **MMMM d, yyyy**, and then click **OK**.

The Text Form Field Options dialog box closes. No matter how users fill in this date field, the date will be displayed as specified, such as July 22, 2004.

Form Field
Shading

Tip   New fields are shaded by default to make it obvious where users should enter information. To remove the shading, click the Form Field Shading button on the Forms toolbar.

7   Press [Ctrl]+[End] to position the insertion point at the end of the document below the word *Comments*.

8   On the Forms toolbar, click the **Text Form Field** button.

A text form field is inserted.

9   Scroll up in the document, click to the right of the phrase *Trees, shrubs, vines, potted plants, starter plants, or seeds*, and then press [Tab].

Check Box
Form Field

10   On the Forms toolbar, click the **Check Box Form Field** button.

A check box is added to the right of the word *seeds*.

11   On the Forms toolbar, click the **Form Fields Options** button.

The Check Box Form Field Options dialog box appears.

Tip You can provide instructions for filling out a field by adding help text to form fields. In any Form Field Options dialog box, click Add Help Text, select the "Type your own" option, type the instructions in the box, and then click OK.

12 In the **Check box size** area, select the **Exactly** option, click the up arrow until **12 pt** appears, and then click **OK**.

The check box is now the size of 12-point text and is by default cleared (empty) and highlighted.

Copy

13 On the Standard toolbar, click the **Copy** button.

The check box is copied to the Office Clipboard.

Paste

14 Click to the right of *Garden tools and accessories*, press ⌨Tab, and on the Standard toolbar, click the **Paste** button.

The check box is pasted to the right of the word *Accessories*, directly below the other check box.

Tip To save time, you can copy and paste any type of form field and then change its properties as necessary, instead of having to set up every form field from scratch. A quick way to copy and paste is to use the keyboard combinations ⌨Ctrl+⌨C (copy) and ⌨Ctrl+⌨V (paste).

15 Click to the right of *Instructional books, tapes, or videos*, press ⌨Tab, and click the **Paste** button on the Standard toolbar.

The check box is pasted to the right of the word *videos*, directly below the other check boxes.

16 Select the check box, hold down the ⊡ key, and drag a copy of the selected check box one tab to the right of the word *Yes*.

17 Hold down ⊡, and drag another copy of the selected check box one tab to the right of the word *No*.

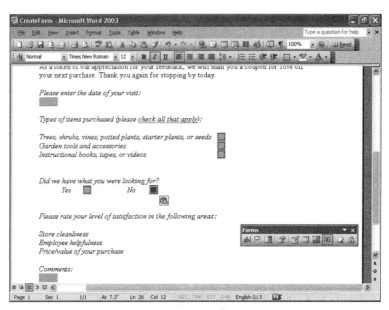

18 Click to the right of *Store cleanliness*, and press the ⊡ key.

19 On the Forms toolbar, click the **Drop-Down Form Field** button.

Drop-Down
Form Field

Word inserts a drop-down form field to the right of the words *Store cleanliness*. (When users fill out the form, they will see a box with a down arrow.)

20 On the Forms toolbar, click the **Form Field Options** button to open the **Drop-Down Form Field Options** dialog box.

21 In the **Drop-down item** box, type Very Satisfied, and click **Add**.

This option is added to the "Items in drop-down list" box.

22 In the **Drop-down item** box, add Somewhat Satisfied, Satisfied, Very Dissatisfied, and Mildly Dissatisfied, clicking **Add** after each entry.

The entries are added to the "Items in drop-down list" box.

23 Click the **Move Up** arrow button once to move the *Mildly Dissatisfied* entry up in the list, and then click **OK**.

The Drop-Down Form Field Options dialog box closes, and the first entry in the drop-down list—*Very Satisfied*—appears in the box.

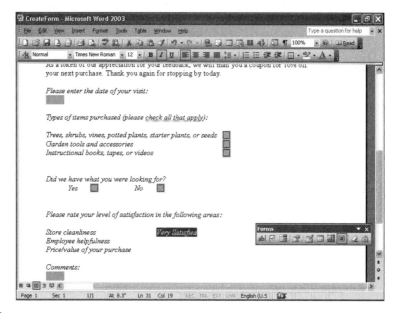

24 If the drop-down box is not active, drag across it to select it. Then on the Standard toolbar, click the **Copy** button.

The drop-down box is copied to the Office Clipboard.

25 Click to the right of *Employee helpfulness* in the next paragraph, press ⇥, and then press Ctrl+V.

A copy of the drop-down box is pasted to the right of the text.

26   Click to the right of *Price/value of your purchase* in the next paragraph, press [Tab],
and then press [Ctrl]+[V].

Another copy is pasted to the right of the text.

27   On the Standard toolbar, click the **Save** button to save the document.

Save

CLOSE the *CreateForm* document.

Modifying and Protecting a Form

*Microsoft
Office
Specialist*

You can enhance the look of a form by changing formatting and adding graphics
just as you would in any other type of Word document. You can also modify form
field properties to change the way the fields look and work.

After you finish a form but before you distribute it to users, you will want to protect
it so that users can fill in the fields but not change the form itself. In fact, you cannot
use a form to gather responses until you protect it. If you need to change the layout
or content later, you will need to unprotect the form. You use the Protect Form button
on the Forms toolbar to turn protection on and off.

Tip   You can add further protection to a form by assigning it a password so that only
people who know the password can unprotect and edit the form. To assign a password,
click Protect Document on the Tools menu to open the Protect Document task pane. In the
"Editing restrictions" area, select "Allow only this type of editing in the document," click
the down arrow to the right of the text box, and then click "Filling in forms." In the "Start
enforcement" area, click "Yes, Start Enforcing Protection" to open the Start Enforcing
Protection dialog box, where you can set the password.

In this exercise, you'll format a text field, change the default value of a check box,
change an item in a drop-down form field, insert a frame, remove the shading from
all the form fields, and then protect the form.

USE the *ModifyForm* document in the practice file folder for this topic. This practice file is located in the
My Documents\Microsoft Press\Word 2003 SBS\CreatingForm\ModifyingForm folder and can also be
accessed by clicking *Start/All Programs/Microsoft Press/Word 2003 Step by Step*.
OPEN the *ModifyForm* document.

1   If the Forms toolbar is not visible, point to **Toolbars** on the **View** menu, and click
Forms.

2   Scroll down the document, and click the text form field below *Please enter the date
of your visit* to select the field.

Border

3 On the Formatting toolbar, click the down arrow to the right of the **Border** button, click **Outside Border** on the button palette, and then click a blank area of the document to deselect the text form field.

The field now has a border.

4 If necessary, scroll down the document, and then double-click the check box to the right of *Yes*.

The Check Box Form Field Options dialog box opens.

5 In the **Default value** area, select the **Checked** option, and click **OK**.

An X is placed in the check box as the default value.

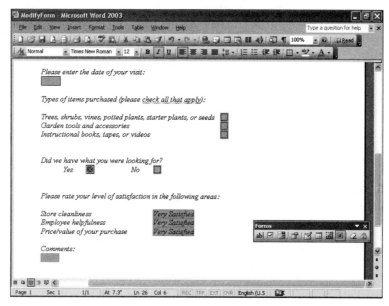

6 If necessary, scroll down until you can see *Store cleanliness*, and then double-click the first drop-down form field.

The Drop-Down Form Field Options dialog box opens.

7 In the **Items in drop-down list** box, click *Mildly Dissatisfied*, and then click **Remove**.

The *Mildly Dissatisfied* option is removed from the "Items in drop-down list" box.

8 In the **Drop-down item** box, type Somewhat Dissatisfied, click **Add**, and then click the **Move Up** arrow button.

The text *Somewhat Dissatisfied* takes the place of *Mildly Dissatisfied* in the list.

Insert Frame

9 Click **OK** to close the **Drop-Down Form Field Options** dialog box.

10 Repeat steps 6 through 9 for the next two drop-down form fields.

11 Click the text form field below the *Comments* heading, and on the Forms toolbar, click the **Insert Frame** button.

Handles around the frame indicate that this object can be moved or sized.

12 Drag the text form field down a bit to add space between *Comments* and the text form field.

13 Drag the frame's lower-right handle down and to the right until the right edge of the frame is aligned with the three check boxes and the frame is about an inch high.

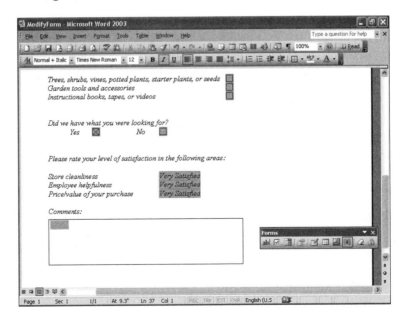

Form Field
Shading

14 On the Forms toolbar, click the **Form Field Shading** button.

The shading is removed from all the form fields.

Protect Form

15 On the Forms toolbar, click the **Protect Form** button.

Word locks all the non-field text and formatting of the form, protecting the form from changes other than to the form fields. The form is now ready for distribution so that it can be filled out.

Save

16 On the Standard toolbar, click the **Save** button.

CLOSE the *ModifyForm* document.

Using a Form

After you have created a form, you can test it by filling it out the same way that the recipients of the form will. Because the form is protected, the responses you enter into the form will not change the form itself.

When you are satisfied that the form is working correctly, you can print it so that users can fill it out manually, or you can distribute it electronically so that users can fill it out in Word. If you distribute the form electronically, you need to save the form as a template so that each user can create a separate document with his or her responses. You can send the form in an e-mail message, or if you work on a network, you can store the form in a central location from which people can access the file. If you have a Web site, you can save the form as a Web page so that people can fill it out online.

See Also   For more information about creating Web pages, see Chapter 9.

In this exercise, you will view and test a form.

USE the *UseForm* document in the practice file folder for this topic. This practice file is located in the *My Documents\Microsoft Press\Word 2003 SBS\CreatingForm\UsingForm* folder and can also be accessed by clicking *Start/All Programs/Microsoft Press/Word 2003 Step by Step*.
OPEN the *UseForm* document.

1 Scroll down the document to the first field, type 6/25/04, and press `Tab`.

The date *June 25, 2004* appears in the date form field, and the first check box on the form is now selected.

2 Click each of the three check boxes below the *Types of items purchased* heading.

The X in each box indicates that it is selected.

Tip   When filling out a form, you can also press `Space` to insert or remove an X in an active check box.

3 Under the *Did we have what you were looking for?* question, clear the **Yes** check box, and select the **No** check box.

The X is removed from the Yes box, and is added to the No box.

Important In a Word form, check boxes are independent of each other. You need to select or clear each check box. Word does not automatically clear one check box when another check box in the same set is selected.

4 Click the field to the right of *Store cleanliness* to reveal its drop-down box, and then click *Somewhat Satisfied* in the list.

The box now contains the *Somewhat Satisfied* option.

5 Click the field to the right of *Employee helpfulness* to reveal its drop-down box, and click *Satisfied*.

This drop-down box now contains the *Satisfied* option.

6 Click the field to the right of *Price/value of your purchase* to reveal its drop-down box, and click *Somewhat Dissatisfied*.

The *Somewhat Dissatisfied* option appears in this drop-down box.

7 Click the upper-left corner of the text form field below the *Comments* heading to select the field, and then type I really wanted the new Buzzcut weed whacker for my garden, but you didn't have it. Can I order one through you?

The form is working as expected, so you can now distribute it.

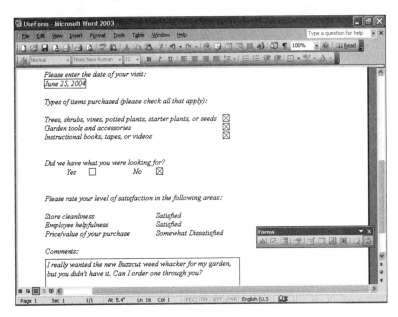

Reset Form
Fields

8 On the **Forms** toolbar, click **Protect Form** to turn off protection, and click the **Reset Form Fields** button to erase the responses you entered and return all the fields to their original state. Then click **Protect Form** to turn protection back on.

9 On the **File** menu, click **Save As**.

The Save As dialog box appears.

10 In the **File name** box, type SendForm.

11 Click the down arrow to the right of the **Save as type** box, and then click **Document Template**.

12 Navigate to the *My Documents\Microsoft Press\Word 2003 SBS\CreatingForm \UsingForm* folder on your hard disk, and then click **Save**.

Word saves the form as a template in the specified folder. You can now send it via e-mail or otherwise distribute it. To fill out the form, double-click the template file to open a Word document based on it, and then save the document with its own file name.

13 Close the Forms toolbar.

CLOSE the *UseForm* document, and if you are not continuing on to the next chapter, quit Word.

Key Points

- A form consists of instructions, questions, and comments that don't change and form fields that are filled out by the form's users.

- You can insert several types of form fields in a form: text form fields for variable information; check boxes for yes/no or true/false responses; and drop-down form fields for lists of predefined choices.

- You can enhance the usability and look of a form by changing formatting, adding graphics, and changing form field properties, such as the length of text form fields or the default setting for a check box.

- Before distributing a form, you need to protect it so that only the form fields can be changed. If you need to change the layout or contents later, you must first unprotect the form.

- You can print a form or distribute it electronically, either as a Word document or as a Web document. If you distribute the form as a Word document, you need to save the form as a template so that each user can create a separate document for his or her responses.

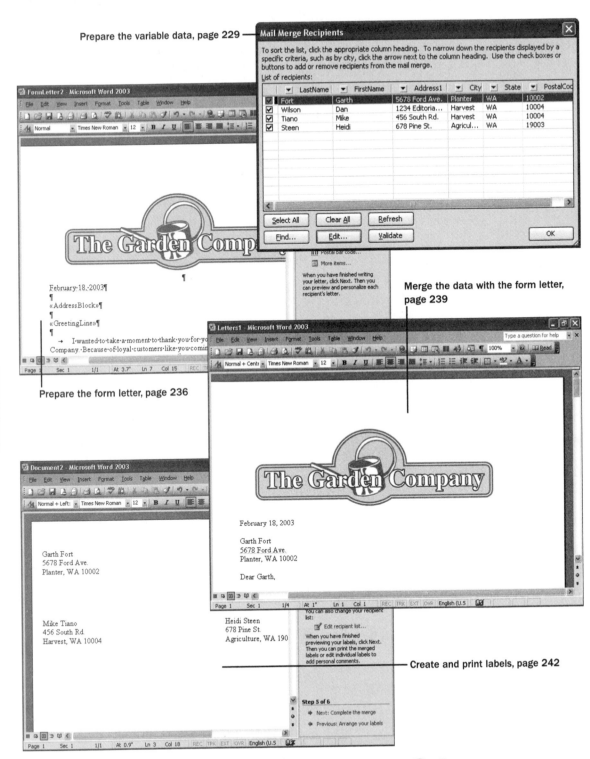

Prepare the variable data, page 229

Merge the data with the form letter, page 239

Prepare the form letter, page 236

Create and print labels, page 242

11 Creating Form Letters and Labels

In this chapter you will learn to:

✔ Understand mail merge.

✔ Prepare the variable data.

✔ Prepare the form letter.

✔ Merge the data with the form letter.

✔ Create and print labels.

Many businesses and other organizations communicate with their customers or members by means of letters, newsletters, and promotional pieces that are sent to everyone on a mailing list. For example, The Garden Company might want to send a letter to everyone on a customer list to advertise the products, services, and classes being introduced to celebrate a new gardening season. The easiest way to generate a set of documents that are identical except for certain information—such as the name, address, and greeting of a letter—is to use a process called *mail merge*. If you have a list of potential recipients stored in a consistent format, you can use the Mail Merge wizard or toolbar in Microsoft Office Word 2003 to easily produce a set of personalized documents and mailing labels.

In this chapter, you will produce a personalized form letter addressed to a specific set of customers. You'll use the Mail Merge Wizard to add a name and address to a mailing list, and you'll sort and filter the list to extract the customers you want to communicate with. You'll then set up the form letter for merging, and preview and save the merged results. Finally, you'll create and print mailing labels for each customer.

See Also   Do you need only a quick refresher on the topics in this chapter? See the Quick Reference entries on pages li–lv.

 Important   Before you can use the practice files in this chapter, you need to install them from the book's companion CD to their default location. See "Using the Book's CD-ROM" on page xiii for more information.

Understanding Mail Merge

Mail merge involves taking information from one document—the *data source*—and combining it with another document—the *main document*. The data source is a document, spreadsheet, database, or other type of file that contains the variable information (such as names, addresses, and phone numbers) that changes from one merged document to the next. The main document contains the text that does not change, as well as *merge fields*, which are placeholders that indicate where Word should insert the variable information from the data source. When you merge the data source and the main document, Word creates one copy of the main document for every set of information in the data source, inserting the data source's information in place of the merge fields.

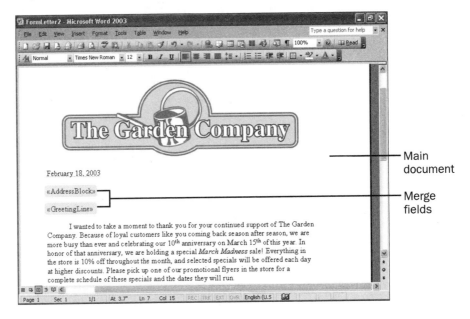

Main document

Merge fields

Tip The main document is sometimes referred to as a *form document*, because it is essentially a form into which variable information will be merged. Like a form, the main document contains fields that indicate where the variable information should be placed. For example, when a letter is used as the main document, it is called a *form letter*.

You can use Word's Mail Merge Wizard to merge a data source, such as a customer list, and a main document, such as a letter, in easy steps. To start the Mail Merge Wizard, you point to Letters and Mailings on the Tools menu, and then click Mail Merge. The Mail Merge task pane appears, showing the first step in the mail merge process, which is to select a document type, such as a letter, e-mail message, envelope, label, or directory list. The document type determines the subsequent steps.

For a letter, the steps are as follows:

■ Specify the document that will be used as the main document.

■ Specify the data source. You can use existing data created in Word or in another program, such as Microsoft Outlook, or you can create the data source as you work through the Mail Merge Wizard.

■ Create the main document by adding merge fields to its text.

■ Preview the letter with the merged data in place. You can exclude data that you don't want to include in the mail merge during this step.

■ Personalize and print the individual letters.

To create the personalized letters, you can merge them into a new document or you can merge them directly to your printer. If you merge them into a new document, Word adds all the letters to a single document so that you can review them and make any individual adjustments before printing. You can also save a permanent copy. If you don't need to save or edit the letters, you can merge directly to the printer. Word prints one personalized letter for each name and address retrieved from the data source. The printed letters are not saved.

Tip   When you have some experience with mail merge, you might want to use the Mail Merge toolbar to create and merge documents, instead of the Mail Merge Wizard. To display the Mail Merge toolbar, point to Toolbars on the View menu, and then click Mail Merge.

Preparing the Variable Data

Microsoft Office Specialist

Before you can merge documents, you need to either specify an existing data source or create one. The data source consists of sets of information structured in columns called *fields* and rows called *records*. Each field is an item of information of a particular type, such as the first name of a customer. Each record is all the items of information belonging to a set, such as the complete name and address of a customer. The data source is arranged with each item of information in a predictable position, as indicated by the set of *field names* in its first row. These field names indicate the type of information in the column.

Tip   Because the field names are also used as the merge fields in the main document, they cannot contain spaces—for example, *FirstName* is an acceptable field name, but *First Name* is not.

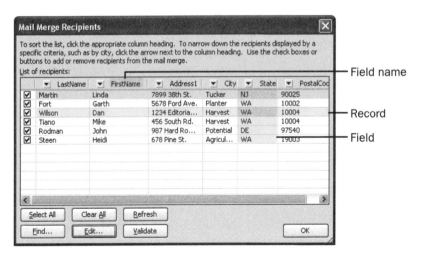

If your mailing list is long and you update it frequently, you might want to create it in a program designed for working with large amounts of data such as Microsoft Access, Microsoft Excel, or Microsoft Visual FoxPro. You can also use the contacts list from Microsoft Outlook or Microsoft Outlook Express. If your data source is short and you don't plan to update it frequently, you can create it in Word. If you are creating the data source in Word, you can use either a table or a list with each part separated by a comma or a tab, as in *Gray, Chris, 4567 Rain St., Buffalo, NY, 98052.*

What if you want to create merge documents for only a subset of the data in the data source? For example, The Garden Company might have mail-order customers from all over the United States, but they might want to target a mass mailing about a store sale to customers with addresses in Washington State. After you specify the data source and create the main document, you can *filter* the data source to create merged documents for only some of its data. You can also set up a simple *query* (a set of selection criteria) to create a data source consisting of only the information you are interested in—for example, all the ZIP Codes for the state of Washington. You can also sort the data source—for example, in ZIP Code order for a bulk mailing. When you use a filter or a query, all the data remains in the data source, but only the data that meets your specifications is used for the mail merge.

In this exercise, you will start the Mail Merge Wizard, specify the main document to be used (a form letter), specify the data source (a mailing list), and then add a record to the data source. You will then sort the records by ZIP Code and create a simple query to select only the records for customers living in Washington State.

BE SURE TO start Word before beginning this exercise.

USE the *FormLetter* and *Data* documents in the practice file folder for this topic. These practice files are located in the *My Documents\Microsoft Press\Word 2003 SBS\CreatingMail\PreparingData* folder and can also be accessed by clicking *Start/All Programs/Microsoft Press/Word 2003 Step by Step*.

OPEN the *FormLetter* document.

1   On the **Tools** menu, point to **Letters and Mailings**, and then click **Mail Merge**.

The Mail Merge task pane opens, showing Step 1 of 6 of the wizard.

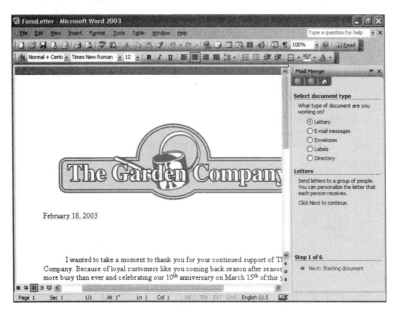

2   In the **Mail Merge** task pane, make sure the **Letters** option is selected, and then click **Next: Starting document** at the bottom of the pane.

Step 2 appears in the Mail Merge task pane.

3   In the **Mail Merge** task pane, make sure the **Use the current document** option is selected, and then click **Next: Select recipients** at the bottom of the pane.

Step 3 appears.

4   In the **Mail Merge** task pane, make sure the **Use an existing list** option is selected, and then click **Browse** in the **Use an existing list** area to open the **Select Data Source** dialog box.

In the Select Data Source dialog box, you can select a Word document, an Excel spreadsheet, or an Access database as the data source.

5 Navigate to the *My Documents\Microsoft Press\Word 2003 SBS\CreatingMail \PreparingData* folder on your hard disk, and then double-click the *Data* file.

The Mail Merge Recipients dialog box opens, displaying the records contained in the data source.

6 In the **Mail Merge Recipients** dialog box, click **Edit**.

The Data Form dialog box opens.

7 Click **Add New** to clear the data fields so that you can add a new record.

8 In the **FirstName** box, type Heidi, and press the ⌨Tab⌨ key.

9 In the **LastName** box, type Steen, and press ⌨Tab⌨.

10 In the **Address1** box, type 678 Pine St., and press ⌨Tab⌨.

11 In the **City** box, type Agriculture, and press ⌨Tab⌨.

12 In the **State** box, type WA, and press ⌨Tab⌨.

13 In the **PostalCode** box, type 19003.

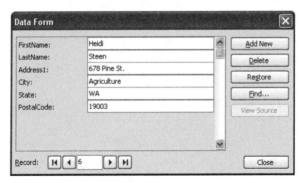

14 Click **Close** to close the **Data Form** dialog box.

Tip To add more new records in the Data Form dialog box, leave the box open, and click Add New after you enter each record.

The new record appears at the bottom of the Mail Merge Recipients dialog box.

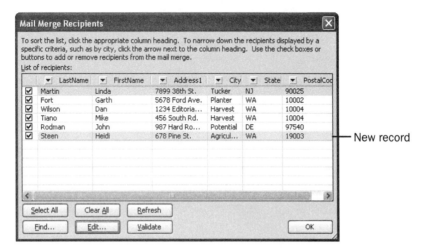

New record

Tip If you need to stop the Mail Merge Wizard before you finish the merge process, simply save the main document. Word retains information about the data source and its merge fields and keeps your place in the Mail Merge Wizard, so you can open the main document and pick up where you left off.

15 Click the down arrow to the left of the **PostalCode** box, and then click **Advanced**.

The Query Options dialog box appears, showing the Filter Records tab.

16 Click the **Sort Records** tab to display the sorting options.

17 Click the down arrow to the right of the **Sort by** box, and then click **PostalCode** (scroll through the list if necessary).

18 Click **Ascending**, if necessary, and then click **OK** to close the **Query Options** dialog box.

The data is sorted in ascending ZIP Code order.

19 In the **Mail Merge Recipients** dialog box, click the down arrow to the left of the **State** box, and then click **Advanced**.

20 In the **Query Options** dialog box, click the down arrow to the right of the **Field** box, scroll the list, and then click **State**.

Several other query options become available.

21 Click the down arrow to the right of the **Comparison** box, and then click **Equal to**.

22 In the **Compare to** box, type WA.

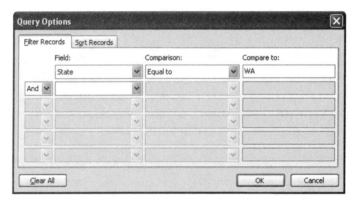

23 Click **OK**.

The Query Options dialog box closes, and the Mail Merge Recipients dialog box is updated to show only Washington State residents in ascending ZIP Code order.

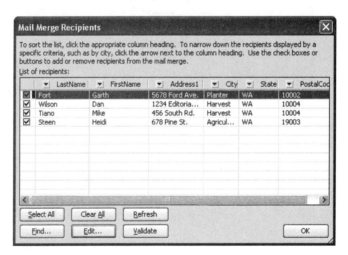

Important Only four records appear now because only those four customers of The Garden Company fit the specified sort criteria. The other records are still in the database—they have just been excluded from this mail-merge process.

24 Click **OK** to close the **Mail Merge Recipients** dialog box.

Save

25 On the Standard toolbar, click the **Save** button to save the document. If Word asks whether you want to save Data, click **Yes**.

CLOSE the *FormLetter* document.

Using an Outlook Contacts List as a Data Source

Using information from an Outlook contacts list as the data source for the merge process requires a few extra steps in the Mail Merge Wizard.

To use Outlook information as the data source for a form letter:

1 On the **Tools** menu, point to **Letters and Mailings**, and then click **Mail Merge** to open the **Mail Merge** task pane.

2 In the **Mail Merge** task pane, select the **Letters** option, and then click **Next: Starting document** at the bottom of the task pane.

3 Select the **Use the current document** option, and then click **Next: Select recipients** at the bottom of the **Mail Merge** task pane.

4 Select the **Select from Outlook contacts** option, and then click **Next: Write your letter** at the bottom of the task pane.

5 If you are prompted to select your Outlook profile, click **OK**.

The Select Contact List Folder dialog box appears.

6 Click a contact list, and click **OK**.

The Mail Merge Recipients dialog box appears, displaying all the contacts from your Outlook Contacts folder.

7 Clear the check boxes in the left column to exclude any contacts you don't want to include in the mail merge.

8 Click **OK** to close the **Mail Merge Recipients** dialog box.

9 In the **Mail Merge** task pane, click **Next: Write your letter** at the bottom of the task pane.

You can then continue with the Mail Merge Wizard's remaining steps for writing and previewing the main document and completing the mail-merge process.

Preparing the Form Letter

Microsoft Office Specialist

The most common type of main document used in the mail merge process is the form letter. This type of document typically contains merge fields for the name and address of each recipient along with text that is the same in all the letters. Each merge field corresponds to a piece of information in the data source. It appears in the main document with *guillemet characters* (« and ») around it. For example the «Address Block» merge field corresponds to name and address information in the data source.

You can create a form letter in two ways: by inserting merge fields into an existing main document, or by creating a new main document as you work through the steps of the Mail Merge Wizard. In either case, you enter the text that will be common to all the letters and then insert the merge fields that will be replaced by the variable information.

In this exercise, you will modify an existing form letter by adding merge fields for a standard inside address and informal greeting line.

USE the *FormLetter2* and *Data2* documents in the practice file folder for this topic. These practice files are located in the *My Documents\Microsoft Press\Word 2003 SBS\CreatingMail\PreparingLetter* folder and can also be accessed by clicking *Start/All Programs/Microsoft Press/Word 2003 Step by Step*. OPEN the *FormLetter2* document, and click Yes to associate the document with a data source.

1 On the **Tools** menu, point to **Letters and Mailings**, and then click **Mail Merge**.

The Mail Merge task pane appears.

2 If Step 3 does not appear in the **Mail Merge** task pane, click the **Next** link until Step 3 appears.

3 In the **Use an existing list** area, click **Select a different list**.

The Select Data Source dialog box opens.

4 Navigate to the *My Documents\Microsoft Press\Word 2003 SBS\CreatingMail \PreparingLetter* folder on your hard disk, and double-click the *Data2* file.

The Mail Merge Recipients dialog box appears.

5 Click **OK** to close the **Mail Merge Recipients** dialog box.

Tip When working with files created on your own computer, steps 3 through 5 are not necessary because the form letter is already associated with the correct data source.

6 At the bottom of the **Mail Merge** task pane, click **Next: Write your letter**.

Step 4 of the wizard appears in the task pane.

Show/Hide ¶

7 If non-printing characters are not visible on your screen, click the **Show/Hide ¶** button on the Standard toolbar to turn them on.

8 In the document window, click the second blank line under the date, and then in the **Mail Merge** task pane, click **Address block**.

The Insert Address Block dialog box appears so that you can specify which fields in the data source should be part of the Address Block merge field.

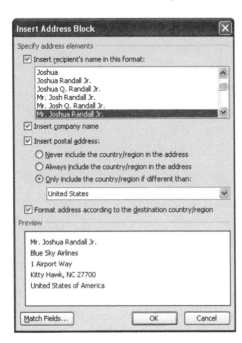

9 Click **OK** to accept the default settings.

The «Address Block» merge field is inserted into the document. When you merge the main document with the data source, Word will substitute the specified name and address information for this merge field.

10 In the document window, click the second blank line after the «Address Block» merge field, and then in the **Mail Merge** task pane, click **Greeting line**.

The Greeting Line dialog box appears so that you can specify how the greeting line should appear in the merged letters.

Insert
Greeting Line

Tip If you are creating a form letter without using the Mail Merge Wizard, you can click the Insert Greeting Line button on the Mail Merge toolbar and then click a style of greeting using the Greeting Line dialog box's drop-down lists.

11 In the **Greeting line format** area, click the down arrow to the right of the second text box, and then click **Joshua**.

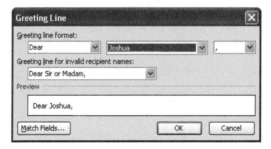

12 Click **OK** to close the **Greeting Line** dialog box.

The «Greeting Line» merge field is inserted in the document. When you merge the main document with the data source, Word will substitute the information in the FirstName field for this merge field.

Merge field for the name and address   Merge field for the greeting line

13 On the Standard toolbar, click the **Show/Hide ¶** button to hide non-printing characters.

14 On the Standard toolbar, click the **Save** button to save the main document.

Save

CLOSE the *FormLetter2* document.

Merging the Data with the Form Letter

Microsoft
Office
Specialist

After you set up a data source and enter merge fields into a main document, you are ready to merge them to create one merged document for each data source record used. These merged documents are either sent directly to the printer or they are merged one after the other into a new document, separated by page breaks. The length of the new document depends on the length of the main document and the number of records being used from the data source. If the main document is two pages long and ten records are being used from the data source, the new document is 20 pages long. You can edit the new document to personalize individual copies of the main document before sending them to the printer, and you can save it.

In this exercise, you will review merged data, add a merge field to personalize a sentence in the body of a letter, and then merge letters into a new document containing one personalized copy of the letter for each recipient.

USE the *FormLetter3* and *Data3* documents in the practice file folder for this topic. These practice files are located in the *My Documents\Microsoft Press\Word 2003 SBS\CreatingMail\MergingData* folder and can also be accessed by clicking *Start/All Programs/Microsoft Press/Word 2003 Step by Step.*
OPEN the *FormLetter3* document, and click Yes to associate the document with a data source.

1 On the **Tools** menu, point to **Letters and Mailings,** and then click **Mail Merge.**

The Mail Merge task pane appears.

2 If Step 3 does not appear in the **Mail Merge** task pane, click the **Next** link until Step 3 appears.

3 In the **Use an existing list** area, click **Select a different list** to open the **Select Data Source** dialog box.

4 Navigate to the *My Documents\Microsoft Press\Word 2003 SBS\CreatingMail \MergingData* folder on your hard disk, and double-click the *Data3* file.

The Mail Merge Recipients dialog box appears.

5 Click **OK** to close the **Mail Merge Recipients** dialog box.

6 At the bottom of the **Mail Merge** task pane, click the **Next** link until Step 5 appears.

The form letter is merged with the specified records in the data source, and the first personalized letter appears in the document window.

Next

7 In the **Mail Merge** task pane, click the **Next** button.

The second personalized letter is displayed.

Tip You can exclude recipients from the mail merge. In Step 5 in the Mail Merge task pane, click the Previous or Next button to display the recipient you want to exclude, and then click "Exclude this recipient" in the "Make changes" area of the Mail Merge task pane.

8 At the bottom of the **Mail Merge** task pane, click **Previous: Write your letter**.

You return to Step 4.

9 In the document window, scroll down to the second paragraph, and then click to the left of the comma at the beginning of the paragraph.

10 In the **Write your letter** area of the **Mail Merge** task pane, click **More items**.

The Insert Merge Field dialog box appears.

11 Select the **Database Fields** option, and then, if necessary, in the **Fields** box, click the **FirstName** field.

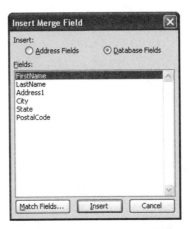

12 Click **Insert**, and then click **Close** to close the **Insert Merge Field** dialog box.

The «FirstName» merge field appears to the left of the comma at the beginning of the second paragraph.

13 At the bottom of the **Mail Merge** task pane, click **Next: Preview your letters**.

The form letter shows the first recipient's name at the beginning of the second paragraph.

Main
document
setup

Tip If you change your mind during the mail-merge process and want to save the main document as a regular document, point to Letters and Mailings on the Tools menu, and click Show Mail Merge Toolbar. On the Mail Merge toolbar, click the "Main document setup" button, click "Normal Word document," and then click OK. You can now save the document without any mail merge information.

14 At the bottom of the **Mail Merge** task pane, click **Next: Complete the merge**.

You move to Step 6 of the wizard.

15 In the **Merge** area of the **Mail Merge** task pane, click **Edit individual letters**.

The Merge to New Document dialog box appears.

16 Select the **All** option, if necessary, and then click **OK**.

Word creates a new document called Letters1 containing personalized copies of the form letter, one for each person in the data source.

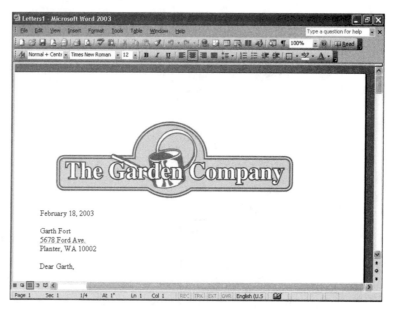

Save

17 On the Standard toolbar, click the **Save** button.

The Save As dialog box appears so that you can save the new document with a more specific name.

18 Navigate to the *My Documents\Microsoft Press\Word 2003 SBS\CreatingMail \MergingData* folder on your hard disk, type MergedLetters in the **File name** box, and then click **Save**.

Word saves the new document with the name *MergedLetters* in the specified folder.

19 Activate the *FormLetter3* window by clicking its button on the Windows taskbar, and on the Standard toolbar, click the **Save** button to save the new version of the form letter main document.

CLOSE the *MergedLetters* and *FormLetter3* documents.

Creating and Printing Labels

Microsoft Office Specialist

You can use a data source with more than one kind of main document. For example, the same data source you use to print form letters can be used to print sheets of mailing labels or to print envelopes.

The mail-merge process for creating mailing labels is similar to the process for creating form letters. You start by preparing the data source and then prepare the main document by selecting the brand and style of labels you plan to use, such as Avery standard 5159. Word then creates a full-page table with cells the size of the labels so that each cell will print on one label in a sheet. You insert merge fields into one cell as a template for all the other cells. When you merge the main document and the data source, you can print the labels or create a new label document that you can use whenever you want to send something to the same set of people.

In this exercise, you use the Mail Merge Wizard to create mailing labels and then print the labels on standard paper to proofread them.

BE SURE TO turn on the printer you will be using before beginning this exercise.
USE the *Data4* document in the practice file folder for this topic. This practice file is located in the *My Documents\Microsoft Press\Word 2003 SBS\CreatingMail\CreatingLabel* folder and can also be accessed by clicking *Start/All Programs/Microsoft Press/Word 2003 Step by Step.*

New Blank
Document

1 On the Standard toolbar, click the **New Blank Document** button.

A new blank document window appears.

2 On the **Tools** menu, point to **Letters and Mailings,** and then click **Mail Merge.**

3 In the **Mail Merge** task pane, select the **Labels** option, and then click **Next: Starting document** to proceed to Step 2.

4 Select the **Change document layout** option, if necessary, and then in the **Change document layout** area, click **Label options.**

The Label Options dialog box appears.

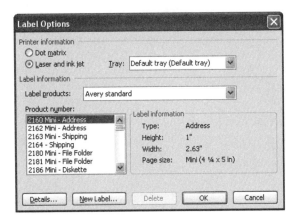

5 Scroll down the **Product number** list, click **5159 - Address**, and then click **OK**.

Word inserts a table that fills the first page of the document with cells the size of the specified labels.

Important The document window might appear blank. The table with label-sized rectangles is there but not visible.

6 At the bottom of the **Mail Merge** task pane, click **Next: Select recipients** to proceed to Step 3.

7 Select the **Use an existing list** option, if necessary, and then click **Browse**.

The Select Data Source dialog box appears.

8 Navigate to the *My Documents\Microsoft Press\Word 2003 SBS\CreatingMail \CreatingLabel* folder on your hard disk, and double-click the *Data4* file.

The Mail Merge Recipients dialog box appears.

9 Make sure that all four recipient check boxes are selected in the first column, and then click **OK**.

The Mail Merge Recipients dialog box closes and the «Next Record» merge field appears in all the labels in the main document.

10 At the bottom of the **Mail Merge** task pane, click **Next: Arrange your labels** to proceed to Step 4, and then drag the scroll box in the horizontal scroll bar all the way to the left.

11 With the insertion point positioned in the upper-left label in the main document window, click **Address block** in the **Mail Merge** task pane.

The Insert Address Block dialog box opens.

12 Click **OK** to accept the default settings and close the **Insert Address Block** dialog box.

Word inserts the «AddressBlock» merge field into the upper-left label in the main document.

13 In the **Replicate labels** area of the **Mail Merge** task pane, click the **Update all labels** button.

The «AddressBlock» merge field is inserted in all the labels.

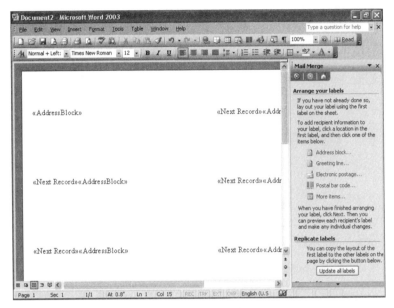

14 Point to the scroll arrow at the bottom of the **Mail Merge** task pane, and then click **Next: Preview your labels** to proceed to Step 5.

Word displays the labels as they will appear after the merge.

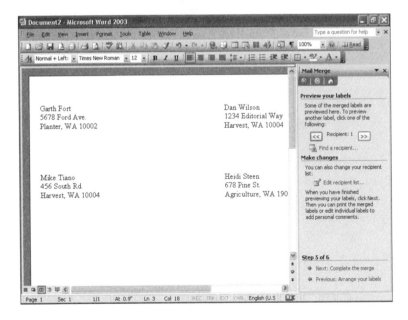

15 At the bottom of the **Mail Merge** task pane, click **Next: Complete the merge**.

The names and addresses from the data source appear in the mailing label document.

16 In the **Mail Merge** task pane, click **Print**.

The Merge to Printer dialog box appears with the All option selected.

17 Click **OK**.

The Print dialog box opens.

18 Check that the name of the printer you want to use appears in the **Name** box, and then click **OK** to print the labels.

The labels are printed on regular paper on the printer you selected. If you wanted to print on label sheets, you would insert the label sheets in the printer's paper tray before clicking OK in the Print dialog box.

19 On the **File** menu, click **Save As**, navigate to the *My Documents\Microsoft Press \Word 2003 SBS\CreatingMail\CreatingLabel* folder, type MergedLabels as the file name, and then click **Save** to save the mailing labels document.

CLOSE the *MergedLabels* document, and if you are not continuing on to the next chapter, quit Word.

Key Points

- You can use the Mail Merge Wizard to merge a data source, such as a database or contact list, and a main document, such as a form letter or labels.

- The information in a data source is organized into records, with each record containing the same set of fields.

- You can use a list from another program, such as Microsoft Access, Microsoft Excel, Microsoft Visual FoxPro, or the contact list from Microsoft Outlook or Microsoft Outlook Express.

- You can sort the information in a data source. You can also filter the data in the data source or exclude specific records so that they are not part of the merge process.

- You can create a main document in two ways: by using an existing document and inserting merge fields into it; or by creating a new main document as you work through the mail merge process, entering the main text of the document, and then inserting the merge fields that you want to use.

- You can review merged data and add a merge field to personalize a sentence in the body of a main document.

- You can use a data source to create mailing labels or envelopes to use with your mailing. After you merge the data source and the main document to create labels, you can print them on standard paper to proofread them or on sheets of adhesive labels.

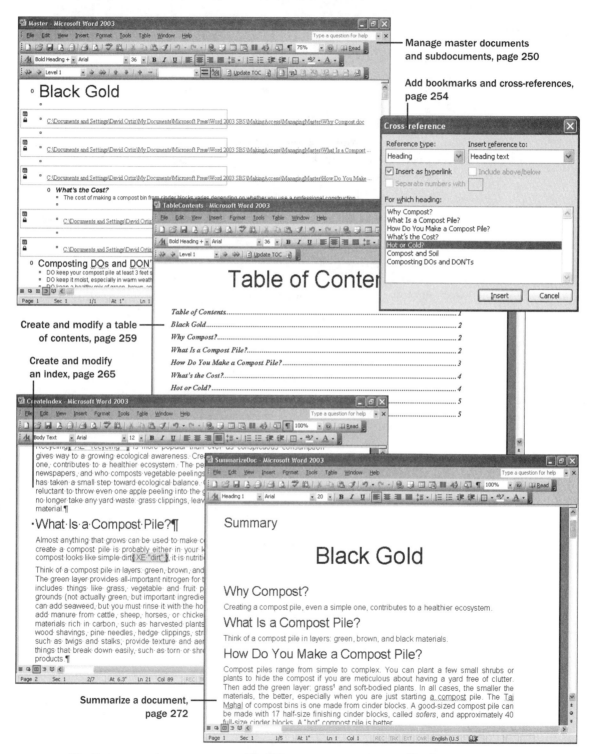

Manage master documents and subdocuments, page 250

Add bookmarks and cross-references, page 254

Create and modify a table of contents, page 259

Create and modify an index, page 265

Summarize a document, page 272

12 Making Information in Longer Documents Accessible

In this chapter you will learn to:

✔ Manage master documents and subdocuments.

✔ Add bookmarks and cross-references.

✔ Create and modify a table of contents.

✔ Create and modify an index.

✔ Summarize a document.

Microsoft Office Word 2003 provides tools to help you create and manage long or complex documents and to help your readers find the information they are looking for.

One way of handling long documents is to break them into a set of *subdocuments* with a *master document*. The master document contains hyperlinks to all the subdocuments, allowing navigation to different parts of the document with the click of a button. However, each subdocument can be worked on independently.

If you are reading a long document and come across an item you think you will want to refer to later, you can flag the item with a *bookmark*. When you can predict that readers will want to jump to a specific location in a document, you can insert a *cross-reference*. Both techniques enable readers to jump quickly to another place in a document.

To make information easy to find, you can include tables of contents and indexes in long documents. You can also use Word's *AutoSummarize* feature to highlight the key points in a document for quick reference.

In this chapter, you'll work with master documents and subdocuments, insert bookmarks and cross-references, create and modify a table of contents and an index, and summarize a document.

See Also Do you need only a quick refresher on the topics in this chapter? See the Quick Reference entries on pages lv–lvii.

Important Before you can use the practice files in this chapter, you need to install them from the book's companion CD to their default location. See "Using the Book's CD-ROM" on page xiii for more information.

Managing Master Documents and Subdocuments

Microsoft Office Specialist

When you must create and manage a long document that involves multiple sections, you can turn the document into a *master document* and *subdocuments* so that you can work on different parts independently. For example, if a team is collaborating on the development of The Garden Company's annual catalog, it might be more efficient to split the catalog document into a master document and subdocuments so that different people can work on different parts simultaneously.

The master document is structured like an outline, with links to all the subdocuments. Clicking a link opens the corresponding subdocument. You can also open each subdocument in the usual way, without going through the master document. After you update and save a subdocument, clicking its link in the master document opens the new version of the subdocument. If you want to create a table of contents, an index, cross-references, and headers and footers for the entire document, you can do so in the master document after working on the subdocuments. For example, you can add index entries to each subdocument, number their pages consecutively, and then create an index from the master document for the entire larger document.

Before you can create a master document and subdocuments, you must switch to Outline view. If your document does not already have heading levels assigned, you can use the buttons on the Outlining toolbar to assign them. Then you select a heading and use the Create Subdocument button on the Outlining toolbar to turn that section of the document into a subdocument. You can also click an insertion point and then click the Insert Subdocument button on the Outlining toolbar to add an existing document to a master document as a subdocument.

After you have assembled the master document and its subdocuments, you can use the buttons on the Outlining toolbar to change your view of the documents. For example, you can click the Collapse Subdocuments button on the Outlining toolbar to hide the contents of subdocuments and display them only as *hyperlinks*. When the subdocuments are collapsed, the master document is easier to view and organize. You can see all the subdocument titles and simply drag them to reorder them, and if you want to edit a subdocument, you can get to it easily by clicking its hyperlink. If you want to work with the master document as a whole—for example, to check its spelling—you can click the Expand Subdocuments button to show the contents of all subdocuments.

In this exercise, you will outline a document in Outline view, create a set of subdocuments and a master document, and then open and modify a subdocument.

BE SURE TO start Word before beginning this exercise.
USE the *Master* document in the practice file folder for this topic. This practice file is located in the *My Documents\Microsoft Press\Word 2003 SBS\MakingAvail\ManagingMaster* folder and can also be accessed by clicking *Start/All Programs/Microsoft Press/Word 2003 Step by Step*.
OPEN the *Master* document.

Outline View

1 In the lower-left corner of the document window, click the **Outline View** button.

Word switches to Outline view, displays the Outlining toolbar, and changes the zoom percentage to 75%. The insertion point appears to the left of the first heading.

Show First
Line Only

2 On the Outlining toolbar, click the **Show First Line Only** button.

The first line of each paragraph appears in the outline.

3 Click the plus sign to the left of the *Why Compost?* heading.

Word selects the heading and its subordinate text.

4 Hold down [Shift], and then click the plus sign to the left of the *Compost and Soil* heading.

Word extends the selection to include the *Compost and Soil* heading and its text and all the text between the two headings.

Demote

5 On the Outlining toolbar, click the **Demote** button. Then click to the right of the *Why Compost?* heading.

The Style box on the Formatting toolbar indicates that the *Why Compost?* heading has been assigned the Heading 2 paragraph style. The Outline Level box on the Outlining toolbar shows that the heading is outline Level 2. In the outline, the text below the heading is indented accordingly.

6 Click the plus sign to the left of the *Why Compost?* heading to select the heading and its subordinate text.

Create
Subdocument

7 On the Outlining toolbar, click the **Create Subdocument** button.

The Subdocument icon appears in the left margin of the document, a light border surrounds the selected text, and the heading and its text become a subdocument of the master document.

Subdocument icon

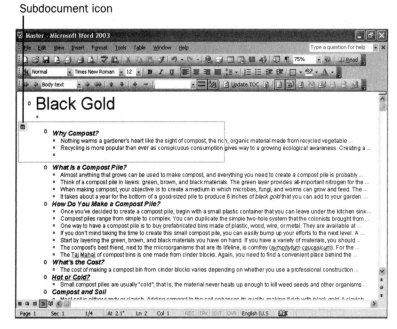

8. Repeat steps 6 and 7 to turn each of the following headings and their text into subdocuments: *What Is a Compost Pile?*, *How Do You Make a Compost Pile?*, *Hot or Cold?*, and *Compost and Soil*.

Collapse Subdocuments

9. On the Outlining toolbar, click the **Collapse Subdocuments** button.

Word asks whether you want to save changes to the master document before collasping the subdocuments.

10. Click **OK**.

Word moves the heading and text of each subdocument to a separate file, saves the file with the heading as its name in the same folder as the master document, and then closes the subdocument. In the subdocument's place in the master document, Word inserts a hyperlink to the subdocument, showing its path.

Tip You can point to a hyperlink to see a ScreenTip with the complete path of the subdocument, including the file name.

Subdocument hyperlink

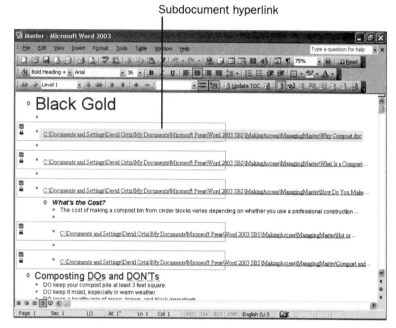

11 Hold down the ⌈Ctrl⌉ key, and click the first hyperlink.

Tip If you want to simply click hyperlinks in Word documents without having to hold down the Ctrl key, click Options on the Tools menu, and on the Edit tab, clear the "Use CTRL + Click to follow hyperlink" check box.

The *Why Compost?* subdocument opens in its own document window. You can edit and format the subdocument just as you would any other document.

Bold

12 At the beginning of the second paragraph, select the word *Recycling*. Then on the Formatting toolbar, click the **Bold** button to make the words stand out.

Save

13 On the Standard toolbar, click the **Save** button, and then click the **Close Window** button to close the subdocument.

Word saves and closes the subdocument, and the master document is now the active document.

Expand
Subdocuments

14 On the Outlining toolbar, click the **Expand Subdocuments** button.

The headings and text of all the subdocuments are displayed in the master document.

15 On the Outlining toolbar, click the **Show First Line Only** button to toggle that button off.

The document expands to show all its text. The change you made to the *Why Compost?* subdocument is reflected in the master document.

16 On the Standard toolbar, click the **Save** button to save the master document.

CLOSE the *Master* document, and turn off the Outlining toolbar.

Adding Bookmarks and Cross-References

*Microsoft
Office
Specialist*

Word provides several tools for navigating long documents, two of which—bookmarks and cross-references—enable you to jump easily to designated places. Both tools require you to mark locations in a document and name them.

See Also   You can also create hyperlinks to enable people to quickly jump to other locations in the same document or to other documents. For information about hyperlinks, see "Adding Hyperlinks" in Chapter 9.

Whether the document you are reading was created by you or by someone else, you can insert bookmarks to flag information to which you might want to return later. Like a physical bookmark, a Word bookmark marks a specific place in a document. To insert a bookmark, you select the text or object you want to mark and assign it a bookmark name by clicking Bookmark on the Insert menu. Then instead of having to scroll through the document to look for the text or object later, you can quickly jump to the bookmark by using the Go To tab of the Find and Replace dialog box.

If you are developing a long document, you can create cross-references to quickly move readers to associated information elsewhere in the document. For example, The Garden Company catalog team might insert the text *For more information about pest control, see "All About Bugs,"* with a link to that section in the catalog. You can create cross-references to headings, figure captions, numbered paragraphs, endnotes, or any other text. If you later delete an item you have designated as the target of a cross-reference, you will need to update the cross-reference.

Important   You can create bookmarks and cross-references only to items within the same document, or within a master document and its subdocuments.

In this exercise, you will insert a bookmark and jump to it in a document. You will also create a cross-reference, move the referenced item, and then update the cross-reference.

USE the *Bookmark* document in the practice file folder for this topic. This practice file is located in the *My Documents\Microsoft Press\Word 2003 SBS\MakingAvail\AddingBook* folder and can also be accessed by clicking *Start/All Programs/Microsoft Press/Word 2003 Step by Step*.
OPEN the *Bookmark* document.

1 Scroll down to the last page in the document, and then click to the left of the *C* in *Composting DOs and DON'Ts* heading.

2 On the **Insert** menu, click **Bookmark** to open the **Bookmark** dialog box.

3 In the **Bookmark name** box, type DOs.

4 Click **Add**.

Troubleshooting   Bookmark names cannot contain spaces. If you enter a space, the Add button will become inactive. To name bookmarks with multiple words, you'll need to run the words together, as in CompostAndSoil.

The Bookmark dialog box closes, and although you can't see it, a bookmark named DOs is inserted into the document.

5 Press Ctrl+Home to move to the beginning of the document.

6 On the **Edit** menu, click **Go To**.

The Find and Replace dialog box appears, with the Go To tab active.

Tip   You can also jump to a bookmark by clicking the Find or Replace commands on the Edit menu and then clicking the Go To tab. Alternatively, you can click Bookmark on the Insert menu, click the bookmark's name in the Bookmark dialog box, and then click Go To. If you prefer to use keyboard shortcuts, press Ctrl+G to access the Go To tab.

7 In the **Go to what** list, click **Bookmark**.

The document's only bookmark, DOs, appears in the "Enter bookmark name" box. When there are several bookmark names from which to select, you can click the down arrow to the right of this box and make your selection in the drop-down list.

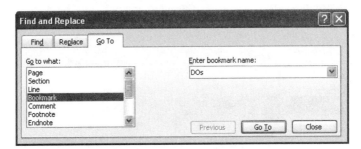

8 Click the **Go To** button.

The insertion point moves to the location of the bookmark. The dialog box remains open in case you want to move somewhere else.

9 Click **Close** to close the **Find and Replace** dialog box.

Tip To delete a bookmark, click Bookmark on the Insert menu, click the bookmark's name, and then click Delete.

10 Scroll up in the document, and click at the end of the first paragraph under the *What Is a Compost Pile?* heading.

11 Press ⌴Space⌴, type For more information, see and then press ⌴Space⌴.

12 On the **Insert** menu, point to **Reference**, and click **Cross-reference**.

The Cross-reference dialog box appears.

13 Click the down arrow to the right of the **Reference type** box, and click **Heading**.

14 If necessary, click the down arrow to the right of the **Insert reference to** box, and click **Heading text**.

15 In the **For which heading** list, click **Hot or Cold?**.

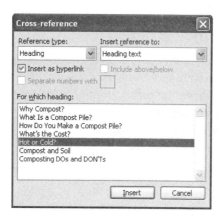

16 Click **Insert**, and then click **Close**.

A cross-reference to the *Hot or Cold?* heading appears in the text.

17 Hold down the [Ctrl] key, and click the *Hot or Cold?* cross-reference.

The insertion point moves to the location of the referenced heading.

18 With the insertion point to the left of the *Hot or Cold?* heading, type **Which Is Best**, and then press [Space].

19 Scroll up to the *What Is a Compost Pile?* section, and select the text of the cross-reference. (Don't select the *For more information, see* introductory text.)

20 Right-click the selected cross-reference, and click **Update Field**.

Word inserts the text *Which Is Best,* updating the cross-reference to reflect the change you made to the heading.

21 Hold down the [Ctrl] key, and click the cross-reference.

The insertion point moves to the location of the referenced heading.

Save

22 On the Standard toolbar, click the **Save** button to save the document.

CLOSE the *Bookmark* document.

Adding Footnotes and Endnotes

Footnotes and endnotes explain, comment on, or provide references for text in a document. *Footnotes* appear at the bottom of the page containing the associated text, whereas *endnotes* appear at the end of a document or at the end of a section in that document. Each footnote and endnote consists of a *reference mark* and *note text*. The reference mark is a number or symbol in the main text of the document that matches a number or symbol next to the footnote or endnote. In most views, this area is divided from the main text by a *note separator* line.

To create a footnote or endnote:

1. With the insertion point where you want the reference mark to be, point to **Reference** on the **Insert** menu, and click **Footnote**.

    The Footnote and Endnote dialog box appears.

2. In the **Location** area, select the **Footnotes** or **Endnotes** option.

3. In the **Format** area, click the down arrow to the right of the **Number format** box, select a number format, and click **Insert**.

    Word inserts the reference mark in the document and, if you are in Print Layout view, you type the note in an area at the bottom of the page or end of the section. (In Normal view, the insertion point moves to the right of the reference mark in the Notes pane.)

4. Type the note text. (If you are working in the **Notes** pane, click **Close** to close the pane.)

To find a footnote or an endnote:

1. On the **Edit** menu, click **Go To** to open the **Find and Replace** dialog box with the **Go To** tab active.

2. In the **Go to what** list, click **Footnote** or **Endnote**.

3. In the **Enter footnote number** box, enter the number of the note you want to see, and click **Go To**.

4. Close the **Find and Replace** dialog box.

Word applies default styles to the reference marks for footnotes and endnotes. By default, footnote reference marks use the 1, 2, 3 format, and endnote reference marks use the i, ii, iii style. To change the number format of existing footnotes or endnotes:

1. On the **Insert** menu, point to **Reference**, and then click **Footnote**.

The Footnote and Endnote dialog box appears.

2 Select the **Footnotes** or **Endnotes** option.

3 In the **Format** area, click the down arrow to the right of the **Number format** box, and click a new number format.

4 Verify that **Whole document** appears in the **Apply changes to** box, and then click **Apply.**

All footnotes change to the new number format.

To change the formatting applied to footnote or endnote reference marks:

1 Select the reference mark for the first footnote or endnote, and apply the character formatting you want.

2 Select another reference mark, and on the **Format** menu, click **Styles and Formatting.**

The Styles and Formatting task pane appears.

3 Click the **Select All** button to select all the footnotes or endnotes in the document, and then in the **Pick formatting to apply** area, click **Footnote Reference.**

All the footnotes or endnotes now appear with the character formatting you applied in step 1.

Creating and Modifying a Table of Contents

Microsoft
Office
Specialist

A *table of contents* generally appears at the beginning of a document, and lists the main headings and subheadings along with corresponding page numbers. A table of contents provides an overview of the topics covered in a document and lets readers navigate quickly to a topic. For example, The Garden Company might add a table of contents to a garden tools catalog that has several sections.

To create and format a table of contents, you designate headings and subheadings and then click Index and Tables on the Reference submenu of the Insert menu. Word then uses the heading styles to identify table of contents entries, and inserts the table at the insertion point. When the table is selected, shading indicates that Word treats it as a single field. Each entry is hyperlinked to the heading it references, and you can hold down the [Ctrl] key and click the entry to go to the corresponding section.

This shading indicates that the table of contents is a single field.

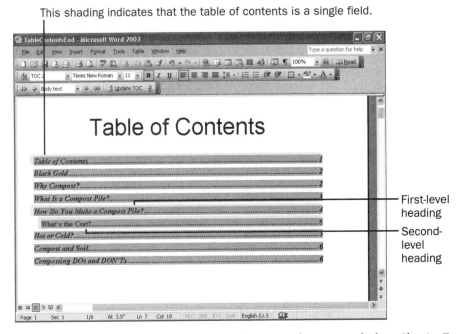

First-level heading

Second-level heading

Word provides several predefined table-of-contents formats, including Classic, Formal, and Simple. The default format is "From template," which takes the table of contents styles from whatever template is attached to the document. If this is the Normal template (the default), the "From template" styles create a table of contents in which the headings are title case (important words have initial capital letters). You can format a table of contents manually as you would any other text in Word—by selecting text and then applying character or paragraph formatting or styles.

Tip You can customize a table of contents format by changing the format's styles. On the Insert menu, point to Reference, click Index and Tables, and click the Table of Contents tab. Click the Modify button. The Style dialog box opens, displaying the nine table of contents styles. You can then change these styles the same way you change any other style.

If you create a table of contents but later make changes to the document that affect its headings or pagination, you can update the table of contents by clicking the Update TOC button on the Outlining toolbar and selecting an update option. Although you can edit the text in a table of contents directly, updating it instead ensures that the entries and headings match exactly.

Tip You can also update the table of contents by clicking anywhere in the table, opening the Index and Tables dialog box from the Insert menu, and clicking OK.

In this exercise, you will open a document that uses heading styles and then create a table of contents. You will then change the document by inserting page breaks and update the table of contents.

USE the *TableContents* document in the practice file folder for this topic. This practice file is located in the *My Documents\Microsoft Press\Word 2003 SBS\MakingAvail\CreatingContents* folder and can also be accessed by clicking *Start/All Programs/Microsoft Press/Word 2003 Step by Step*.
OPEN the *TableContents* document.

1 With the insertion point at the beginning of the document, press <kbd>Ctrl</kbd>+<kbd>Enter</kbd> to insert a new page.

2 Press <kbd>Ctrl</kbd>+<kbd>Home</kbd> to move to the beginning of the document.

3 Type Table of Contents, and press <kbd>Enter</kbd>.

4 On the **Insert** menu, point to **Reference**, and then click **Index and Tables**.

The Index and Tables dialog box appears.

5 Click the **Table of Contents** tab to display table of contents settings.

6 Click the down arrow to the right of the **Formats** box, and click **Distinctive**.

The Distinctive table of contents format appears in the preview boxes.

7 Click the down arrow to the right of the **Tab leader** box, and click the dotted line (the second option) in the drop-down list.

The preview box changes to display dotted tab leaders.

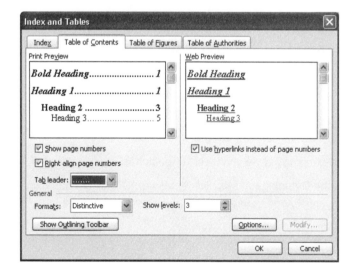

8 Click **Show Outlining Toolbar**, and click **OK**.

Word inserts a table of contents with the Distinctive format modified to include dotted leaders. It also displays the Outlining toolbar.

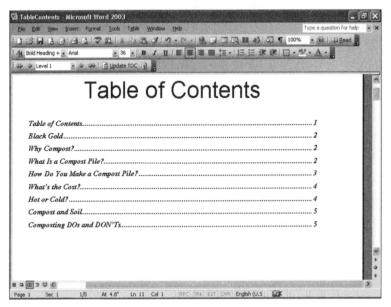

9 Scroll down to page 2, click to the left of the *What Is a Compost Pile?* heading, and press Ctrl+Enter to start a new page.

The *What Is a Compost Pile?* heading is now on page 3.

10 Scroll down, click to the left of the *How Do You Make a Compost Pile?* heading, and press Ctrl+Enter to start another new page.

The *How Do You Make a Compost Pile?* heading is moved to page 4.

11 Scroll down to page 5, and select the *What's the Cost?* heading.

12 On the Formatting toolbar, click the down arrow to the right of the **Style** box, and then click **Heading 2** in the drop-down list.

The heading's style changes to Heading 2.

Go to TOC

13 On the Outlining toolbar, click the **Go to TOC** button to select the table of contents on page 1, and then scroll up to display the entire table.

14 On the Outlining toolbar, click the **Update TOC** button.

The Update Table of Contents dialog box appears with the "Update page numbers only" option selected.

15 Select the **Update entire table** option, and then click **OK**.

Word updates the table of contents to reflect the new page numbers and headings.

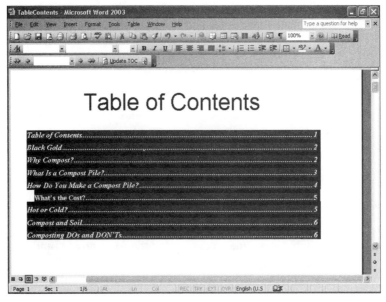

Save

16 On the Standard toolbar, click the **Save** button to save the document.

CLOSE the *TableContents* document, and turn off the Outlining toolbar.

Creating Other Types of Tables

Microsoft Office Specialist

If a document includes figures or tables that have descriptions, or *captions*, you can use the Index and Tables dialog box to create a *table of figures*. If a legal document contains items such as regulations, cases, and statutes that are designated with legal citations, you can use the Index and Tables dialog box to create a *table of authorities*. Word uses the captions or citations to create these types of tables the same way it uses headings to create a table of contents.

To insert captions and create a table of figures:

1   Click where you want the caption to appear, and on the **Insert** menu, point to **Reference**, and then click **Caption**.

2   In the **Caption** dialog box, click the **New Label** button, type the default text for the caption (for example, *Figure*), and click **OK**.

3   In the **Caption** box, click to the right of your label and its number, type the caption, and click **OK**.

The caption is added to the document.

4   Repeat steps 1 and 3 for each caption.

5   Click where you want to insert the table of figures, and on the **Insert** menu, point to **Reference**, and click **Index and Tables**.

The Index and Tables dialog box appears.

6   Click the **Table of Figures** tab.

7   Click the down arrow to the right of the **Caption label** box, and click the type of caption you want to include in the table.

8   Click the down arrow to the right of the **Formats** box, and click the format you want for the table.

9   Select any additional options you'd like, and click **OK**.

Word inserts the table of figures in the specified format.

To insert citations and create a table of authorities:

1   Select the first legal reference that you want to mark with a citation.

2 Press Alt+Shift+I.

The Mark Citation dialog box appears.

3 In the **Selected text** box, edit the citation to reflect the way you want it to appear in the table.

4 In the **Category** box, click the category that applies to the citation.

5 In the **Short citation** box, edit the text as necessary to match the entry in the **Selected text** box.

6 To mark a single citation, click **Mark**. To mark all citations that match the selected citation, click **Mark All**.

7 Repeat steps 1 through 6 for each citation you want to include in the table of authorities.

8 Click **Close** to close the **Mark Citation** dialog box.

9 Click where you want the table of authorities to appear, and on the **Insert** menu, point to **Reference**, and then click **Index and Tables**.

The Index and Tables dialog box appears.

10 Click the **Table of Authorities** tab.

11 In the **Category** list, click the category you want in your table of authorities, or click **All** to include all categories.

12 Select formatting options for the table, and then click **OK**.

Word inserts the table of authorities in the specified format.

Creating and Modifying an Index

Microsoft Office Specialist

An *index* typically appears at the end of a document and alphabetically lists the main topics, names, and terms used in a document, along with the page numbers where they're found. The items in the list are called *index entries*. You can create an index entry for a word, phrase, or topic that appears on a single page or is discussed for several pages. An index entry can have related *subentries*. For example, the main index entry *lawn* might have below it the subentries *installing, maintaining*, and *mowing*. An index might also include cross-reference entries that direct readers to related entries. For example, the main index entry *lawn* might have below it a cross-reference to *grasses*.

Entry   Subentry   Cross-reference   Page number

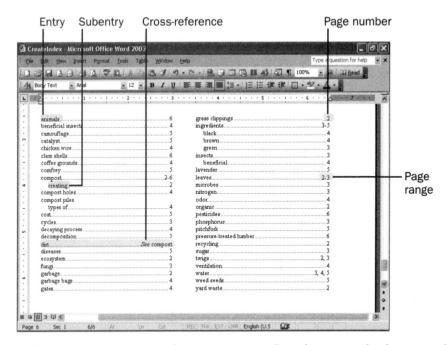

Page range

Before you can create an index, you must mark each entry and subentry in the document. You select the text you want to mark, and press [Alt]+[Shift]+[X] to open the Mark Index Entry dialog box. The selected text appears in the "Main entry" box. You can use this text as is for the entry, or you can change it. You can also format the entry directly in the "Main entry" box—for example, to make it appear bold or italic in the index—by right-clicking it and choosing Font from the shortcut menu. When you are satisfied with the entry, you can choose to mark just the selected text or every occurrence of the selected text in the document. After you mark an entry, the Mark Index Entry dialog box stays open so that you can select and mark more index entries. You can also mark cross-reference entries in the Mark Index Entry dialog box. By default, the cross-reference text is *See*, but you can type any text, such as *See also*. After the cross-reference text, you type the index entry to which you want to refer readers.

Tip   When building an index, you should choose the text you mark carefully, bearing in mind what terms readers are likely to look up. One reader might expect to find information about fertilizing houseplants by looking under *fertilizing*, whereas another might look under *houseplants*. A good index will provide entries for both, and might also include a cross-reference telling readers to also look under the names of individual houseplants.

When you mark an index entry, Word inserts an index entry field adjacent to the text you selected in the document. To be able to hide the field using the Show/Hide ¶ button on the Standard toolbar, click Options on the Tools menu, click the View tab, and clear the "Hidden text" check box. When the field is visible, it appears in the document with a dotted underline, indicating that the field is formatted as hidden and will not print with the document unless you tell Word to print hidden text.

The dotted underline indicates that this index entry field is formatted as hidden.

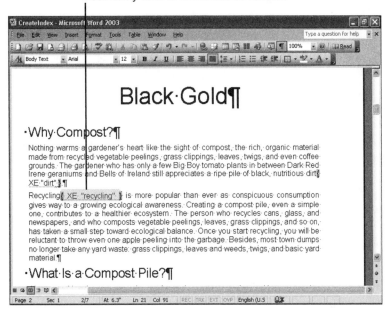

Tip You can hide any text in a document by selecting it, clicking Font on the Format menu, selecting the Hidden check box, and clicking OK. When you print the document, Word will not include the hidden text unless you click Options in the Print dialog box and select the "Hidden text" check box.

To change an index entry after you have marked it, you click anywhere between the quotation marks surrounding the actual text of the field and then edit the text as you would any other. To delete an index entry, you select the entire hidden field (you can drag through just part of it and Word will select the entire field) and press the Del key. You can also move and copy index entries using the techniques you would use for regular text.

After you finish marking entries, subentries, and cross-references, you click the document where you want the index to appear, and then click Index and Tables on the Reference submenu of the Insert menu. To determine the look of the index, you can specify the following:

- You can choose from a number of preset formatting options, including Classic, Fancy, Modern, Bulleted, Formal, or Simple, each of which is displayed in the preview box when you select the format.

- If you're using right-aligned page numbers, you can specify whether the *tab leader*, which separates the entry from the page number associated with it, should be a dotted, dashed, or solid line.

- You can use an *indented index*, which starts each subentry on a separate line below the main entries, or a *run-in index*, which starts subentries on the same line as the main entries.

When you click OK in the Index and Tables dialog box, Word calculates the page numbers of all the entries and subentries, consolidates them, and inserts the index as a single field, shaded when selected, in the specified format at the specified location in the document. To format the text of an index after you have created it, you can select it and then format text as you would any other text. You can also use the Index and Tables dialog box to change the index format. If you make changes to the document that affect its index entries or page numbering, you can update the index by clicking it, opening the Index and Tables dialog box, and then clicking OK.

In this exercise, you will first mark a few index entries, subentries, and cross-references. Then you'll create and format an index, delete an index entry from the document, and update the index.

USE the *CreateIndex* document in the practice file folder for this topic. This practice file is located in the *My Documents\Microsoft Press\Word 2003 SBS\MakingAvail\CreatingIndex* folder and can also be accessed by clicking *Start/All Programs/Microsoft Press/Word 2003 Step by Step*.
OPEN the *CreateIndex* document.

Show/Hide ¶

1 If non-printing characters are not displayed on your screen, click the **Show/Hide ¶** button on the Standard toolbar to turn them on.

2 Hold down the Ctrl key, and click the *Why Compost?* entry in the table of contents at the top of the document.

Page 2 appears in the document window.

3 In the first paragraph below the *Why Compost?* heading, select the word *dirt*.

4 On the **Insert** menu, point to **Reference**, and then click **Index and Tables**.

The Index and Tables dialog box appears.

5 Click the **Index** tab, and then click **Mark Entry**.

The Mark Index Entry dialog box appears, with the word *dirt* in the "Main entry" box.

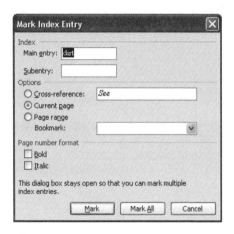

Tip You can also press Alt + Shift + X to open the Mark Index Entry dialog box without going through the Index and Tables dialog box.

6 Click **Mark All**.

Word inserts hidden index entry fields adjacent to every occurrence of the word *dirt* in the document.

7 In the second paragraph on page 2, select the word *Recycling*, and click the title bar of the **Mark Index Entry** dialog box to activate it.

8 In the **Main entry** box, change the entry to recycling, and click **Mark All**.

9 In the second paragraph under *What Is a Compost Pile?*, select the word *materials*, and click the title bar of the **Mark Index Entry** dialog box to activate it.

Troubleshooting You might have to move the dialog box to see and select the words you want to mark.

The word *materials* appears in the "Main entry" box.

10 In the **Page number format** area, select the **Bold** check box, and then click **Mark All**.

When Word creates the index, it will show the page numbers for the *materials* entry in bold.

11 In the same paragraph, select the word *soil*, and click the title bar of the **Mark Index Entry** dialog box to activate it.

12 In the **Options** area, click the **Cross-reference** option.

The insertion point moves to the space after the word *See* in the Cross-reference box.

13 Type dirt. (including the period), clear the **Bold** check box, and click **Mark**.

A cross-reference to the *dirt* index entry appears for the *soil* entry. When Word creates the index, it will enter *soil. See dirt.* (Notice that a period appears after the word *dirt*, just as you typed it.)

14 Click **Close** to close the **Mark Index Entry** dialog box.

Cross-reference index entry

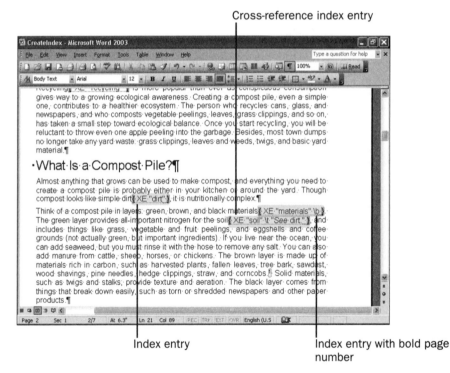

Index entry   Index entry with bold page number

15 Press Ctrl+End to move to the end of the document, and then press Ctrl+Enter to insert a new page.

The insertion point moves to the top of the new page.

16 Type Index, press Enter twice, and then make this heading bold and 18 points.

17 Press the ⬇ key twice, and then on the Standard toolbar, click the **Show/Hide ¶** button.

Troubleshooting   Before you create an index, make sure that the document is paginated correctly by hiding text formatted as hidden, such as the index entries and field codes. If the XE (index entry) fields are visible, click Show/Hide ¶ on the Standard toolbar. To hide field codes, click Options on the Tools menu, click the View tab, and clear the "Field codes" check box.

18 On the **Insert** menu, point to **Reference**, and then click **Index and Tables**.

The Index and Tables dialog box appears.

19 On the **Index** tab, click the down arrow to the right of the **Formats** box, and click **Formal** as the index format.

20 Clear the **right align page numbers** check box, and then click the down arrow to the right of the **Columns** box until its setting is **1**.

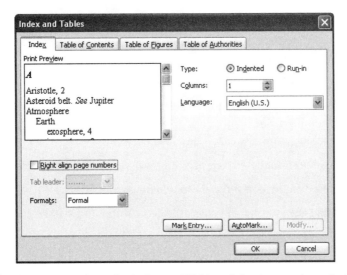

21 Click **OK** to close the **Index and Tables** dialog box and create the index.

The index is formatted in one column with the page numbers adjacent to their index entries. (This short index shows you how the feature works; a fully indexed document would obviously produce a much longer index.)

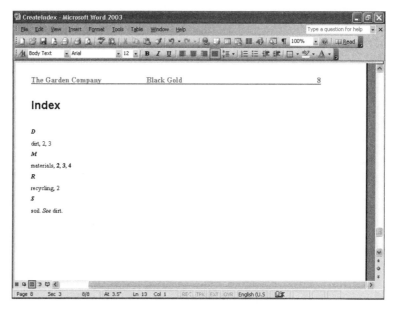

22 Scroll up to page 2, and select the cross-reference entry /t "See dirt." in the index entry after *soil*, and press ⌫.

The cross-reference entry is deleted from the document.

23 Press Ctrl+End to move to the end of the document, click anywhere in the index, and on the **Index** menu, point to **Reference**, click **Index and Tables**, clear the **Right align page numbers** check box, and click **OK**.

The index is updated to reflect that you have deleted the cross-reference.

24 When Word asks if you want to replace the index, click **OK**.

25 On the Standard toolbar, click the **Save** button to save the document.

Save

CLOSE the *CreateIndex* document.

Summarizing a Document

Microsoft Office Specialist

New In Office 2003

AutoSummarize feature
Readability Statistics

Whenever you develop a new document, you might want to take advantage of some of Word's summarizing capabilities. With Word, you can get summary information about a document in a variety of ways. One of these ways is by clicking Properties on the File menu to display the document's Properties dialog box, which can store the following *document properties*:

■ The General tab displays the document's name, location, and size; and the dates of creation, modification, and last access. This information is stored by default.

■ The Summary tab can display the title, subject, and author, as well as the category and any relevant keywords or comments. You enter this information to remind you at a glance what the document is about.

■ The Statistics tab displays the number of times the document has been revised and the amount of time it has been open on the screen for editing, as well as the number of pages, paragraphs, lines, words, and characters the document contains.

Tip Another way to get information about the number of pages, paragraphs, lines, words, and characters in a document is by clicking Word Count on the Tools menu.

■ If the document has been styled with heading styles and you have selected the "Save preview picture" check box on the Summary tab, the Contents tab displays an outline of the document.

■ The Custom tab lists custom fields you can associate with the document, together with the text you have entered. For example, you can enter a client's name or the document's status.

You don't have to open a document and display its Properties dialog box to see how you described the document. The information you enter in the Properties dialog box is displayed in a ScreenTip when you point to the document in My Computer or Windows Explorer.

If you are writing for a specific audience, such as children, you might want to summarize your documents in terms of their readability. On the Spelling & Grammar tab of the Options dialog box, you can tell Word to compile *readability statistics* for your documents by applying a couple of standard statistical tests. Then whenever you tell Word to check a document's spelling and grammar, it also displays such statistics as the average number of characters in a word, the average number of words in a sentence, and the reading level of the document (in terms of U.S. school grades 1 through 12).

If you are concerned that people might be too busy to read a long and detailed document, you can use Word's *AutoSummarize* feature to extract the key points of the document. AutoSummarize works best on well-structured documents with headings and subheadings, such as reports. The feature works by analyzing the document to determine which words are used frequently, and then assigning a score to each sentence based on the number of high-frequency words it contains. You determine what score is necessary for a sentence to be included in the summary, which can be inserted in the document as an executive summary or abstract that can be quickly scanned. You can also have Word copy the high-frequency words to the Summary tab of the Properties dialog box as keywords, and the high-scoring sentences as comments.

In this chapter, you will use the Word Count command to take a quick look at the number of words in a document. Then you will look at this and other document properties. You will change a property and display the document's readability statistics. Finally, you'll insert a summary of key concepts at the beginning of the document.

USE the *SummarizeDoc* document in the practice file folder for this topic. This practice file is located in the *My Documents\Microsoft Press\Word 2003 SBS\MakingAvail\SummarizingDoc* folder and can also be accessed by clicking *Start/All Programs/Microsoft Press/Word 2003 Step by Step*.
OPEN the *SummarizeDoc* document.

1 On the **Tools** menu, click **Word Count**.

The Word Count dialog box opens, displaying the count information.

Tip If you need to keep a close watch on the number of words or characters in a document as you edit text, you can display the Word Count toolbar by clicking Show Toolbar in the Word Count dialog box or by pointing to Toolbars on the View menu and then clicking Word Count. As you edit, you can click Recount on the Word Count toolbar to quickly update count information.

2 Click **Close** to close the **Word Count** dialog box.

3 On the **File** menu, click **Properties**, and then click the **Statistics** tab.

4 Compare the counts with those displayed in the **Word Count** dialog box, and then click the **Summary** tab.

5 In the **Subject** box, type Composting.

6   In the **Comments** box, type An instructive overview of composting for the home garden, and then click **OK** to close the **Properties** dialog box.

Tip   When you point to a closed Word document in Windows Explorer, the author, title, subject, and first 126 characters of a comment entered on the Summary tab of the Properties dialog box will appear in a ScreenTip. If you have many Word documents stored on your computer, this information can help you find the one you need.

7   On the **Tools** menu, click **Options**.

8   Click the **Spelling & Grammar** tab, and in the **Grammar** area, select the **Show readability statistics** check box, and click **OK**.

Spelling and
Grammar

9   On the Standard toolbar, click the **Spelling and Grammar** button, and work your way through the document, clicking **Ignore Once** each time Word stops on a suspected error.

When Word finishes the spelling and grammar check, it displays the Readability Statistics dialog box, which summarizes the readability of the document.

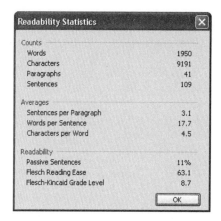

10 Click **OK** to close the summary.

11 Press `Ctrl`+`Home` to move to the top of the document, and on the **Tools** menu, click **AutoSummarize**.

The AutoSummarize dialog box appears.

12 In the **Length of summary** area, click the down arrow to the right of the **Percent of original** box, and click **25%** in the drop-down list.

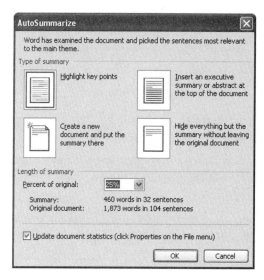

13 With **Highlight key points** selected in the **Type of Summary** area, click **OK**.

Word displays the AutoSummarize toolbar and highlights in yellow the 25 percent of the document it considers to be the most important.

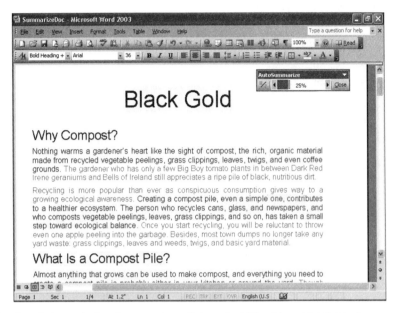

14 Scroll through the document, noticing what Word has highlighted.

15 On the AutoSummarize toolbar, click the vertical line in the **Percent of original** box, and drag it to the left until it displays **10%**.

Ten percent of the document is now highlighted.

16 On the **Tools** menu, click **AutoSummarize**.

17 In the **Type of summary** area, click **Insert an executive summary or abstract at the top of the document**.

18 In the **Length of summary** area, confirm that **Percent of original** is set to 10%, and then click **OK**.

Troubleshooting   If you have entered keywords or comments on the Summary tab of the Properties dialog box, Word will replace them with its own information when you use the AutoSummarize feature. To prevent this, clear the "Update document statistics" check box in the AutoSummarize dialog box.

Word closes the AutoSummarize toolbar and inserts a summary at the beginning of the document. The summary highlighting is no longer displayed.

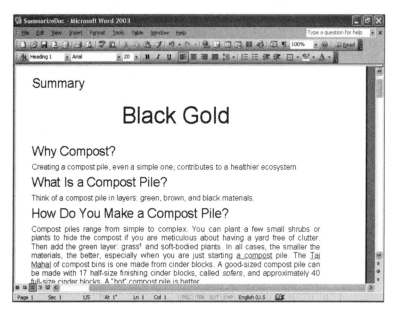

Save

19 On the Standard toolbar, click the **Save** button to save the document.

CLOSE the *SummarizeDoc* document, and if you are not continuing on to the next chapter, quit Word.

Key Points

- If you are collaborating on a large document with other people, you can split the document by creating a master document and subdocuments. You can then work on the subdocuments independently of each other.

- You can quickly navigate to specific points in a document using bookmarks and cross-references. You can use bookmarks to flag information you might want to look up later, and you can use cross-references to quickly jump to related information.

- You can use a table of contents to provide an overview of the topics covered in a document and to let readers navigate quickly to a topic. You can format the table of contents by selecting a predefined format or by changing individual table of content styles.

- You can create an index of key concepts, words, and phrases. After marking the entries you want, you use the Index and Tables command to tell Word to compile the index.

■ Word keeps track of summary information such as word and character count, and you can also have Word calculate readability statistics for a document.

■ You can attach summary information, such as a subject, keywords, and comments to a document by entering it in the Properties dialog box. You can tell Word to summarize the content of a document by using the AutoSummarize feature. The AutoSummarize results can be inserted in the document as an abstract or executive summary.

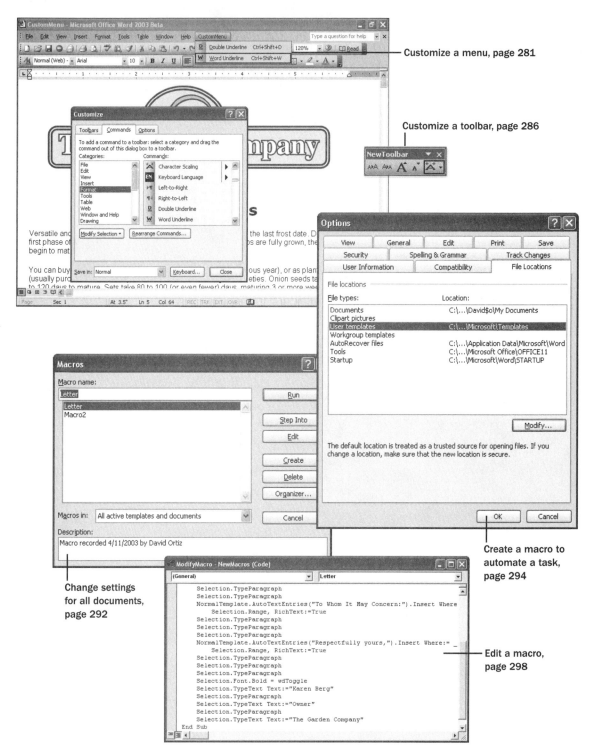

Customize a menu, page 281

Customize a toolbar, page 286

Create a macro to automate a task, page 294

Edit a macro, page 298

Change settings for all documents, page 292

13 Increasing Efficiency

In this chapter you will learn to:

✔ Customize a menu.

✔ Customize a toolbar.

✔ Change settings for all documents.

✔ Create a macro to automate a task.

✔ Edit a macro.

As you work with Microsoft Office Word 2003, you'll develop your own preferences and styles for working with documents. To match the way that you like to work, you can customize Word by adjusting its menus and toolbars, changing the default setting for new documents, and using macros to automate repetitive tasks.

In this chapter, you will get an idea of the ways in which you can customize Word. Specifically, you will learn to modify the existing Word toolbars and menus to show the buttons and commands you use most frequently, and you'll create custom toolbars and menus that show only the commands you frequently choose. You will also change the default storage location for templates and the default font used for the Normal style in new Word documents. Finally, you will create, run, edit, and delete macros.

See Also   Do you need only a quick refresher on the topics in this chapter? See the Quick Reference entries on pages lvii-lix.

 Important   Before you can use the practice files in this chapter, you need to install them from the book's companion CD to their default location. See "Using the Book's CD-ROM" on page xiii for more information.

Customizing a Menu

Microsoft Office Specialist

The first time you start Word, the menus on the menu bar list only the basic commands. For example, the File menu lists the New, Exit, Save, Save As, and Print commands, but not the Versions and Properties commands. To see the full menu, you can click the chevrons at the bottom of the menu, or simply wait a few seconds until Word expands the menu for you. As you work, the menus adjust so that the commands you use most often appear on the short menus—in other words, Word arranges your menus to suit the way you work.

Tip To show only long menus, not shortened menus, click Customize on the Tools menu, click the Options tab, and select the "Always show full menus" check box.

If you want to control which commands appear on the menus, you can customize the menus by clicking Customize on the tools menu and using the Commands tab of the Customize dialog box to make adjustments. You can remove commands you never use and add commands that you use often. You can even create new menus for specialized tasks—for example, you might want to create a menu for a particular project and then delete it when you have finished.

Tip If you delete one of Word's built-in menus and later need it back, click the Commands tab of the Customize dialog box. Then in the Categories list, scroll down to "Built-in Menus," click the menu you want, and drag it back where you want it on the menu bar. If you've deleted your Tools menu, you can still open the Customize dialog box by right-clicking a toolbar and clicking Customize on the shortcut menu.

In this exercise, you'll add and delete commands on Word's menus, create and then delete a custom menu, and then restore the original menu settings.

BE SURE TO start Word before beginning this exercise.
USE the *CustomMenu* document in the practice file folder for this topic. This practice file is located in the *My Documents\Microsoft Press\Word 2003 SBS\IncreasingEfficiency\CustomizingMenu* folder and can also be accessed by clicking *Start/All Programs/Microsoft Press/Word 2003 Step by Step*.
OPEN the *CustomMenu* document.

1 On the **Tools** menu, click **Customize** to open the **Customize** dialog box, and then click the **Options** tab if it's not already active.

Tip You can add animation effects, such as a sliding or unfolding effect, to menus. On the Options tab of the Customize dialog box, click the down arrow to the right of the "Menu animations" box and then click an animation in the drop-down list.

2   Click **Reset menu and toolbar usage data**, and then click **Yes**.

Word resets your menus and toolbars to their default settings so that they appear the way they did when you first started the program.

3   Click the **Commands** tab, and then in the **Categories** list, click **Drawing**.

The Drawing commands appear in the Commands list.

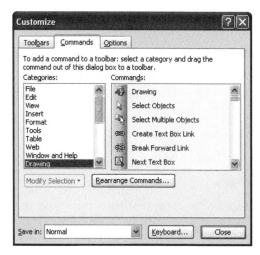

4   Scroll down the **Commands** list, click **WordArt Shape**, and drag the command over **Format** on the menu bar, without releasing the mouse button.

As you drag, an insertion bar follows the pointer.

5   When the **Format** menu opens, drag the insertion bar below the **Object** command at the bottom of the menu, and then release the mouse button to lock this position.

6   Click the **Format** menu's name to close it.

The WordArt Shape command is now available on the Format menu for the documents that are currently open and those that you open in the future.

7   Scroll down to the end of the **Categories** list, and click **New Menu**.

The New Menu appears in the Commands list.

8 Drag **New Menu** from the **Commands** list to the end of the menu bar (to the right of the Help menu).

9 On the menu bar, right-click **New Menu**. Then in the **Name** box on the shortcut menu, select the words *New Menu*, and type CustomMenu.

10 Press the [Enter] key to change the menu name to *CustomMenu*.

11 On the menu bar, click **CustomMenu**.

A blank menu drops down.

12 Scroll up in the **Categories** list of the **Customize** dialog box, and click **Format**.

The Format commands appear in the Commands list.

13 Scroll down in the **Commands** list, click **Double Underline**, and drag the command up to the menu bar (don't release the mouse button yet).

14 Hold the pointer over the words *CustomMenu*, and when the empty **CustomMenu** menu drops down, drag the pointer onto the empty menu and release the mouse button.

The Double Underline command appears on the CustomMenu menu.

15 In the **Commands** list, drag **Word Underline** onto the **CustomMenu** menu, and position it below the **Double Underline** command.

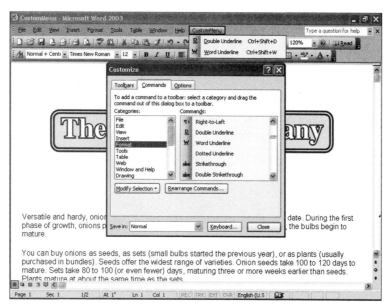

16 Click **Close** to close the **Customize** dialog box.

17 In the document window, scroll down and select the text heading *Preparation and Planting*, and then on the **CustomMenu** menu, click **Double Underline**.

18 Right-click any toolbar, and then click **Customize** to open the **Customize** dialog box.

19 On Word's menu bar, right-click the **CustomMenu** menu, and then click **Delete** in the shortcut menu to delete the menu.

> **Tip** You can move any menu by holding down the ⎇ key while you drag the menu to a new location. You can delete any menu by holding down the ⎇ key and dragging it into an open document window. Click "Built-in Menus" in the Categories list and then drag the menu back to the menu bar to restore it.

20 Click the **Format** menu to open it.

21 Drag the **Word Art Shape** command to a blank area in the open document.

The Word Art Shape command is removed from the Format menu.

22 Click the **Format** menu again to close it.

23 Click **Close** to close the **Customize** dialog box.

24 On the Standard toolbar, click the **Save** button to save the document.

Save

CLOSE the *CustomMenu* document.

Customizing a Toolbar

The screens in this book show the Standard and Formatting toolbars on two rows at the top of the screen, but by default, they appear on one row. When they occupy just one row, Word arranges the toolbars just as it arranges menus, showing only the buttons you use most often. To see all buttons on a toolbar, you can click the Toolbar Options button at the right end of a toolbar. You also can hide or change the order of visible buttons by dragging them to different positions on the toolbar.

Tip   To switch between displaying toolbars on one row and two rows, click the Toolbar Options button, and then click "Show Buttons on One Row" or "Show Buttons on Two Rows."

Microsoft Office programs have two states for toolbars:

■   A *docked toolbar* is attached to the top, bottom, left, or right edge of the Word window. By default, the Standard and Formatting toolbars are docked at the top on one row.

■   A *floating toolbar* is not attached to an edge of the Word window, but can be dragged anywhere on the screen by its title bar. By default, the Picture toolbar is a floating toolbar.

When you dock more than one toolbar on a row, they usually overlap. Some of the first toolbar's buttons will be obscured by the second toolbar, whose buttons might be obscured by the third toolbar, and so on. (You probably won't want more than three toolbars on a row.)

You can configure toolbars in any of the following ways to make them more convenient to work with:

■   With multiple toolbars on one row, control which buttons are visible by dragging the *move handle* (the four vertical dots) of the second or third toolbar to the left or right. As you drag the move handle, the preceding toolbar's less frequently used buttons are hidden or revealed.

■   Turn a docked toolbar into a floating toolbar by dragging it away from the edge of the window by its move handle.

■   Dock a floating toolbar by double-clicking its title bar to restore it to its previous location, or by dragging it to an edge of the document window.

■ Change the shape of a floating toolbar by dragging its frame. The arrangement of the buttons within the toolbar shifts accordingly.

■ Close a floating toolbar by clicking its Close button.

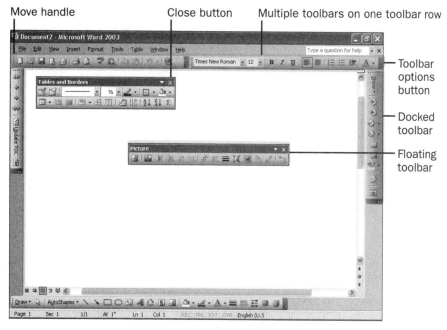

You can customize toolbar buttons by adding, removing, or arranging them using the following methods:

■ On a docked toolbar, click the Toolbar Options button at the end of the toolbar, and then click Add or Remove Buttons. Point to the toolbar's name to see a list of all the buttons that can appear on the toolbar. In the list, the buttons that currently appear on a toolbar are checked. You can select or deselect buttons to add them to or remove them from a toolbar.

■ On a floating toolbar, click the Toolbar Options down arrow at the right end of the title bar, and then click Add or Remove Buttons. Then follow the procedure for docked toolbars.

■ Use the Customize command to add buttons to toolbars. Right-click any toolbar, click Customize, click the Commands tab, click a category, and then drag the button to the desired toolbar, positioning the insertion bar where you want the button to appear. Then release the mouse button.

■ Use the Customize command to remove a button from a toolbar. Right-click any toolbar, click Customize, drag the button from the toolbar to a blank area of the window, and then release the mouse button.

Tip If the Customize dialog box is not open, you can remove a button from a toolbar or alter the sequence of buttons on a toolbar by holding down the [Alt] key while dragging the button.

You can also use the Customize dialog box to create a custom toolbar that displays the buttons you use most frequently. By using a custom toolbar, you can avoid having to jump between multiple menus or toolbars to complete your work.

In this exercise, you will hide and show a toolbar, switch the Standard and Formatting toolbars between one row and two rows, remove some buttons from the Standard toolbar and add others, and then restore the Standard toolbar to its default settings. You will also create a custom toolbar, use its buttons to format a document, and then delete it.

USE the *CustomToolbar* document in the practice file folder for this topic. This practice file is located in the *My Documents\Microsoft Press\Word 2003 SBS\IncreasingEfficiency\CustomizingTool* folder and can also be accessed by clicking *Start/All Programs/Microsoft Press/Word 2003 Step by Step*.
OPEN the *CustomToolbar* document.

1 On the **View** menu, point to **Toolbars**, and then click **Drawing**.

The Drawing toolbar appears at the bottom of the screen.

2 Right-click any toolbar, and then click **Drawing** to close the Drawing toolbar.

3 If the Standard and Formatting toolbars are currently displayed on two rows at the top of your screen, click either of their **Toolbar Options** buttons and then click **Show Buttons on One Row**.

4 Point to the move handle (the four vertical dots) at the left end of the Formatting toolbar, and when the pointer changes to a four-headed arrow, drag the toolbar to the left or right.

The number of buttons displayed on the Standard and Formatting toolbars changes depending on how much room each toolbar occupies on the row.

5 Point to the Standard toolbar's move handle, and drag it down into the document window.

The Standard toolbar becomes a floating toolbar.

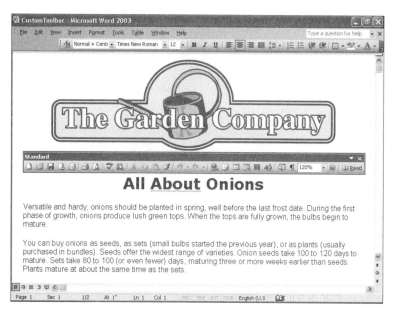

6 Point to the title bar of the Standard toolbar, and drag it to the right edge of the document window.

The toolbar docks itself at the right side of the window.

7 Drag the Standard toolbar back to the left of the Formatting toolbar.

8 At the right end of the Standard toolbar, click the **Toolbar Options** button.

Toolbar Options

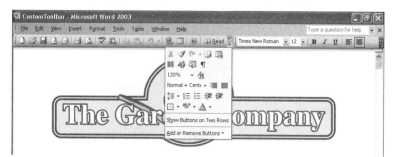

9 Point to **Add or Remove Buttons**, and then point to **Standard**.

Word displays a submenu of all the Standard toolbar buttons. (The checked buttons are the ones that currently appear on the Standard toolbar.)

10 Clear the **Format Painter, Drawing,** and **Document Map** check boxes.

11 Scroll down the list, select the **Close** and **Envelopes and Labels** check boxes, and then click away from the submenu.

The Standard toolbar is updated to reflect your changes.

Close button Envelopes and Labels button

12 On the Standard toolbar, click the **Toolbar Options** button, point to **Add or Remove Buttons**, point to **Standard**, scroll down the list, and click **Reset Toolbar**.

The Standard toolbar is restored to its default settings.

13 Right-click any toolbar, and click **Customize** on the shortcut menu.

The Customize dialog box opens.

14 Click the **Toolbars** tab, and then click **New** to open the **New Toolbar** dialog box.

15 In the **Toolbar name** box, type NewToolbar.

16 Click the down arrow to the right of the **Make toolbar available to** box, and click **CustomToolbar**.

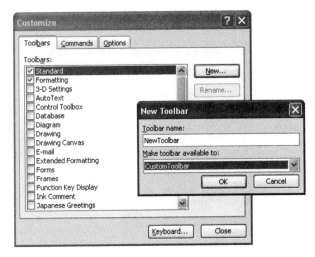

Important The new toolbar will be available only when you are working on this document.

17 Click **OK**.

A small, empty floating toolbar called NewToolbar appears next to the Customize dialog box. (Only part of the NewToolbar title might be showing.)

18 In the **Customize** dialog box, click the **Commands** tab.

19 In the **Categories** list, click **Format**, scroll down the **Commands** list, and drag the **Grow Font** button to the NewToolbar toolbar.

20 Drag the **Shrink Font**, **Grow Font 1 Pt**, **Shrink Font 1 Pt**, and **Character Scaling** buttons from the **Commands** list to the NewToolbar toolbar.

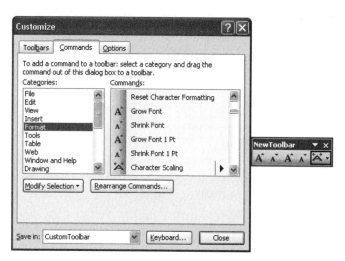

21 Click **Close** to close the **Customize** dialog box.

Grow Font 1 Pt

22 In the document window, scroll the document, select the *Preparation and Planting* heading, and then on the NewToolbar toolbar, click the **Grow Font 1 Pt** button twice.

The text increases in size by 2 points.

23 Right-click any toolbar, and then click **NewToolbar** on the shortcut menu to turn it off.

24 Right-click any toolbar, click **Customize** on the shortcut menu to open the **Customize** dialog box, and then click the **Toolbars** tab.

25 Scroll down the **Toolbars** list, click **NewToolbar**, and click **Delete**.

26 Click **OK** to confirm the deletion, and then click **Close** to close the **Customize** dialog box.

The NewToolbar toolbar is deleted.

Save

27 On the Standard toolbar, click the **Save** button to save the document.

BE SURE TO display the Standard and Formatting toolbars on two rows if you want all the buttons on both toolbars to be visible.
CLOSE the *CustomToolbar* document.

Changing Settings for All Documents

Microsoft Office Specialist

You can change several Word settings to make it faster or easier to do your job. A couple of these settings are relatively easy to change and can save you several keystrokes each time you create a new file.

An organization might want to have one location where all its business templates are stored to make it easy to quickly locate them. You can change the default locations where Word looks for templates so that you don't have to go searching every time you want to use one as the basis for a new document. You can also change the default locations of other types of files.

If you open a new blank document without basing it on a specific template, Word applies the Normal template to the document and assigns the Normal style to all regular paragraphs. This style produces text in 12-point regular Times New Roman, with left alignment and single line spacing. You might prefer to create most of your documents in a different font or font size, and instead of manually adjusting the font or size in every document you create, you can simply set the font and font size in the Normal template to the setting you prefer.

In this exercise, you'll change the default location for templates and modify default font settings.

USE the *SettingsDoc* document in the practice file folder for this topic. This practice file is located in the *My Documents\Microsoft Press\Word 2003 SBS\IncreasingEfficiency\ChangingSetting* folder and can also be accessed by clicking *Start/All Programs/Microsoft Press/Word 2003 Step by Step*.
OPEN the *SettingsDoc* document.

1 On the **Tools** menu, click **Options**.

The Options dialog box appears.

2 Click the **File Locations** tab.

3 In the **File types** list, click **User templates**, and then click **Modify**.

The Modify Location dialog box appears.

Important Before you modify any default setting, it is a good idea to make a note of the original setting in case you want to restore it later. So that you will remember the original location for templates, click the down arrow to the right of the "Look in" box, and write down the current location (probably *C:\Documents and Settings\(your name)\Application Data\Microsoft\Templates*) before you specify a new location.

4 Click the down arrow to the right of the **Look in** box, and then click the folder just above the current folder in the list.

If you haven't changed the default location before, you will click the Microsoft folder above the Templates folder.

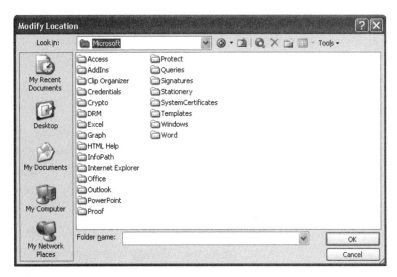

5   Click **Cancel** to close the **Modify Location** dialog box without actually changing the default template location, and then click **Close** to close the **Options** dialog box.

6   On the **Format** menu, click **Font**.

The Font dialog box appears, showing that the current font is Times New Roman, the font style is Regular, the font size is 12, and the font color is Automatic (meaning whatever is specified for the active style in the current template.)

Troubleshooting   If you've inadvertently clicked somewhere in the document since beginning this exercise, the current font might be Arial, not Times New Roman. Ignore this and go on to step 7.

7   Change the **Font** to **Verdana**, the **Size** to **11**, and the **Font color** to **Dark Green**.

A sample of the font settings you have selected appears in the Preview box.

8   In the lower-left corner of the dialog box, click **Default**.

A message box asks you to confirm that you want to change the default font for new documents to the settings currently in the Font dialog box.

9   Click **Yes**.

Both the message box and the Font dialog box close, and the text of the open document changes to reflect the new default font.

Save

10 On the Standard toolbar, click the **Save** button.

BE SURE TO restore your previous default font settings (Times New Roman font, Regular style, size 12, and Automatic color) if you don't want the new settings to apply to your work in Word from now on. CLOSE the *SettingsDoc* document.

Add a Custom Dictionary

Microsoft
Office
Specialist

If you work in an industry that uses terms not included in standard dictionaries, such as medicine or law, you can add a specialized dictionary to the supplemental dictionaries Word uses. That way, your industry terms will not be flagged as misspellings. (Supplemental dictionary files should have the file name extension *.dic*.) If you use this dictionary more than any other, you can make this dictionary the default supplemental dictionary.

To add a custom dictionary and make it the default supplemental dictionary:

1 On the **Tools** menu, click **Options**, and click the **Spelling & Grammar** tab.

2 Click **Custom Dictionaries**, and then in the **Custom Dictionaries** dialog box, click **Add**.

3 Navigate to the folder that contains the dictionary you want to use, and double-click the dictionary's file name.

Word adds the dictionary to the Dictionary list box

4 If the check box to the left of the dictionary's name is not checked, select the check box.

5 If you want this dictionary to be the default supplemental dictionary, click the **Change Default** button.

6 Click **OK** to close the **Custom Dictionaries** dialog box.

7 In the **Spelling** area of the **Spelling & Grammar** tab of the **Options** dialog box, make sure that the **Suggest from main dictionary only** check box is cleared, and then click **OK**.

Creating a Macro to Automate a Task

Microsoft
Office
Specialist

When performing a task requires a series of commands, you can create a macro to automate the process, which will reduce the number of steps involved in a task and save you time. A *macro* is a recorded series of commands (keystrokes and instructions) that are treated as a single command.

You can use macros to automate many tasks in Word, such as creating form letters, inserting AutoText, formatting text, creating tables, and turning command options on and off. For example, suppose The Garden Company uses a special design for tables or charts that appear in marketing materials and correspondence. Instead of employees having to manually create and format a table—insert it, add shading and borders, apply character formatting to column and row headings, and then adjust the line spacing—each time they write a new document, a macro, executed at the click of a button, could perform all these steps, saving time and reducing the chances of error.

Important   Macros can contain viruses—destructive computer programs that can destroy information and other programs on your computer. If you frequently run macros created by other people, you should purchase and install special anti-virus software. To further reduce the risk of virus infection in Word files, set your computer's macro security level to High or Medium by pointing to Macro on the Tools menu, clicking Security, clicking the Security Level tab, and then selecting the security level you want.

The simplest way to create a macro is to record the steps required to complete the desired task. You can then repeat the steps at any time by running the macro. You start by pointing to Macro on the Tools menu and clicking Record New Macro. In the Record Macro dialog box, you specify a name and storage location for the macro. (Macros are not separate files; they are stored and work only in conjunction with the document or template for which they were created.) You then carry out the steps for completing the task, clicking the Stop Recording button when you have finished.

Tip   By default, new documents are based on the Normal template. If you associate macros with the Normal template, they will always be available to new documents (unless you base them on a different template).

Before you run a macro, you position the insertion point where you want the result of the macro to be displayed. For example, if the macro inserts a table, you click where you want the table to appear. To run a macro, you point to Macro on the Tools menu and click Macros to display the Macros dialog box. You click the macro you want, and then click Run. (Or you can double-click the macro name.)

Tip   You can place a button for a macro you use frequently on a toolbar, or you can assign it a shortcut key combination so that the macro is readily available and easily executed.

In this exercise, you will create a macro that formats the basic elements of a letter, and then you'll run the macro.

USE the *RecordMacro* document in the practice file folder for this topic. This practice file is located in the *My Documents\Microsoft Press\Word 2003 SBS\IncreasingEfficiency\CreatingMacro* folder and can also be accessed by clicking *Start/All Programs/Microsoft Press/Word 2003 Step by Step*.
OPEN the *RecordMacro* document.

1 Press ⌃+End to move the insertion point to the blank line below the logo for The Garden Company.

2 On the **Tools** menu, point to **Macro**, and then click **Record New Macro** to open the **Record Macro** dialog box.

3 In the **Macro name** box, type Letter.

4 Click the down arrow to the right of the **Store macro in** box, and click **RecordMacro (document)**.

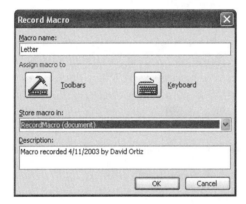

Tip You can assign a macro to a toolbar or menu before or after you record the macro. If you aren't sure that you want to assign your macro, you can create it first and assign it to a toolbar or menu later.

5 Click the **Keyboard** button to open the **Customize Keyboard** dialog box, press Alt+L (the lowercase *el*) to place that key combination in the **Press new shortcut key** box, click **Assign**, and click **Close**.

Word closes the Customize Keyboard dialog box and displays the Stop Recording toolbar, which has buttons you can click to stop or pause the recording.

6 In the document, type The Garden Company, and press Enter.

7 Type 1234 Oak Street, and press Enter.

8 Type Seattle, WA 10101, and press Enter three times.

9 On the **Insert** menu, point to **AutoText**, point to **Salutation**, and click **To Whom It May Concern:**.

The words *To Whom It May Concern:* are inserted into the document.

10 Press ⏎Enter three times.

11 On the **Insert** menu, point to **AutoText,** point to **Closing,** and then click **Respectfully yours,.**

The words *Respectfully yours,* are inserted into the document.

12 Press ⏎Enter three times.

13 Type Karen Berg, and press ⏎Enter.

14 Type Owner, and press ⏎Enter.

15 Type The Garden Company.

Stop Recording

16 On the Macro toolbar, click the **Stop Recording** button.

The macro stops recording, and the Stop Recording toolbar closes.

17 On the **Tools** menu, point to **Macro,** and click **Macros.**

The Macros dialog box appears.

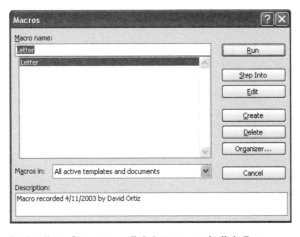

18 In the list of macros, click **Letter,** and click **Run.**

The placeholders for a second letter are inserted in the document, below the ones you typed while recording the macro.

Save

19 On the Standard toolbar, click the **Save** button to save the document.

CLOSE the *RecordMacro* document.

Editing a Macro

Microsoft Office Specialist

Sometimes a macro does not work as you expect, and you need to modify it. You can rerecord the macro to correct the problem, or because macros are instructions written in *Microsoft Visual Basic for Applications (VBA)*, you can edit it in the *Visual Basic Editor*.

Word macros are stored in *modules* within a Visual Basic *macro project* that is stored in a document or template. To edit a macro, you display the Macros dialog box, click the macro, and then click Edit. The Visual Basic Editor program window opens, and you can then select the module you want to work on and make changes.

When you no longer need a macro, you can delete it from the document or template where it is stored by selecting it in the Macros dialog box and clicking Delete.

Tip If you create a toolbar button or menu command for a macro and then delete the macro from the document or template, you can delete the macro's button or command by holding down the ⎇ key and dragging it into any blank space in the document window.

In this exercise, you will edit an existing macro to add character formatting, and then you'll delete the macro.

USE the *ModifyMacro* document in the practice file folder for this topic. This practice file is located in the *My Documents\Microsoft Press\Word 2003 SBS\IncreasingEfficiency\EditingMacro* folder and can also be accessed by clicking *Start/All Programs/Microsoft Press/Word 2003 Step by Step*.
OPEN the *ModifyMacro* document. If Word asks you whether you want to enable macros or disable macros, click Enable Macros.

1 On the **Tools** menu, point to **Macro**, and then click **Macros** to open the **Macros** dialog box.

2 In the list of macros, click **Letter**, and click **Edit**.

The macro's instructions are displayed in the Visual Basic Editor code window.

3 Scroll to the bottom of the ModifyMacro - NewMacros (Code) window.

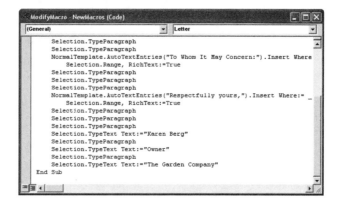

Troubleshooting   You might have to move this window by dragging its title bar, or resize it by dragging its lower-right corner.

4   Click to the left of *Selection.TypeText Text:="Karen Berg"*, and press ⌈Enter⌉ to insert a blank line before that instruction.

5   Press the ⌈↑⌉ key, and type Selection.Font.Bold=wdToggle.

As you type, the Visual Basic Editor displays a menu of possible commands. You can select a command from the menu instead of typing the entire command. When you've finished, the new instruction appears in the code.

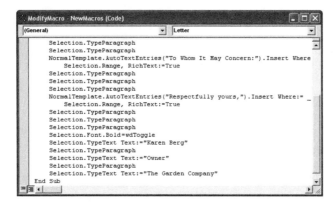

The new instruction tells the program that the following text should be displayed in bold.

Important   For information about inserting and editing macro commands in the Visual Basic Editor or about creating macros that perform complicated tasks that cannot be recorded, use the Help menu in the Visual Basic Editor window.

6   On the **File** menu, click **Close and Return to Microsoft Word**.

The Visual Basic Editor closes, and the macro is saved with the change.

7   Close any floating toolbars, and press ⌈Ctrl⌉+⌈End⌉ to move to the end of the document.

8   On the **Tools** menu, point to **Macro**, and then click **Macros** to open the **Macros** dialog box.

9   Click the down arrow to the right of the **Macros in** box, and click **ModifyMacro (document)**.

Tip   You don't have to open the Macros dialog box and select a macro to run it. You can simply press ⌈Alt⌉+⌈L⌉ (lowercase *el*), the keyboard shortcut assigned to the Letter macro when it was originally created.

10   In the list of macros, click **Letter**, and then click **Run**.

Troubleshooting If Word tells you that the macros in this project are disabled, your Security level is probably set to High. On the Tools menu, point to Macro, and then click Security to open the Security dialog box. On the Security Level tab, click Medium, and then click OK. Now save, close, and reopen the ModifyMacro document, clicking Enable Macros when asked. After completing this exercise on editing a macro, be sure to return your security setting to High if you do not want to have the option to run unsigned macros, which could contain viruses. (Unsigned macros do not have digital signatures that guarantee their source.)

A set of letter placeholders appears at the end of the document.

11 On the **Tools** menu, point to **Macro**, and then click **Macros** to open the **Macros** dialog box.

12 Make sure the setting in the **Macros in** box is **ModifyMacro (document)**.

13 In the list of macros, click **Letter**, and then click **Delete**.

An alert box asks you to confirm that you want to delete the Letter macro.

14 Click **Yes**.

Word deletes the Letter macro.

15 Close the **Macros** dialog box.

Save

16 On the Standard toolbar, click the **Save** button to save the document.

CLOSE the *ModifyMacro* document, and quit Word.

Key Points

- You can customize menu content by removing commands you don't use and adding ones you do use. You can also create new menus for specialized tasks.

- You can display toolbars docked along the edge of the document window or floating over it. You can hide and display buttons and change their order. You can also create a custom toolbar containing the buttons you use most frequently.

- You can change the default settings for many Word operations, including the locations of templates and other types of documents and the default font used in documents created when you click the New Blank Document button on the Standard toolbar.

- You can record the set of commands and keystrokes needed to perform a task and save it as a macro. You can then run the macro to carry out the task.

- You can rerecord a macro to correct any problems, or you can edit the macro in the Visual Basic Editor. When you no longer need a macro, you can delete it.

Glossary

absolutely   The designation of a picture whose position is determined by measurements you set.

attribute   A characteristic, such as size, style, or color, that changes the look of individual characters.

AutoCorrect   A feature that corrects commonly misspelled words as you type.

AutoSummarize   This feature in Word identifies the main points in a document and sets them apart for quick reference.

AutoText   A feature similar to AutoCorrect that makes corrections as you tell it to, rather than automatically.

axis   A common element in a chart. The x-axis (usually horizontal) plots the categories, and the y-axis (usually vertical) plots the values.

bookmark   A location in a document that marks text so that it can be found quickly.

bullet   A small graphic, such as a dot, that introduces a line or paragraph in a list.

caption   The expository text associated with a graphic or other type of figure.

case   The capitalization (uppercase or lowercase) of a word or phrase. Title case has the first letter of all important words capitalized. Sentence case has only the first letter of the first word capitalized. *ZIP* is all uppercase, and *zip* is all lowercase. Toggle case changes uppercase to lowercase and vice versa.

cell   In a table or datasheet, the intersection of a column with a row.

cell address   A combination of the column letter and the row number at the intersection where the cell is located.

character formatting   Collectively, a font and the attributes used to vary its look.

character spacing   The space between letters and other characters in words and sentences. Character spacing can be adjusted so that words and letters are closer together or farther apart.

character style   A set of attributes that can be applied to selected characters by selecting the style from a list.

chart   A graphic that uses lines, bars, columns, pie slices, or other markers to represent numbers and other values.

chart area   The entire area within the frame displayed when you click a chart.

check-box form field   A form field that enables you to provide several options, which users can click to indicate their choices.

Click and Type   A way to insert text, graphics, or other items in a blank area of a document. When you double-click a blank area, Click and Type will automatically apply the paragraph formatting to align the item where you double-clicked.

column   One of the vertical sections or stacks of information in a table or spreadsheet.

column headings   The gray buttons (A, B, C, etc.) across the top of a datasheet. See also *row headings*.

comment   An electronic note that can be placed in a document during editing or reviewing and made visible or hidden.

comment balloon   In Word's Track Changes feature, a text box that appears in the margin of the document.

cross-reference   An entry that refers the reader to another entry.

data marker   A graphical element, such as a bar or area, in a chart that represents a value in a datasheet.

data series   A group of related data points in a datasheet.

data source   A document that is combined with the main document in the mail merge process.

data table   A grid attached to a chart that shows the data used to create the chart.

datasheet   A numerical representation of data in cells that form rows and columns.

date and time fields   These fields supply the date and time from your computer's internal calendar and clock, so that you don't have to look them up.

demote   In an outline, to change a heading to body text or to a lower-level heading.

desktop publishing   A process that combines text and graphics in an appealing and easy to read format, such as a report, newsletter, or book.

destination file   A file into which you insert information created in another program.

diagram   A relational representation of information, such as an organization chart.

digital signature   A secure electronic stamp of authentication on a document.

docked toolbar   A toolbar that is attached to the edge of the Word window.

Document Map   A pane on the left of the screen that displays a document's headings. Clicking a heading in the Document Map moves to that heading in the document.

document properties   Information about a document, including the document's creation and modification date, size and location, author and subject.

document window   The part of a Word program where you enter and edit text.

drag-and-drop editing   A method for moving or copying selected text by dragging it to a new location. To copy selected text, hold down the [Ctrl] key as you drag.

drawing canvas   An area that contains drawing objects.

drawing object   An image created within Word—an AutoShape, a diagram, a line, or a WordArt object.

drop-down form field   A form field with which you can provide predefined answers so that users are limited to specified choices.

embedded object   An object that becomes part of the destination file and is no longer a part of its source file.

endnote   A note or citation that appears at the end of a document to explain, comment on, or provide references for text in a document. See also *footnote*.

Extensible Markup Language (XML)   A system for defining, validating, and sharing Web document formats.

extension   A period followed by a three-letter program identifier. Examples of extensions are .doc for Word, and .xls for Excel.

field name   A first-row cell in a datasheet that identifies data in the column below.

fields   The columns in a datasheet.

file   Information, such as a document, that a program saves with a unique name.

file format   The way that a program stores a file so that the program can open the file later.

filter   To exclude records from a data list in a mail merge.

floating toolbar   A toolbar that is not attached to an edge of the Word window.

folder   A logical place on a hard disk for storing documents and programs. Folders can contain files and subfolders.

font   A complete set of characters that all have the same design.

font color   One of a range of colors that can be applied to text.

font effect   An attribute, such as superscript, small capital letters, or shadow, that can be applied to a font.

font size   The size of text, usually expressed in points.

font style   An attribute that changes the look of text. The most common font styles are regular (or plain), italic, bold, and bold italic.

footer   A region at the bottom of a page whose text can be applied to all or some of the pages in a document.

footnote   A note or citation that appears at the bottom of a page to explain, comment on, or provide references for text in a document. See also *endnote*.

form   A printed or online document with instructions, questions, and fields (blanks) where users can enter responses.

form field   A predefined place where users enter answers to the questions on a form.

form field properties   Settings with which you can change form field attributes, such as text field length or the check box default setting.

formula   A mathematical expression that performs calculations, such as adding values.

frame   A window region on a Web page.

frames page   A special page for viewing multiple elements, including Web documents.

graphic   A picture or a drawing object.

gridlines   Lines that appear in a chart to make it easier to view the data.

guillemets   The « and » characters that surround each merge field in a main document.

header   A region at the top of a page whose text can be repeated on all or some of the pages in a document.

hover   To pause the pointer over an object, such as a menu name or button, for a second or two to display more information, such as a submenu or ScreenTip.

HTML   See *Hypertext Markup Language (HTML)*.

hyperlinks   Links to a location in the same file, another file, or an HTML page that are represented by colored and underlined text or by a graphic.

Hypertext Markup Language (HTML)   A tagging system used to code documents so that they can be viewed as pages in a Web browser.

indent markers   Markers shown along the horizontal ruler that are used to control how text is indented on the left or right side of a document.

indented index   An index that uses subentries on separate lines below main entries.

index   An alphabetical list of the topics, names, and terms used in a document along with the page numbers where they are found.

index entry   An entry in the body of a document that tags terms to be included in the Word's automated construction of an index. See also *XE*.

insertion point   The blinking vertical line that appears in the document window.

key combination   Two or more keys that perform an action when pressed together.

label   Text that identifies what each data series represents.

landscape   Horizontal orientation in which the page is wider than it is tall.

legend   A chart element that identifies the patterns or colors assigned to the data.

line break   A manual break that forces the text that follows it to the next line. Also called a text wrapping break.

link   A hyperlink. Text that is a link is usually colored and underlined to distinguish it from surrounding text.

linked object   An object that maintains a direct link to its source file.

lowercase   Small letters, as opposed to capital, or uppercase, letters.

macro   A command or series of commands (keystrokes and instructions) treated as a single command and used to automate repetitive or complicated tasks.

macro project   A group of components, including code, that constitute a macro.

mail merge   A process used to personalize individual documents in a mass production.

main document   The document that is combined with the data source in the mail merge process.

manual page break   A page break that you insert in a document. A manual page break appears as a dotted line across the page with the label *pagebreak*.

master document   A document that contains a set of subdocuments.

merge fields   Placeholders that indicate where Word inserts personalized information from a data source.

Microsoft Visual Basic for Applications (VBA)   A high-level programming language developed for creating Windows applications.

module   A location within a Visual Basic project where a macro is stored.

move handle   The four vertical dots at the left end of a toolbar with which you can move the toolbar.

Normal style   Word's default predefined paragraph style.

Normal template   Word's default document template.

Normal view   A stripped-down editing view, used to write and edit documents.

note separator   The line that divides the notes from the body of the document.

note text   The contents of a footnote or endnote.

object   An item, such as a graphic, video or sound file, or worksheet, that can be inserted in a Word document and then selected and modified.

Office Assistant   A tool that answers questions, offers tips, and provides access to the Help system for Microsoft Office System 2003 features.

Office Clipboard   A storage area shared by all Office programs where multiple pieces of information from one or more sources are stored.

OLE Linking and Embedding   A feature that allows you to insert a file created in one program into a document created in another program.

orientation   The direction—vertical or horizontal—in which a page is laid out.

orphan   The first line of a paragraph printed by itself at the bottom of a page.

Outline view   A view that shows the structure of a document, which consists of headings and body text.

paragraph   In word processing, text that ends when you press the [Enter] key.

paragraph formatting Collectively, the settings used to vary the look of paragraphs.

paragraph style A set of formatting that can be applied to the paragraph containing the insertion point by selecting the style from a list.

permissions Authorization that allows access to designated documents or programs.

picture A scanned photograph, clip art, or another type of image created with a program other than Word.

plot area The area that includes the data markers and the category (x) and value (y) axes in a chart.

point A measurement for the size of text. A point is equal to about 1/72 of an inch.

portrait Vertical orientation in which the page is taller than it is wide.

Print Layout view A view that shows a document as it will appear on the printed page.

program window The main window in a program that includes many of the menus, tools, and other features found in all Microsoft Office program windows, as well as some features that are unique to a specific program or version.

promote In an outline, to change body text to a heading, or to change a heading to a higher-level heading.

query A set of selection criteria that indicate how to filter recipients in a mail merge.

readability statistics Information about the reading level of a document determined by the average number of syllables per word and words per sentence in relation to various U.S. reading scales.

Reading Layout view A view that allows you to see and read the document as it will appear on paper without needing to print it.

read-only Available for viewing but protected from alterations.

records Sets of fields of information about a single item in a data source.

reference mark A number or character in the main text of a document that indicates additional information is included in a footnote or endnote.

relatively The designation of a picture whose position is determined by its relation to another element of a document, such as a margin, page, column, or character.

Research service A feature that enables you to access the reference material included in Word, materials you add to the service, and Internet resources.

revision marks Underlines, strike-through marks, and colored text that distinguishes revised text from original text.

row One of the horizontal sections or strings of information in a table or spreadsheet.

row headings The gray buttons (1, 2, 3, etc.) along the left side of a datasheet. *See also* column headings.

run-in index An index that lists subentries on the same line as the main entries.

section break   A portion of a document that you can format with unique page settings, such as different margins. A section break appears as a double-dotted line with the words *Section Break* and the type of section break in the middle.

select   To highlight an item in preparation for making some change to it.

selection area   A blank area to the left of a document's left margin that you can click to select parts of the document.

ScreenTip   A pop-up box that tells you the name of or more information about a button, icon, or other item on the screen when you place the pointer over it.

Smart Tag   A flag that helps you control the result of certain actions, such as automatic text correction, automatic layout behavior, or copying and pasting.

soft page break   A page break that Word inserts in a document when the text reaches the bottom of the specified text column. In Normal view, a soft page break appears as a dotted line across the page.

source file   A file created in a source program that is inserted in a destination file.

Spelling and Grammar   A feature that finds errors and suggests and makes corrections.

Standard Generalized Markup Language (SGML)   A system for coding the structure of text and other data so that it can be used in a variety of environments.

style   A set of character and paragraph formatting applied by selecting it from a list.

subdocument   A subordinate document that is used in master documents.

subentry   A subtopic index listing.

tab leader   A repeating character (usually a dot or dash) that separates an entry from the page number associated with it. Tab leaders are often found in a table of contents and can be dotted, dashed, or solid lines.

tab stops   Locations across a page that you use to align text.

table autoformat   A set of 18 predefined table formats that include a variety of borders, colors, and attributes.

table of authorities   A table used in legal papers and other types of official documents that lists statutes, citations, case numbers, and similar information.

table of contents   A list of the main headings and subheadings in a document along with corresponding page numbers.

table of figures   A list of graphics, pictures, or figures and their corresponding captions.

tag   A command inserted in a document that specifies how the document, or a portion of the document, should be formatted.

task pane   A pane that enables you to quickly access commands related to a specific task, without having to use menus and toolbars.

template   A document that stores text, styles, formatting, macros, and page information for use in other documents.

text form field   A form field with several types of text boxes where users enter text.

text wrapping break   A manual break that forces the text that follows it to the next line. Also called a *line break*.

theme   A unified look in a document that incorporates heading and text styles.

Thesaurus   A Word feature that looks up alternative words or synonyms for a word.

thumbnail   A small image that represents a page in a document and that you can click to navigate to that page.

toggle   An on/off button or command that is activated when you click it and deactivated when you click it again.

Uniform Resource Locator (URL)   A unique address for a page on the Web, such as *http://www.microsoft.com*.

uppercase   Capital letters, as opposed to lowercase letters.

version   A document that has been altered from the original; Word records changes from version to version to help you track the editing history of a document.

Visual Basic Editor   The environment in which VBA programs are written and edited.

watermark   A picture or text that appears faintly in the background of a document.

Web browser   A program such as Microsoft Internet Explorer that is used to locate and display web pages.

Web Layout view   A view that shows a document as it will appear as a Web page.

Web page   A special document in HTML designed to be viewed in a Web browser.

Web site   A collection of Web pages with navigation tools and a designed theme.

widow   The last line of a paragraph printed by itself at the top of a page.

wildcard characters   When using the Find and Replace dialog box, characters that serve as placeholders for a single character, such as *?ffect* for *affect* and *effect*, or multiple characters.

Word document window   A window that displays a document, along with the tools most frequently used when creating, editing, and formatting a document.

word processing   A process by which you create, edit, and format text documents.

word wrap   The movement of text to the next line when typing goes beyond the right margin.

WordArt   A feature that creates fancy text objects for use as banners or titles.

workgroup template   A template stored in a central location to be used over a network.

XE   An index entry field code that defines the text and page number for an index entry and other options, such as a subentry text. See also *index entry*.

XML   *See* Extensible Markup Language (XML).

XML schema   A description of a document's structure.

Index

A

absolute positioning of pictures, 137, 140, 301
abstracts, 277
Accept Change button (Reviewing toolbar), 171
accepting changes, xlv, 169, 171
Actual Page button (Reading Mode toolbar), 21
Advanced Layout dialog box, 138
Align Right button, 117
aligning
    paragraphs, xxxvi
    pictures with text, 137–38
    text, 117
    WordArt, 141
animating
    menus, 283
    text, 57
animation effects, 57
    adding, xxxv
applying
    styles, xxxvii
    themes, 92
arranging windows, 15
Arrow button (Drawing toolbar), 161
arrows
    adding to organization chart lines, 132
    inserting in charts, 161
attaching
    documents to e-mail messages, xlvii
    templates to existing documents, 83
attributes, 301
AutoCorrect, 31, 301
    adding entries, 32
    cancelling, 31
    capitalization, turning off, 32
    customizing, 31
AutoCorrect dialog box, 74
AutoCorrect Options button, 31, 73
AutoFormat options, specifying, xxxvii

AutoFormats, 72, 114, 117
    applying to tables, xlii
automatic repagination, 99
automating tasks. *See macros*
AutoRecover, 6
AutoShapes
    curves, 146
    setting defaults, 145
AutoSum button (Tables and Borders toolbar), 122
AutoSummarize, 273, 276, 301
AutoText, 31, 296, 301
    creating text abbreviations with, xxxiii
    inserting, 31, 33

B

backgrounds, 87–90
    color, adding, xxxviii
    color, changing, 88
    fill effects, applying, 89
    watermarks *(see watermarks)*
balloons, comment. *See comments*
bar charts, 156
Bold button (Formatting toolbar), 56, 116, 253
bolding text, xxxv, 56, 116, 253
bookmarks, 249, 254–57, 301
    deleting, 256
    inserting, lv, 255
    jumping to, 255
    naming conventions, 255
borders
    adding to paragraphs, xxxvi, 67
    applying to charts, 161
    form field, 221
    table, 114, 117
Borders and Shading dialog box, 67, 116
Break dialog box, 101
breaking columns, 126
brightness, picture, 133, 135
Browse by Page button, 14
browsing documents, 14

bulleted lists, 69. *See also numbered lists*
    bullets, formatting, xxxvii
    converting into outlines, 69
    creating, 69
    creating styles for, 75
    formatting automatically, 73
    indent, changing, 71
    sorting, 70
bullets, 301
Bullets and Numbering dialog box, 69
Bullets button (Formatting toolbar), 71
By Column button (Graph Standard toolbar), 164

C

calculations in tables, 107, 119
cameras, inserting pictures from, 133
capitalization, turning off automatic, 32
captions, 264, 301
case, 301
cell addresses, 301
cells, datasheet, entering data in, 152
cells, table, 107, 301
    borders, 114
    merging, xli, 109–11
    referencing in formulas, 119
    selecting, 108
    shading, 114, 116
    splitting, 109
Center button (Formatting toolbar), 62, 103, 116, 202
centering
    paragraphs, 66
    text, 62, 116
change tracking, 168–72. *See also revision marks*
    accepting changes, xlv, 169, 171
    changing name displayed as author, 171
    moving among changes, 169
    rejecting changes, xlv, 169, 171

T

table of contents